Activists, Alliances, and Anti–U.S.

No other country maintains a global military presence comparable to that of the United States. Yet outside the United States, considerable debate exists about what this presence is about and how well it serves national and global interests. Anti–U.S. base protests, played out in parliaments and the streets of host nations, continue to arise in different parts of the world. In a novel approach fusing international relations theory with social movement perspectives, this book examines the impact of anti-base movements and the important role bilateral alliance relationships play in shaping movement outcomes. The author explains not only when and how anti-base movements matter but also how host governments balance between domestic and international pressure on base-related issues. Drawing on interviews with activists, politicians, policymakers, and U.S. base officials in the Philippines, Japan (Okinawa), Ecuador, Italy, and South Korea, the author finds that the security and foreign policy ideas held by host-government elites act as a political opportunity or barrier for anti-base movements, influencing their ability to challenge overseas U.S. basing policies.

Andrew Yeo is Assistant Professor of Politics at the Catholic University of America in Washington, D.C. His research and teaching interests include international relations theory, social movements and transnational politics, East Asian security, and U.S. global force posture. His research has appeared in *Comparative Politics*, *International Studies Quarterly*, *Peace Review*, and *Journal of East Asian Studies*.

To Mom and Dad

Cambridge Studies in Contentious Politics

Editors

Ronald Aminzade et al., *Silence and Voice in the Study of Contentious Politics*

Javier Auyero, *Routine Politics and Violence in Argentina: The Gray Zone of State Power*

Clifford Bob, *The Marketing of Rebellion: Insurgents, Media, and International Activism*

Charles Brockett, *Political Movements and Violence in Central America*

Christian Davenport, *Media Bias, Perspective, and State Repression*

Gerald F. Davis, Doug McAdam, W. Richard Scott, and Mayer N. Zald, *Social Movements and Organization Theory*

Jack A. Goldstone, *States, Parties, and Social Movements*

Tamara Kay, *NAFTA and the Politics of Labor Transnationalism*

Joseph Luders, *The Civil Rights Movement and the Logic of Social Change*

Doug McAdam, Sidney Tarrow, and Charles Tilly, *Dynamics of Contention*

Sharon Nepstad, *War Resistance and the Plowshares Movement*

Kevin J. O'Brien, and Lianjiang Li, *Rightful Resistance in Rural China*

Silvia Pedraza, *Political Disaffection in Cuba's Revolution and Exodus*

Eduardo Silva, *Challenging Neoliberalism in Latin America*

Sarah Soule, *Contention and Corporate Social Responsibility*

Yang Su, *Collective Killings in Rural China during the Cultural Revolution*

Sidney Tarrow, *The New Transnational Activism*

Ralph Thaxton, Jr., *Catastrophe and Contention in Rural China: Mao's Great Leap Forward Famine and the Origins of Righteous Resistance in Da Fo Village*

Charles Tilly, *Contention and Democracy in Europe, 1650–2000*

Charles Tilly, *Contentious Performances*

Charles Tilly, *The Politics of Collective Violence*

Stuart A. Wright, *Patriots, Politics, and the Oklahoma City Bombing*

Deborah Yashar, *Contesting Citizenship in Latin America: The Rise of Indigenous Movements and the Postliberal Challenge*

Activists, Alliances, and Anti–U.S. Base Protests

ANDREW YEO
Catholic University of America

CAMBRIDGE UNIVERSITY PRESS

CAMBRIDGE UNIVERSITY PRESS
Cambridge, New York, Melbourne, Madrid, Cape Town,
Singapore, São Paulo, Delhi, Tokyo, Mexico City

Cambridge University Press
32 Avenue of the Americas, New York, NY 10013-2473, USA

www.cambridge.org
Information on this title: www.cambridge.org/9780521175562

First published 2011

Printed in the United States of America

A catalog record for this publication is available from the British Library.

Library of Congress Cataloging in Publication Data
Yeo, Andrew, 1978–
Activists, alliances, and anti–U.S. base protests / Andrew Yeo.
   p.   cm.
Includes bibliographical references and index.
ISBN 978-1-107-00247-0 (hardback) – ISBN 978-0-521-17556-2 (paperback)
   1. Military bases, American – Foreign countries.   2. Military bases, American – Political
aspects.   3. Military bases, American – Social aspects.   4. Protest movements.
5. United States – Military relations – Foreign countries.   I. Title.
UA26.A2Y46   2011
355.7–dc22   2010048075

ISBN 978-1-107-00247-0 Hardback
ISBN 978-0-521-17556-2 Paperback

Contents

Figures

Tables

Preface and Acknowledgments

I originally titled this book "Yankee Go Home? Activists, Alliances, and Overseas U.S. Military Bases." I presumed the title would grab readers' attention. As the book moved closer to completion, however, I began to think harder about the ramifications of publishing a book with the said title. Based on the title alone, some might dismiss the book as another left-wing manifesto denouncing U.S. militarism and avoid reading it. Meanwhile, those most eager to read the book – namely, those in the activist community – might walk away sorely disappointed by my findings and tell others to leave the book on the shelf. Picturing the book (or myself as the author) getting flak from both ends of the political spectrum, I prepared to open the preface with the old saying "Never judge a book by its cover."

I imagine my paranoia has something to do with teaching and residing inside the Washington beltway. Thus, after a brief discussion with my editor, Lew Bateman, I decided to choose the more neutral title that now graces the cover: *Activists, Alliances, and Anti–U.S. Base Protests*. This title more accurately reflects the subject matter as well as my intentions in writing a book about security alliances and anti-base movements.

As a graduate student studying international relations in the early 2000s, I was perplexed by various anti-U.S. protests taking place in countries I assumed were generally "pro-American." What the media labeled as "anti-American," however, was actually more complex. Some protests were geared broadly against U.S. foreign policies, or the policies of the George W. Bush administration. Others were specific to the Iraq War. Still others focused on U.S. bases and the presence of American troops on sovereign soil. The last was particularly interesting because countries hosting U.S. bases were often allied with the United States. Despite long-standing alliance partnerships in some cases, anti-base protests nevertheless erupted.

Were anti-base protests isolated incidents? Were they relatively insignificant events? I was rather skeptical about the impact of anti-base protests. How could ordinary people challenge not only their own national security policies but the foreign and military interests of the most powerful country in the world? As I probed for answers, it became increasingly clear that I would have to look beyond the boundaries of international relations theory to present an accurate, but still coherent, argument. Thus, I turned to the study of social movements. This resulted in an interdisciplinary approach, fusing social movement theories with international relations perspectives to explain when and how anti-base movements mattered and how host governments responded to domestic and international pressures on alliance issues.

I approached this study as an academic scholar and have attempted to write about the subject of anti-base movements as objectively as possible. I am not an activist-scholar. Nor do I pretend to be one. Although I am somewhat detached from the normative debate, I have learned a great deal about base politics from anti-base activists, and I have come to respect their lifelong commitment to peace and social justice. I am sympathetic to many of their arguments, particularly the grievances of local residents affected by U.S. bases. However, in the interest of full disclosure, I do not fully agree with the strategic logic presented by anti-base activists regarding the presence and purpose of overseas U.S. bases. There is certainly much room for discussion, even among anti-base activists, but especially (and hopefully) between the activist and policy communities.

U.S. military interventions in Iraq and Afghanistan have continued to fuel anti-base sentiment well into the twenty-first century as parts of the world grow wary of U.S. militarism. But even while waging two bloody wars, the U.S. military saved countless lives in Indonesia and Haiti following apocalyptic natural disasters in 2004 and 2010, respectively. The network of U.S. bases, and the men and women in uniform they host, are neither inherently good nor bad. Neither are the residents and activists on the street who are shouting at U.S. soldiers to go home. In the process of piecing together a narrative based largely on the account of numerous activists, government policymakers, and military officials, I discovered there were no "right" or easy answers, much less a solution. Perhaps this is why political scientists find it much easier to explain than prescribe. In presenting my argument about activists, alliances, and overseas U.S. military bases, however, I hope others will come to understand the claims made by anti-base activists that are often taken for granted, and the reasons why U.S. bases – as much as activists may wish – cannot just simply disappear.

I owe an enormous debt of gratitude to many individuals and institutions that provided intellectual, financial, emotional, and spiritual support during different stages of the project. The intellectual inspiration behind this book rests on the shoulders of two academic giants on top of a hill: I thank Peter Katzenstein for his continual support and encouragement in work and in life since my graduate student days at Cornell University. Peter's generosity as a mentor is legendary, and I hope the successful completion of this work adds to that legend. I also owe Sidney Tarrow a big thank-you for drawing me into the social movement camp. Sid, noting my disciplinary identity crisis between international relations and social movements, recommended on more than one occasion that I stop worrying about how others would interpret my work and instead let the argument speak for itself. I have carried that piece of advice with me to this day.

At Cornell, I also want to extend a heartfelt thank-you to Matthew Evangelista, who enthusiastically supported this project from start to finish. His encouragement helped me overcome several bouts of frustration and doubt during the early phases of the project. Chris Way's knack for analytical rigor and the expertise of J. J. Suh (now at SAIS–Johns Hopkins) on alliance relations also helped sharpen the theoretical and empirical arguments found in the book. Several friends and colleagues in the Government Department provided advice and comments during early phases of the project or just made the long Ithaca winters bearable. I extend a warm thank-you to Stephanie Hofmann, Stephen Nelson, Jennifer Hadden, Maria Zaitseva, Jennifer Erickson, Jai-Kwan Jung, Yuriko Takahashi, Seo-hyun Park, Il-hyun Cho, Israel Waismel-Manor, Sean Boutin, Devarshee Gupta, and Noelle Brigden.

Other colleagues provided valuable feedback on conference papers and draft chapters that helped refine the final product. I thank Richard Bensel, Jon Brown, Kent Calder, Alexander Cooley, Joseph Gerson, Amy Holmes, Yuko Kawato, Paul MacDonald, and Sheila Smith for their comments.

Much of the manuscript was revised at my new home at the Catholic University of America, where I have been welcomed by several wonderful colleagues. I thank my fellow junior colleagues in the Politics Department, Matthew Green and Christopher Darnton, for their friendship and support. Our lunch conversations on life as an assistant professor have given me some great laughs, if not occasional reasons for despair! I would also like to thank Phil Henderson, Wallace Thies, Claes Ryn, David Walsh, Dennis Coyle, and Jim O'Leary for their professional advice and camaraderie. I thank Lawrence Poos, Dean of the School of Arts and Science, for his academic and financial support.

My research was made possible with generous financial and logistical support from several institutions. I gratefully acknowledge funding from the U.S. Fulbright Program and the Korean-American Education Commission; Cornell University's East Asia Program, Peace Studies Program, Graduate School, and Department of Government; and finally Seoul National University's East Asia Institute.

In the Philippines, I would like to thank the staff and researchers at the Third World Studies Center (TWSC) at the University of Philippines–Diliman for their friendship and support during my visiting fellowship. A special thank-you goes out to Sharon Quinsaat, Josephine Diosno, Teresa S. Encarnacion Tadem, Zurdaida Mae Cabilo, Joel Ariate Jr., and Ate Bien (Bienvenida C. Lacsamana), who warmly welcomed me into the TWSC community.

In South Korea, Professor Young-chool Ha helped secure my visiting research fellowship at Seoul National University's Center for International Studies and provided me with office space at the Unification Forum (now the Center for Unification Studies). I thank Professor Keun-sik Jung for inviting me into his Okinawa research seminar at Seoul National University and allowing me to join the group research trip to Okinawa. Wang-hui Lee and Seung-joo Cha at the Unification Forum always had their doors open for me, and Misook Kwon provided helpful research assistance and language tutoring. Fellow Fulbrighters Irene Hahn, Laura Pohl, and Jennifer Manne helped keep my intellectual (and not so intellectual) spirits up!

I am grateful to Lew Bateman at Cambridge University Press for making this book project a reality. In addition, I would like to express my sincere gratitude to Anne Lovering Rounds, Helen Wheeler, and Mark Fox for guiding me through the production and copyediting process. Two anonymous reviewers for Cambridge University Press provided invaluable suggestions that not only strengthened the arguments found in several chapters but reminded me of the significance and timeliness of anti-U.S. base protests.

This book would not have been possible without the willingness of activists to share their stories and insights. In South Korea, I would like to single out three individuals and their respective organizations in particular: Jiseon Koh and other members of Green Korea United introduced me to the world of South Korean activism; Father Junghyeon Moon and members of Peace Wind hosted me several times in Pyeongtaek as they relayed their account of Korean anti-base movements into the wee hours of the morning; and Youkyoung Ko of the National Campaign for Eradication of Crimes by U.S. Troops in Korea provided important insights and data related to South Korean anti-base movements. In the Philippines, Cora Valdez Fabros dug out old documents on anti-base movements from the Nuclear Free Philippines Coalition's library and her own personal collection for me. Roland Simbulan provided expert feedback on my rendition of anti-base movements in the Philippines. Lastly, Herbert Docena graciously fulfilled several of my requests for information on U.S. military involvement in the Philippines and the transnational anti-base network.

I extend my gratitude to Stefano Osti for hosting my stay in Vicenza, Italy, and Helga Serrano for coordinating interviews and providing contacts with Ecuadorian activists. Personal correspondence and valuable updates from Enzo Ciscato in Vicenza and Stephanie Westbrook in Rome helped keep me informed on anti-base resistance in Italy even after I concluded my formal research. Needless to say, at all my field research sites, numerous activists, scholars, and current and former government and military officials shared with me their perspectives on base politics, which in turn helped shape my own understanding of alliances, anti-base movements, and the politics of overseas bases. There are too many names to acknowledge individually, but I am grateful to each one who contributed their time to this project.

Although this book has largely been an academic endeavor, close friends and family have supported me throughout the research and writing process with their encouragement and prayers. I thank Kwangtaik Kim for being a great listener all these years. I also thank Kyonga Kim, Daniel Johnson, Christine Kim, Heather MacLachlan, and Thea Sircar for their support and prayers at various stages of this project. I met my wife, Yoon Cho, around the time I was seeking out publishers for my manuscript (Yoon insists she was my lucky charm). I am grateful for her encouragement, wisdom, humor, and grace as she supports me through the finish line. Finally, I thank my wonderful parents, who have shown me much love and support. They have had a profound impact on my pursuit to become a respectable scholar and teacher, and it is to them I dedicate this book.

Abbreviations

ABAKADA	Anti-Baseng Kilusan
ABC	Anti-Bases Coalition
ACBT	Airborne Combat Brigade Team
ACJ	Asociación Cristiana de Jóvenes (Young Men's Christian Association)
ACSA	Acquisition and Cross-Servicing Agreement
AEW	Airborne Early Warning
AFP	Armed Forces of the Philippines
AFSC	American Friends Service Committee
ALDHU	Latin American Association of Human Rights
ATM	Anti-Treaty Movement
AWACS	Airborne Warning and Control System
CAM	National Solution Committee to Abolish the Maehyangri Air Force Training Range
CC	Coordinamento Comitati
CEDHU	Ecumenical Commission of Human Rights
CLB	Cabinet Legislative Bureau
CONAIE	Confederation of Indigenous Nationalities
CPP	Communist Party of the Philippines
CSL	Cooperative Security Location
CSP	Campaign for a Sovereign Philippines
DFAA	Defense Facilities Administration Agency
DND	Department of National Defense
DOD	Department of Defense
DPJ	Democratic Party of Japan
EASR	East Asian Strategic Review
FARC	Revolutionary Armed Forces of Colombia
FLAG	Free Legal Assistance Group
FMF	Foreign Military Financing
FOL	Forward Operating Location

FOTA	Future of the Alliance Policy Initiative
FTA	Free Trade Agreement
GAO	Government Accountability Office
GDPR	Global Defense Posture Review
GKU	Green Korea United
GNP	Grand National Party
INREDH	Regional Foundation of Consultant's Office in Human Rights
IOC	International Organization Committee
JDA	Japanese Defense Agency
KCPT	Pan-National Solution Committee to Stop the Expansion of U.S. Bases
KCTU	Korean Confederated Trade Union
KIDA	Korean Institute for Defense Analysis
KPD	Kilusansa Pambansang Demokrasya
LPP	Land Partnership Plan
MBA	R.P.-U.S. Military Bases Agreement
MDP	Millennium Democratic Party
MILF	Moro Islamic Liberation Front
MITI	Ministry of International Trade and Industry
MLSA	Mutual Logistics Support Agreement
MND	Ministry of National Defense
MNLF	Moro National Liberation Front
MOF	Ministry of Finance
MOFA	Ministry of Foreign Affairs
MOFAT	Ministry of Foreign Affairs and Trade
NATO	North Atlantic Treaty Organization
NCCP	National Council of Churches in the Philippines
ND	National Democrat
NDF	National Democratic Front
NDPO	National Defense Program Outline
NFPC	Nuclear Free Philippines Coalition
NGO	Nongovernmental Organization
NIMBY	Not In My Backyard
NL	National Liberation
NPA	New People's Army
OBC	Overseas Basing Committee
OIPAZ	International Observance for Peace
OPP	Okinawa People's Party
OTA	Okinawa Teachers Association
OWAAMV	Okinawan Women Act against Military and Violence
PACT	Philippine American Cooperation Talks
PADH	Andean Program of Human Rights

PAR-SOFA	People's Action for Reform of the Unjust Status of Forces Agreement
PdCI	Party of Italian Communists
PKP	Partido Komunista ng Pilipinas
PLANEX	National Plan of Foreign Policy
PnB	Partido ng Bayan
PNSMS	Patto Nazionale di Solidarietà e Mutuo Soccorso
PO	People's Organizations
POS	Political Opportunity Structure
PRC	Communist Refoundation Party
PSOE	Partido Socialista Obrero Español
PSPD	People's Solidarity for Participatory Democracy
PTFBC	People's Task Force for Bases Cleanup
QDR	Quadrennial Defense Review
REDHER	Network of Friendship and Solidarity with Colombia
ROK	Republic of Korea
RP	Republic of the Philippines
SACO	Special Action Committee on Okinawa
SCM	Security Consultative Meeting
SD	Social Democrat
SDC	Subcommittee for Defense Cooperation
SDF	Self-Defense Force
SERPAJ	Peace and Justice Service of Ecuador
SOFA	Status of Forces Agreement
SOUTHCOM	U.S. Southern Command
SPARK	Solidarity for Peace and Reunification of Korea
SWS	Social Weather Station
UPOCAM	Provincial Union of Farmers' Organization of Manabí
USCAR	United States Civilian Administration of the Ryukyu Islands
USFJ	United States Forces, Japan
USFK	United States Forces, Korea
USIA	United States Information Agency
VFA	Visiting Forces Agreement
WSF	World Social Forum

Introduction

Activists, Alliances, and the Politics of Overseas U.S. Bases

Step along the paved village path lining a South Korean rice field at dawn. Stare out into the vast expanse of land under a reddish-orange sky. The distant hills behind the fog will certainly conjure an image befitting the nation known as the "land of the morning calm." This was my last image of Daechuri village on a brisk February morning as I said farewell to a group of activists over breakfast.

After a three-month research stint in the Philippines, I returned in May 2006 to a strikingly different scene. The South Korean government had cordoned off all roads into Daechuri. Unable to access the village via public transportation, I made my way by foot. I passed through the first three police checkpoints with a U.S. passport, and the final checkpoint only after revealing my A-level semi-diplomatic visa status and berating the checkpoint supervisor for obstructing "official business." Inside the village, thousands of riot police, complete with helmet, face mask, and shield, stood in front of a trench bordered by a double layer of barbed wire surrounding rice fields.

Only a week earlier, anti-base activists had clashed with South Korean soldiers and riot police to block the expansion of Camp Humphreys, the future headquarters of United States Forces, Korea (USFK). The South Korean government had acquired the land through eminent domain by the end of 2005 but faced fierce resistance from activists and local residents. Wedded to their farmland, local residents had joined hands with South Korean nongovernmental organizations (NGOs) and activists in a national effort to stop the expansion of a U.S. base. On May 4–5, 2006, riot police used brute force to remove activists from the designated land expropriated for the base, bulldozing their headquarters and partitioning the expansion area with barbed wire. At the end of the violent melee, over one hundred protestors, police, and soldiers were injured, and 524 protestors were taken into custody.

Witnessing the violent clashes from a rooftop, South Korean National Assembly member Lim Jong-in noted the tragic irony of events: South Korean security forces battled fellow Korean citizens for control of land to be given to USFK as U.S. soldiers observed the drama outside from the safety of their base. Why did the South Korean government resort to coercion to remove activists?

For Seoul, the future of the U.S.–South Korean alliance rested on base expansion at Camp Humphreys in Pyeongtaek. Seoul and Washington had already signed an agreement to relocate USFK headquarters and the 2nd Infantry Division to the Pyeongtaek area. Thus, fearing further delays by local residents and activists, the government resorted to strategies of co-optation and coercion to destroy anti-base opposition.

If the movement episode in Daechuri were a single, isolated incident, the story of activists, alliances, and overseas military bases would likely have faded into the annals of activist lore and newspaper archives. However, similar anti-base movements have erupted in different parts of the world. In July 2009, Italian riot police blocked roads, fired tear gas, and scuffled with anti-base activists opposed to base expansion and the consolidation of the 173rd U.S. Airborne Brigade in Vicenza. Like the Pyeongtaek anti-base movement, the No Dal Molin campaign in Vicenza began as a local initiative, but with support from national and trans-national actors, it eventually erupted onto the national scene. During President Barack Obama's visit to Prague in March 2009, anti-base activists in the Czech Republic staged mass protests in objection to Washington's plan to build a radar base as part of a U.S. missile defense system for Europe. A month later, activists declared a tactical victory when the Czech government withdrew its proposal to ratify a U.S.-Czech agreement regarding the radar station, fearing its likely rejection in the lower house of the Czech Parliament.

Anti-base movement outcomes vary. On more than one occasion, anti-base activists were able to claim movement victory by shutting down U.S. bases. In other cases, movement episodes concluded with government forces quashing anti-base opposition. Still other episodes fizzled as a mixture of carrots and sticks presented by host governments split anti-base movements into different factions.

Why do some movements succeed whereas others fail? When and how do social movement actors abroad thwart the strategic basing preferences of the most powerful military in the world? In the wake of massive anti-base protests, how do host governments balance between domestic tension and international pressure from the United States on foreign policy issues? How do international security relations affect host-government responses to anti-base pressure? This book examines these questions in an effort to understand the impact of social movements on base politics and the important role bilateral alliance relationships play in shaping movement outcomes.

BASE POLITICS

Two Boards, Three Players

Base politics is analogous to a two-level board game with three players. The two boards are the domestic and international arenas. The three actors are the sending state, the receiving state, and the domestic constituents within the receiving state (or civil society).

The sending state projects power beyond its own territory by establishing bases overseas. The United States, Russia, Great Britain, France, and China are contemporary examples. With close to 900 overseas bases in 45 countries, the United States is by far the largest sending state. The receiving state hosts foreign military bases. In 2010, Afghanistan hosted over one hundred foreign bases as U.S.-led coalition forces battled Taliban insurgents to stabilize the country. Germany and Japan, two countries at peace, host the largest number of U.S. bases in the world, at 235 and 123 sites, respectively.[1] In addition to more well-known countries hosting U.S. bases, overseas bases exist in some of the most remote parts of the world, including Djibouti, Diego Garcia, Antigua, Tajikistan, and Greenland.

Civil society includes a diverse cross section of the host-state polity. Local communities, activists, and various interest groups have a stake in either keeping open or shutting down foreign bases. On the one hand, overseas bases provide public goods in the form of security or economic stability. Bases also provide jobs and boost the local economy. On the other hand, bases present externalities, such as noise or environmental pollution, crime, accidents, and prostitution. Some also view foreign military bases as the basis for violence and insecurity, and a violation of host-nation sovereignty. Often lacking formal government channels to address overseas U.S. base issues, civil societal actors resort to informal, contentious politics – including protests, social movements, and other forms of collective action – to influence basing policy decisions.[2]

The common assumption in international politics is that the rules of the game are determined by the first two players. After all, basing agreements are bilateral agreements signed between the sending and receiving states. Moreover, from a legal, diplomatic standpoint, foreign governments cannot negotiate basing agreements with members of civil society. Sending and receiving states may also prefer isolating civil societal actors from the base decision-making process. Given the sensitive nature of "high politics," government and military officials are often insulated from civil society when making decisions concerning national security.[3]

---

[1] United States Department of Defense, *Base Structure Report: A Summary of the Department of Defense's Real Property Inventory* (Washington, D.C.: Office of the Deputy Under-Secretary of Defense, 2009), 7.

[2] Civil societal actors in favor of U.S. bases, as part of the status quo, are often tied to the political establishment. Therefore, pro-base actors are likely to engage in base politics through formal channels. However, they are less prevalent and not as well organized. Driven by economic profit, they often mobilize in reaction to anti-base protests.

[3] Lawrence Jacobs and Benjamin Page, "Who Influences U.S. Foreign Policy?" *American Political Science Review* 99, no. 1 (2005): 107–23; and Stephen D. Krasner, *Defending the National Interest: Raw Materials Investments and U.S. Foreign Policy* (Princeton, N.J.: Princeton University Press, 1978), 11. Often, domestic security institutions particular to the state further isolate security policymakers from civil society. For instance, in South Korea, the National Security Laws, the institutionalization of the U.S.-ROK Combined Forces Command, and the subordinate role of the ROK military in the chain-of-command system limits the role civil society plays in security policy.

Yet, social movements,[4] as a subset of civil society, challenge several well-established assumptions underpinning dominant international relations paradigms. The nuclear freeze movement in the 1980s and the campaign to ban anti-personnel land mines in the 1990s are two of the better-known examples highlighting the impact domestic and transnational activists place on security issues.[5] Despite the autonomous nature of security policy decisionmaking, intense anti-base protests in different corners of the world have also produced a range of policy shifts and outcomes on military matters. Thus one might question whether security politics is really devoid of societal influence. Given certain political opportunities, social movements have the power to induce change in basing policy outcomes.[6] The assumption that civil society bears little impact on security politics needs to be reexamined.

Why Base Politics Matters

Grand Strategy and Alliances

Why should anyone care about U.S. military bases and anti-base movements? The network of overseas military bases is intimately linked to U.S. national security strategy. The presence of forward-deployed troops, equipment, and supplies, and the portfolio of bilateral arrangements permitting a global U.S. military presence, are not mere policy choices but an extension of strategy itself.[7] Overseas bases exist as "the skeleton upon which the flesh and muscle of operational capability will be molded."[8] More specifically, bases provide strategic deterrence, territorial control, logistics and transportation capabilities, and alliance support.[9] They facilitate communication, command, and control, and

---

[4] Social movements are defined as "sequences of contentious politics that are based on underlying social networks and resonant collective action frames, and which develop the capacity to maintain sustained challenges against powerful opponents." See Sidney G. Tarrow, *Power in Movement: Social Movements and Contentious Politics*, 2nd ed. (Cambridge: Cambridge University Press, 1998), 2.

[5] Thomas Rochon and David Meyer, eds., *Coalitions and Political Movements: The Lessons of the Nuclear Freeze* (Boulder, Colo.: Lynne Rienner, 1997); David Meyer, *A Winter of Discontent: The Nuclear Freeze and American Politics* (New York: Praeger, 1990); Richard Price, "Reversing the Gun Sights: Transnational Civil Society Targets Landmines," *International Organization* 52, no. 3 (1998): 613–44; and Matthew Evangelista, *Unarmed Forces: The Transnational Movement to End the Cold War* (Ithaca, N.Y.: Cornell University Press, 1999).

[6] Doug McAdam, "Political Opportunities: Conceptual Origins, Current Problems, Future Directions," in *Comparative Perspectives on Social Movements: Political Opportunities, Mobilizing Structures, and Cultural Framings*, edited by Doug McAdam, John D. McCarthy, and Mayer N. Zald (Cambridge: Cambridge University Press, 1996); and David Meyer and Debra Minkoff, "Conceptualizing Political Opportunity," *Social Forces* 82, no. 4 (2004): 1457–92; and Tarrow, *Power in Movement*.

[7] Overseas Basing Committee (OBC), *Interim Report of the Commission on Review of Overseas Military Facility Structure of the United States* (Arlington, Va.: Overseas Basing Committee, 2005), 4.

[8] Ibid.

[9] Kent E. Calder, *Embattled Garrisons: Comparative Base Politics and American Globalism* (Princeton, N.J.: Princeton University Press, 2007), 39; and Robert E. Harkavy, *Bases Abroad: The Global Foreign Military Presence* (New York: Oxford University Press, 1989), 17.

intelligence-gathering. Overseas bases are the physical units generating the basic structure of the U.S. global defense posture. However, global defense posture is more than the sum of U.S. bases and troops. It encompasses cooperation with key strategic partners who provide logistical and diplomatic support for forward-deployed troops. Therefore, an overhaul in global force posture reflects not only operational changes, such as greater flexibility and enhanced rapid-deployment capabilities, but an expanded role for alliance partners.[10]

This book speaks directly to the last category – the role of alliance partners. The global force posture of the United States both "presupposes and determines" the network of political relations forged between the United States and alliance partners.[11] The ability to build or share facilities, place troops, store munitions, or pre-position equipment implies a bilateral relationship between the host nation and the United States. Bases not only fulfill a military function; they represent a *political* arrangement with "bilateral, international, cultural, and economic consequences."[12] Unfortunately, U.S. strategic needs and the political realities presented by host-nation politics are not always congruent, resulting in bilateral and internal domestic friction. As Kent Calder argues, bases are "embattled garrisons": strategically important but politically vulnerable.[13]

Resistance and Blowback

For much of the Cold War era, U.S. allies provided diplomatic and logistical support to the United States in exchange for open markets, regime legitimacy, and security. Overseas military bases played a central part in this postwar global security bargain as states ceded a part of their sovereignty to the hegemonic patron. The system of alliances and bases critical to U.S. power projection was originally established to meet the exigencies of the Cold War. While old Cold War alliances have remained remarkably intact, changes in the international environment and the evolution of domestic politics in several countries have challenged the political bargain struck between host-nation polities and the United States.

Although global force posture requires security cooperation with allies through different legal arrangements, U.S. power projection, most visibly manifest in overseas bases, has heightened the domestic political sensitivity of U.S. military activity in several host nations. In Turkey, U.S. officials expressed frustration after Ankara's month-long vacillation and eventual denial of basing access for U.S. aircraft prior to the 2003 Iraq invasion. In the Czech Republic, peace activists in 2008 demanded a national referendum in hopes of blocking plans to construct a U.S. missile defense radar base on Czech soil. In Ecuador, anti-base activists applauded President Rafael Correa's pledge not to renew a

---

[10] Calder, *Embattled Garrisons*, 9.
[11] OBC, *Interim Report of the Commission on Review of Overseas Military Facility Structure of the United States*, 8.
[12] Ibid., 10.
[13] Calder, *Embattled Garrisons*, 9.

base agreement, denying the U.S. access to a key air base in the war on drugs. And on June 30, 2009, Iraqis declared a new holiday, National Sovereignty Day, to celebrate the withdrawal of U.S. combat troops from Iraqi cities.

An analysis of base politics sheds light on these issues while challenging two conventional understandings of world politics. First, the political contestation against U.S. military bases, played out in parliaments and the streets of host nations, blurs the distinction between high and low politics. Host nations and the United States must face different trade-offs between security, sovereignty, and social issues. Thus, overseas military bases, although used to project power, fight wars, house nuclear weapons, and maintain a global defense posture, are no longer just an issue of high politics in the twenty-first century. Second, overseas military bases constitute the most important form of extraterritoriality in the modern world of *sovereign* states. In the formative Cold War years, the breach in sovereignty remained relatively unproblematic. However, the recent surge of anti-base and anti-American protests, even among alliance partners, may be indicative of fundamental changes and resistance to a U.S.-led political order. If U.S. power projection rests on stable alliance relationships with host nations, a clear understanding of anti-base movements and their impact on security policy is imperative.

No other country maintains, or has ever maintained, a global military presence comparable to that of the United States. Yet outside the United States there is considerable dispute about what this presence is about and how well it serves national or global interests.[14] To some, the U.S. forward presence acts as an "offshore" balance that provides stability and security to different regions.[15] Others, however, question the necessity of maintaining such a vast network of bases and point out the potential "blowback" associated with U.S. military activity abroad.[16] Regardless of which side of the debate one falls on, policy-makers and the general public are too often unaware of the unintended consequences generated by overseas U.S. bases and the conflict that erupts between ordinary people and governments. Those generally supportive of U.S. global leadership indignantly wonder why protestors are shouting "Yankee go home!" These chants cannot simply be dismissed as a form of blanket anti-Americanism.[17] Behind each protest movement lies a narrative filled with politics and drama, and more poignantly, hope and despair. This story must also be told.

[14] I thank an anonymous reviewer at Cambridge University Press for this point.

[15] John J. Mearsheimer, *The Tragedy of Great Power Politics* (New York: Norton, 2001).

[16] See Chalmers A. Johnson, *Blowback: The Costs and Consequences of American Empire* (New York: Metropolitan Books, 2000); and Chalmers A. Johnson, *The Sorrows of Empire: Militarism, Secrecy, and the End of the Republic* (New York: Metropolitan Books, 2004).

[17] On anti-Americanism, see Giacomo Chiozza, *Anti-Americanism and the American World Order* (Baltimore: Johns Hopkins University Press, 2009); and Peter J. Katzenstein and Robert O. Keohane, *Anti-Americanisms in World Politics* (Ithaca, N.Y.: Cornell University Press, 2007).

A SECURITY CONSENSUS FRAMEWORK

Several recent volumes on base politics have already provided rich analyses on the subject.[18] Yet, to date, few studies have attempted to systematically explore base politics through the lens of social movements.[19] This lacuna partially stems from a lack of fit between questions germane to social movements and answers found at the level of international politics, and vice versa. Outside the transnational movement literature, there is a general lack of theoretically informed scholarship linking international relations with social movement approaches. The bias toward systemic international relations theorizing often marginalizes the roles civil society and social movements play in security politics. Likewise, social movement theories generally look inward at movement dynamics or domestic political structures, thereby neglecting important implications social movements may have on international relations.

Using case examples from the Philippines, Japan (Okinawa), Ecuador, Italy, and South Korea, I develop a theoretical framework explaining when and how anti-base movements matter and how host governments respond to activist pressure at the domestic and international levels. The framework takes on a novel, multidisciplinary approach by synthesizing various strands of international relations theory with social movement perspectives.

Within the context of U.S. alliance relations, I explore the process of interaction between host governments and anti-base movements that leads to varying base policy outcomes. Elite ideas or perceptions regarding the security relationship with the United States – what I refer to as the *security consensus* – play a key role in determining anti-base movement effectiveness and the type of response elicited by host governments when faced with anti-base opposition.

When host-government elites are ambivalent or divided over the role of bilateral security relations with the United States – a condition of "weak security consensus" – anti-base movements are more likely to impact base policy decisions. Under a weak security consensus, political elites remain unwedded to any particular ideas or beliefs about U.S. alliance relations, enabling activists to reframe the public debate regarding U.S. bases. By taking advantage of this political opportunity, anti-base activists "penetrate" the state and form ties

[18] Calder, *Embattled Garrisons*; Alexander Cooley, *Base Politics: Democratic Change and the U.S. Military Overseas* (Ithaca, N.Y.: Cornell University Press, 2008); Catherine Lutz, *The Bases of Empire: The Struggle against U.S. Military Posts* (New York: New York University Press, 2009); Sheila A. Smith, *Shifting Terrain: The Domestic Politics of U.S. Military Presence in Asia* (Honolulu: East-West Center, 2006); Robert E Harkavy, *Strategic Basing and the Great Powers, 1200–2000* (London: Routledge, 2007); and Michael O'Hanlon, *Unfinished Business: U.S. Overseas Military Presence in the 21st Century* (Washington, D.C.: Center for a New American Security, 2008).

[19] One notable exception is the volume by Lutz. However, the author focuses on the problem of U.S. bases and anti-base resistance rather than offering a comparative analysis examining the impact of anti-base movements on base politics. See Lutz, *Bases of Empire*.

with sympathetic elites, providing these elites with a domestic support base and greater political leverage at the domestic and international levels. Moreover, activists influence base policy outcomes by pressuring and altering the political calculations of elites who, in the absence of significant base opposition, would otherwise tolerate the status quo on basing issues. In short, a weak security consensus, coupled with effective movement mobilization strategies, leads to significant shifts in base policy outcomes.

Conversely, when a powerful collective consensus regarding security relations with the United States exists among domestic political elites, anti-base movements are unable to bring about major changes in basing policy outcomes. Dominant ideas and beliefs favoring positive relations with the United States permeate the foreign policy and security establishments, creating obstacles for anti-base voices. With a dominant consensus crowding out alternative ideas, activists find it difficult to gain elite access, form ties with political allies, or reframe the broader bases debate. Instead, political elites, in an effort to maintain positive alliance relations with the United States, employ various strategies and tactics to coerce, co-opt, and weaken anti-base movements. The government will unleash its own public media campaign, drag out negotiations with activists until the movement loses steam, or make minimal concessions to mitigate any potential crisis between the state and civil society. The confrontation between activists and government officials leads at best to token concessions amounting to marginal changes in basing policies and, at worst, movement defeat and the status quo. As a result, base policy outcomes are decided between the host government and the United States, with little influence from anti-base movements. Social movements therefore have little effect on base policy outcomes under conditions of a strong security consensus. Movements may use all the right frames, exhibit a high degree of cohesion, and rally hundreds of thousands of protestors in a broad coalition but still end up empty-handed.

In sum, I find that the level of security consensus among host-state political elites, particularly those within the foreign policy and security establishments, influences (1) how host states respond to domestic pressure against bases and (2) the relative success of anti-base movements in gaining significant concessions from the host state and the United States on base policy decisions. Thus, the degree of security consensus shapes or constrains the strategies employed by movement and government actors, thereby affecting policy outcomes.

ALTERNATIVE EXPLANATIONS

By synthesizing social movement analysis and international relations theory into a single framework, the arguments in this book differ from standard variants of realism, liberalism, or constructivism found in international relations theory, or from social movement explanations offered by sociologists. But what advantages does the security consensus framework have over existing accounts of base politics? Are there alternative explanations that challenge or refute the arguments offered here?

Power and interest-based arguments offer the simplest and most appealing account for base politics. Rooted in the realist perspective of international relations, U.S. geopolitical interests largely determine basing policy outcomes. Focusing on strategic objectives and the distribution of power in the international system, realists explain the closure of bases as a result of declining threats or a shift in the strategic environment. Social movements, for the most part, are irrelevant.

In many instances, power-based theories are correct, and I certainly do not ignore the role of power. Nor are realist explanations entirely antithetical to my own argument. My theoretical framework draws from realist insights that take into account domestic factors and the role of perceptions.[20] If an elite security consensus is partially based on threat perceptions, we could address "balance of threat" within the security consensus framework.[21] Differences in the distribution of material capabilities would lead to higher or lower threat perceptions. Under low threat perceptions, the host government may feel ambivalent about its security relationship with the United States, enabling activists to form ties with elites in bringing down U.S. bases.

However, an understanding of an elite security consensus focused solely on threat perceptions is misleading at best, and in some cases inaccurate. Taking a more eclectic approach, I argue that an elite consensus is shaped not only by material-based threat perceptions but by existing ideology, norms, and institutions. More importantly, power-based theories, particularly the systemic variant, do not provide the proper theoretical tools to assess the role of social movements in cases where they seemed to make a difference in base politics. Civil societal actors are simply ignored. Even statist realists, when acknowledging civil societal pressure, will treat social movements as a domestic interest group without revealing interactive effects between mobilization strategies and other international relations variables such as alliances.

Moving past power-based explanations, more recent studies in base politics have treated the tension, dilemma, and conflict faced by both the United States and host-nation actors with greater nuance. In these studies, regime type appears as an important variable explaining base politics.[22] For instance, Alexander Cooley contends that the stability of basing agreements, and hence base policy outcomes, is shaped by the contractual environment (i.e., the credibility of

---

[20] See, for example, Jack L. Snyder, *Myths of Empire: Domestic Politics and International Ambition* (Ithaca, N.Y.: Cornell University Press, 1991); Randall L Schweller, *Unanswered Threats: Political Constraints on the Balance of Power* (Princeton, N.J.: Princeton University Press, 2006); William Wohlforth, *The Elusive Balance: Power and Perceptions During the Cold War* (Ithaca, N.Y.: Cornell University Press, 1993); Thomas J. Christensen, *Useful Adversaries: Grand Strategy, Domestic Mobilization, and Sino-American Conflict, 1947–1958* (Princeton, N.J.: Princeton University Press, 1996); and Thomas Christensen, "Perceptions and Alliances in Europe: 1865–1940," *International Organization* 51, no. 1 (1997): 65–97.

[21] Stephen Walt, *The Origins of Alliances* (Ithaca, N.Y.: Cornell University Press, 1987).

[22] Calder, *Embattled Garrisons*; Cooley, *Base Politics*; and Alexander Cooley, "Base Politics," *Foreign Affairs* 84, no. 6 (2005): 79–92.

democratic institutions) and the host regime's level of political dependence on U.S. bases. Cooley finds that basing agreements are most stable under consolidated democracies. Overseas bases are less contested in solidly democratic countries where credible political institutions legitimize bilateral basing agreements.[23] However, when host governments are relatively independent from U.S. security arrangements and transitioning from an autocratic to a democratic regime – conditions where the contractual environment is most unstable – U.S. bases become much more politicized. We expect to find greater anti-base activity and the possibility of major base policy shifts during democratization.

Although regime type explanations offer a compelling account of base politics, they deemphasize the role of bilateral security alliances when accounting for basing outcomes.[24] Host-government elites, particularly those operating under a strong security consensus, are under constant pressure to maintain positive alliance relations as they attempt to address domestic criticism against bases. A focus on regime type skirts this important dilemma faced by host governments, one where elites are tied to international obligations but challenged from below by civil societal actors. How this dilemma is resolved requires closer investigation of both bilateral security relations and social movements.

To counter regime type explanations, I must demonstrate that the security consensus affects elite response to domestic base opposition irrespective of regime type. For example, under conditions of strong security consensus, regardless of regime type or orientation, anti-base movements should remain ineffective, with basing policies remaining relatively unchanged.[25] For the security consensus framework to hold up against Cooley's argument, the empirical cases need to demonstrate that major domestic opposition to bases and base policy changes were determined by anti-base movement pressure under conditions of weak security consensus rather than weak domestic political institutions. Conversely, the stability of base agreements should derive from the security consensus rather than the contractual credibility of political institutions under democracies. While recognizing that both approaches have something unique to offer in the analysis of base politics, I contend that, on the whole, the security consensus subsumes regime type explanations.[26] I return to this point in the concluding chapter.

---

[23] Cooley, *Base Politics*, 15.

[24] Ibid., 9; and Calder, *Embattled Garrisons*, 69–70.

[25] As I will argue, anti-base movements are largely a post-democratization phenomenon, making this argument harder to test. Movement episodes in Ecuador and Italy in Chapter 4, however, help clarify this issue.

[26] Rather than pitting regime type and security consensus as competing arguments, some scholars may find it more constructive to explore parallels and avenues for synthesis. Regime type may actually help inform whether a security consensus exists among host-government elites. For instance, one might argue ceteris paribus that the security consensus shared by host-state elites appears stronger in autocratic rather than democratic regimes given the decentralized domestic structure of democracies. As the following chapters demonstrate, many of the predictions found in the regime type analysis of base politics correspond with my own theoretical framework. However, the mechanisms that explain or predict base policy outcomes differ.

Following this introductory chapter, Chapter 1 outlines the theory and methods used to advance the book's argument. Chapter 2 focuses on the interaction between anti-base movements and the host government under conditions of weak security consensus. The primary case in this chapter is the 1990–91 Anti-Treaty Movement (ATM) against Subic Bay Naval Station in the Philippines. Conversely, Chapter 3 examines base politics under strong levels of security consensus, illustrated by Okinawan anti-base movements. Chapter 4 extends the application of my theory to Europe and Latin America. Using two contrasting cases, I investigate recent anti-base movements in Manta, Ecuador and Vicenza, Italy. Chapter 5 tests the security consensus framework in South Korea. I examine how the Pyeongtaek anti-base movement episode resulted in a status quo outcome under a resilient security consensus. Chapter 6 explores in greater depth how variation in the security consensus over time altered movement and government strategies and subsequent policy outcomes. Through a paired comparison between the Philippines and Japan, I illustrate how the reemergence of a security consensus in the mid- to late 1990s weakened the impact of Philippine protests against the U.S. military presence. I also discuss more recent trends concerning anti-base movements in Okinawa. Finally, Chapter 7 summarizes the findings presented in the book. I also evaluate the security consensus framework by discussing competing explanations in the base politics literature, highlighting both points of tension and areas of complement. I conclude by providing insights for anti-base activists and drawing lessons for policymakers on basing strategy in the post-9/11 period.

I

Anti-Base Movements and the Security Consensus Framework

A vigil, sit-in, demonstration, or protest is taking place outside a U.S. base somewhere around the world at this very moment. Do these pockets of protest, varying in size, shape, and form, make any difference in base politics? When and how do anti-base movements matter? How do host governments react to anti-base opposition with U.S. security relations at stake?

Unfortunately, existing theories of international relations are ill equipped to help us understand when and how anti-base movements matter. Nor do they help us accurately predict the type of response produced by host states when balancing between international and domestic forces. For instance, a realist approach to base politics contends that, regardless of domestic opposition, bases are likely to endure if national security interests are at stake. But empirical examples – most notably the closure of the strategically important Subic Bay Naval Station in 1991 – pose significant problems for realism. Commonly explored concepts in international relations, such as the balance of power, threat perceptions, or alliance relations, certainly shape basing policy decisions. However, an analysis of overseas bases at the systemic level fails to capture the dynamics of base politics played across two boards (the domestic and international levels) with three players (the United States, host government, and civil society).

Whereas international relations perspectives privilege systemic-level factors, social movement scholars tend to focus on domestic political structures, or mobilization resources and strategies found within movements.[1] Favorable circumstances, such as the presence of sympathetic political allies or a dramatic crisis that grabs media attention, provide movements with greater opportunities for successful mobilization and movement outcomes. Basing policy concessions might be explained by strong movements mobilized through powerful frames and sustained by pooling large amounts of political and material resources to

[1] John McCarthy and Mayer N. Zald, "Resource Mobilization and Social Movements: A Partial Theory," *American Journal of Sociology* 82, no. 6 (1977): 1212–41; Meyer and Minkoff, "Conceptualizing Political Opportunity"; and Tarrow, *Power in Movement*.

challenge host governments and the U.S. military. Conversely, those movements suffering from internal problems and divisions may suggest that failed anti-base movements were simply too weak to ever influence U.S. basing policies.

However, successful mobilization does not sufficiently lead to successful outcomes or, in this case, major changes to U.S. basing policy. Movements may rally hundreds of thousands of protestors, use all the right frames, remain relatively united, and even find allies inside the government. However, movements must still sway political elites who not only contend with domestic opposition but also take stock of national security issues and existing international alliance obligations. If the key to anti-base movement success lies with the vitality of movements, then we should find elite support for U.S. bases wavering in the wake of domestic pressure and a greater degree of anti-base movement success. Yet this has not been the case across several movement episodes in Europe or Asia. Successful mobilization is obviously a necessary component of any successful anti-base outcome. However, social movement factors must work in conjunction with other structures in the international environment.

Addressing a gap in the study of base politics and anti-base movements, I draw on two different sets of literature rarely examined together in a single theoretical framework. For social movement scholars who tend to focus on domestic political structures, the security consensus framework I offer suggests that international factors, such as bilateral alliances, shape or constrain movements. For international relations scholars, my theoretical framework highlights the role of social movements in world politics, a group often undertheorized in the literature.[2] I do not naively suggest that civil society always matters in security politics. However, anti-base movements on several occasions have extracted concessions from powerful states. Such empirical puzzles warrant a study on the role of anti-base movements in the politics of bases.

SECURITY CONSENSUS FRAMEWORK

The security consensus framework I present provides a theoretical frame outlining the conditions in which we expect social movement success (or failure) in changing overseas basing policies. In brief, anti-base movement effectiveness and host-government response to anti-base pressure are largely shaped by domestic elites' ideas and perceptions about U.S.–host-state relations. More concretely, government response and social movement outcomes vary based on the degree of elite consensus regarding bilateral security ties to the United States.

I explore base politics in two stages. First, I examine structural factors – the elite security consensus built around bilateral alliances. I then move toward agency, evaluating how structural conditions shape patterns of interaction between government and anti-base movement actors. For anti-base movements

---

[2] But see Richard Price, "Transnational Civil Society and Advocacy in World Politics," *World Politics* 55, no. 4 (2003): 579–606; and David Meyer, "Political Opportunity and Nested Institutions," *Social Movement Studies* 2, no. 1 (2003): 17–35.

to have any influence on basing policy outcomes, activists must take advantage of an open political window – in this case, a weak security consensus. Activists must jump through the open window by forming selective ties with elites to gain leverage in basing policy decisions. As Bear Braumoeller argues when investigating multiple paths of nonoccurrence of policy change, either a closed window (a strong security consensus) or the inability of activists to jump through an open window (mobilize and form ties with sympathetic elites) precludes any major change in base policy outcomes.[3]

Defining the Security Consensus

I define *security consensus* as the shared perception and intersubjective understanding of the concept of national security held by host-government elites.[4] For the purpose of my argument, "security consensus" is construed more narrowly as a pro-U.S. security consensus based on the shared perception and understanding of U.S.–host-state relations among national elites. For example, do political elites agree that U.S. alliance relations function as an integral component of their national security strategy? Do host-government elites value a long-term strategic partnership with the United States? As a corollary, states characterized by a high degree of security consensus tend to accept the hosting of U.S. military bases as an important component of their relationship with the United States.

Although all national elites may hold particular beliefs about U.S.–host-state relations, the relevant "holders" of the security consensus are government or political elites within the foreign policy or national security establishments.[5] These elites include heads of state or government such as the president or the prime minister; cabinet officials with a stake in foreign relations; bureaucrats in relevant agencies, such as those in the ministries of foreign affairs or defense; and government advisors, such as members of the national security council. Elites also include politicians and lawmakers, especially in cases where parliament ratifies the budget that appropriates funds for U.S. bases or the basing agreement itself. Opposition politicians who occasionally make their way into the foreign policy establishment may also be considered as legitimate holders of the security consensus.

As I elaborate on the concept of a security consensus, three important points are worth keeping in mind. First, the security consensus is an ideational rather

---

[3] Bear Braumoeller, "Causal Complexity and the Study of Politics," *Political Analysis* 11, no. 3 (2003), 212.

[4] In a similar vein, Randall Schweller introduces an "elite consensus" variable when examining balancing behavior among states. He describes elite consensus as "a measure of the similarity of elites' preferences over outcomes and their beliefs about the preferences and anticipated actions of others." See Schweller, *Unanswered Threats*, 48–49.

[5] I define "foreign policy and national security establishment" as a broad set of political elites capable of influencing foreign policy and national security decisions.

than material concept.[6] Second, the security consensus is intersubjective in nature. Third, although it is important to understand how a security consensus arises, the theoretical framework I present is more concerned with evaluating the strength (or weakness) of the consensus rather than its origins.[7] Nevertheless, I provide a brief overview outlining the basic foundations of the security consensus.

The security consensus is partially a function of alliance relations. Therefore, the security consensus is associated with many of the same factors that lead to security alliances. Threat perceptions play a central role in shaping bilateral alliances. Threat perception itself is based on the material capabilities of adversaries.[8] It is also rooted in identity and ideological differences.[9]

Likewise, an elite security consensus is shaped by both material-based threat capabilities such as the distribution of power at the global level and nonmaterial factors such as identity at the domestic level. Figure 1.1 illustrates several factors that help form and perpetuate an elite consensus supporting the U.S. alliance and U.S. bases.

Internal factors, including domestic ideology, institutions, and historical legacies, that reify or magnify threat perceptions inform an elite consensus. For example, regarding ideology, Mark Haas writes, "Ideological variables shape leaders' understandings of the security environment in which they operate, in terms of which states constitute the greatest threats to leaders' key interests and the level of this perceived threat."[10] In addition to their intervening effect, these internal domestic factors also directly shape or sustain the security consensus. Once formed, the security consensus profoundly affects the domestic and foreign policy choices of elites.

---

[6] The following works were particularly useful when thinking about "security consensus" as an ideational variable: Judith Goldstein and Robert O. Keohane, *Ideas and Foreign Policy: Beliefs, Institutions, and Political Change* (Ithaca, N.Y.: Cornell University Press, 1993); Jeffrey Legro, *Rethinking the World: Great Power Strategies and International Order* (Ithaca, N.Y.: Cornell University Press, 2005); Mark L. Haas, *The Ideological Origins of Great Power Politics, 1789–1989* (Ithaca, N.Y.: Cornell University Press, 2005); Albert Yee, "The Causal Effects of Ideas on Policies," *International Organization* 50, no. 1 (1996): 69–108; and Sheri Berman, *The Social Democratic Moment: Ideas and Politics in the Making of Interwar Europe* (Cambridge, Mass.: Harvard University Press, 1998).

[7] In other words, the security consensus is treated as an independent rather than dependent variable throughout the book. The formation of an elite security consensus in specific countries is discussed in greater detail in the empirical chapters and Chapter 6.

[8] Walt, *Origins of Alliances*; and Patricia A. Weitsman, *Dangerous Alliances: Proponents of Peace, Weapons of War* (Stanford, Calif.: Stanford University Press, 2004).

[9] Michael Barnett, "Identity and Alliances in the Middle East," in *The Culture of National Security: Norms and Identity in World Politics*, edited by Peter J. Katzenstein (New York: Columbia University Press, 1996), 413. For ideological differences and threat perception, see Haas, *Ideological Origins of Great Power Politics*. For identity and threat construction, see Jutta Weldes, "Constructing National Interests," *European Journal of International Relations* 2, no. 3 (1996): 275–318; and Alexander Wendt, *Social Theory of International Politics* (Cambridge: Cambridge University Press, 1999), Chap. 6.

[10] Haas, *Ideological Origins of Great Power Politics*, 2.

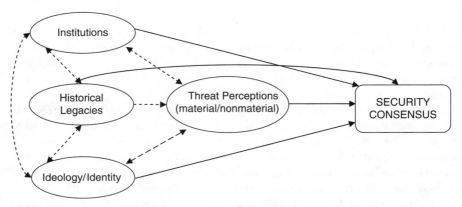

FIGURE 1.1. Subfactors Leading to the Security Consensus.

In studying elite consensus, I am interested in collective rather than individual perceptions and beliefs.[11] This is not to argue that perceptions of individuals are unimportant or unrelated to group ideas. However, as Jeffrey Legro notes, "Dominant ideas are often embedded in public discourse and symbols that also represent intersubjective phenomena that attach to group, not individual, orientation."[12] The security consensus functions as a "dominant idea" precisely because it is held by the majority of key elites within the state. A consensus identifying particular threats, and favoring strong ties to the United States as an appropriate response, may reify over time through processes of institutionalization.[13] Furthermore, powerful actors or groups, either within or outside the foreign policy and national security establishments, may develop vested interests in maintaining the security consensus. The interests of powerful elites may become embedded in the institutionalization process.

Alternative ideas to national security that are less reliant on the U.S. alliance and its basing network may certainly coexist within the polity. However, political, institutional, and normative forces perpetuating a powerful consensus will often drown out these alternative security views at the policy decisionmaking level. Even if numerous individuals hold ideas contrary to the consensus, the "collective orthodoxy" may still prevail, shaping state responses.[14] This is particularly true if ideas, values, and beliefs central to the consensus are wrapped within legal and institutional frameworks. For example, the North Atlantic Treaty Organization (NATO) and the U.S.-Japan Mutual Defense Treaty play an important role in sustaining elite perceptions and beliefs about the U.S.

[11] Legro's discussion of collective ideas in international relations is particularly instructive. See Legro, *Rethinking the World*, 4–7. Also see Wendt, *Social Theory of International Politics*, 150–64.

[12] Legro, *Rethinking the World*, 5.

[13] On the impact of institutionalized ideas, see Kathryn Sikkink, *Ideas and Institutions: Developmentalism in Brazil and Argentina* (Ithaca, N.Y.: Cornell University Press, 1991).

[14] Legro, *Rethinking the World*, 26.

alliance in Italian or Japanese defense policy, respectively. This is not to argue that the security consensus never changes over time, an issue raised in Chapter 6. However, the intersubjective nature of the security consensus, shared across a group of powerful elites, gives the concept an inherent "stickiness."

In sum, the elite security consensus, although often derived from external threats in the international system, is also driven by internal factors. Moreover, the intersubjective nature of the security consensus implies that material and ideational variables often interact as actors interpret their security environment.[15] For instance, ideology or historical legacies may reinforce or heighten existing threat perceptions. These perceptions may persist long after material threat capabilities subside. Furthermore, external threat perceptions may strengthen over time, constructing particular identities between actors. For example, in South Korea, the reproduction of identities based on hostile interaction with North Korea, and the security dependence formed after the Korean War between South Korea and the United States, bear significant influence today on South Korean security policy and the U.S.-ROK alliance. Japan's defeat in World War II and its renouncement of the use of force in settling global disputes has also significantly shaped Japanese security policy. Reliance on the U.S security umbrella and its existing network of bases has become an accepted part of Japanese national security.

The concept of security consensus may strike readers as a bit unsettling; it acts as a catch-all variable, encompassing everything from threat perceptions, to domestic institutions, to identity and norms. As argued earlier, however, my theoretical framework only needs to demonstrate whether a strong or weak consensus exists among host-government elites. Moreover, what constitutes a consensus will undoubtedly vary within the specific context of each country and the historical trajectory of U.S.–host-state relations. For example, the role of norms and domestic institutions will be much more pronounced in Japan, whereas the dominance of internal over external security concerns in the Philippines will play prominently in Philippine elites' understanding of their security alliance with the United States. Later in this chapter, I explain how I measure and code the security consensus.

Anti-Base Movement Mobilization

Before explaining how the security consensus relates to social movement outcomes, I briefly turn our discussion to overseas anti-base movements. I borrow

---

[15] If nonmaterial and ideational factors play such a large role, one might wonder why I choose to focus narrowly on host-government elites while ignoring mass perceptions of national security. After all, if the security consensus is based on shared intersubjective understandings, mass public opinion should also factor into the security consensus. To a certain degree, mass perceptions are reflected in the policy preferences of political elites and vice versa. Thus a common consensus regarding national security issues will often pervade both elites and the masses, particularly in a democratic polity. For the purposes of the book, however, I privilege an elite security consensus because it is elites who make and ultimately implement national security decisions.

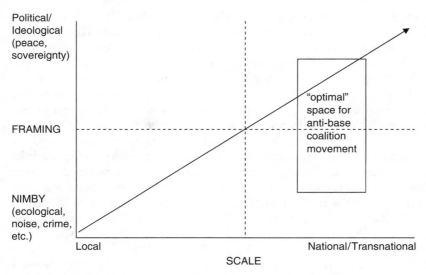

FIGURE 1.2. Typology and Trajectory of Anti-Base Movements.

extensively from the political process model in the social movement literature to explain mobilization patterns.[16] This school of thought contends that the political context surrounding movement mobilization significantly impacts movement development and outcomes. In particular, open political systems, divisions among elites, the presence of elite allies, and reduced state repression all help facilitate social movements.[17] Often referred to as political opportunity structure (POS), these exogenous factors enhance or constrain a movement's ability to mobilize, advance particular claims, build alliances, use certain strategies and tactics, and influence policy.[18] It is important to note, however, that POS does not completely determine outcomes. Other factors, particularly the role of movement actors, must be calculated into the equation. Thus, POS functions as a variable that "influences the choice of protest strategies and the impact of social movements on their environments."[19]

Anti-base movements are comprised of NGOs, grassroots actors, local residents, and civic groups protesting against bases because of various claims of injustices. As Figure 1.2 suggests, various types and levels of anti-base

[16] Tarrow, *Power in Movement*; Marco Giugni, Doug McAdam, and Charles Tilly, *How Social Movements Matter* (Minneapolis: University of Minnesota Press, 1999); and McAdam, McCarthy, and Zald, *Comparative Perspectives on Social Movement*.

[17] McAdam, "Political Opportunities."

[18] David Meyer, "Protest and Political Opportunities," *Annual Review of Sociology* 30 (2004): 125–45 at 125–26.

[19] Herbert Kitschelt, "Political Opportunity Structures and Political Protest: Anti-Nuclear Movements in Four Democracies," *British Journal of Political Science* 16, no. 1 (1986): 57–85 at 58.

activism exist.[20] Some anti-base movements operate primarily at the local level as a simple NIMBY protest. Military bases generate negative externalities such as noise pollution, environmental degradation, crime, safety hazards, and the growth of bars and brothels, which exploit women. Grievances run aplenty. Schoolchildren pause for ten minutes as jets roar by schoolhouses. Misguided bombs damage private property. Chemicals are dumped into nearby waters. Women are raped. Taxicab drivers are beaten. Farmers are evicted from fertile lands.

The lack of formal channels for addressing grievances related to U.S. or other foreign bases often leads to contentious forms of political action. At the local level, the framing of anti-base grievances remains central to coordinated action. The collective action frame will vary depending on the particular grievance caused by the presence of a specific military base. Whether the issues deal with the environment, crime, or disputes over property rights, an underlying commonality in the framing of anti-base contention is the notion of injustice.[21]

Although many anti-base movements begin at the local level, successful campaigns are generally shaped into broader coalition movements at the national or transnational level. "Movement brokers" with ties to actors at different levels of contention help facilitate a process of "scale shift," leading to an increase in the "number and level of coordinated contentious actions to a different focal point."[22] As anti-base movements shift from the local to the national level, movement leaders introduce new frames or modify existing ones to capture a wider audience. Moving beyond simple NIMBY grievances, these frames often resonate at a higher level of abstraction. Activists adopt frames evoking claims of sovereignty, peace, or national respect, which have the potential effect of arousing nationalist sentiment. The arrow in Figure 1.2 represents the typical trajectory of anti-base movements. Different movement sectors, such as peace groups, labor unions, environmental groups, student unions, farmers, religious groups, or women's groups, usually coalesce under a common, albeit loose, umbrella coalition against foreign bases.

The union between local and national or transnational anti-base actors is a strategic decision. By forming ties with a broad range of activists and NGOs at the national level, local anti-base actors increase the size and scope of their struggle. "Outside" activists provide moral and logistical support, mobilize additional actors into the anti-base cause, and draw greater media attention, vaulting local anti-base movements onto the national radar screen. Conversely, by latching onto an issue such as foreign military bases, NGOs and civic groups

[20] For an alternative typology of anti-base protests, see Calder, *Embattled Garrisons*, 84. Calder identifies three varieties of anti-base protests based on actors' motives: ideological, nationalistic, and pragmatic.

[21] Andrew Yeo, "Not in Anyone's Backyard: The Emergence and Identity of a Transnational Anti-Base Network," *International Studies Quarterly* 53, no. 3 (2009): 571–94.

[22] Doug McAdam, Sidney Tarrow, and Charles Tilly, *Dynamics of Contention* (Cambridge: Cambridge University Press, 2001), 331; and Sidney G. Tarrow, *The New Transnational Activism* (Cambridge: Cambridge University Press, 2005).

initially outside the anti-base fold draw on a powerful, tangible symbol associated with their own cause. For example, peace activists identify military bases as instruments of war and imperialism. Supporting local anti-base struggles or joining a broad anti-base coalition provides anti-war groups with another means of promoting their group's particular agenda, with the added advantage of a direct target around which to organize protests. Likewise, environmental groups pushing for more stringent standards or environmental cleanup after base closures join anti-base coalitions to advocate their agenda while supporting local anti-base initiatives.

The formation of a broad anti-base coalition between local and national or transnational actors is generally advantageous to anti-base movements. However, the increase in scope and size of the movement may come at the expense of movement unity. Multiple agendas and different ideas about strategy and tactics create internal tension within movements. Also, local residents more concerned with NIMBY issues may eventually grow wary of "outside" groups with hidden political agendas. Successful mobilization thus entails forming a broad-based coalition across different sectors at the local and national levels.[23] However, it requires movement leaders to incorporate broader frames and expand at the national level without neglecting the local origins of anti-base movements.[24] The "optimal" space for anti-base movement mobilization is represented by the rectangular box in Figure 1.2.

Are overseas foreign anti-base movements distinct from domestic anti-base movements within the United States? Although domestic and foreign anti-U.S. base movements may appear to follow similar mobilization patterns at first blush, particularly if they take on largely NIMBY characteristics, overseas anti-base movements are qualitatively different from domestic ones for four reasons.[25] The most obvious distinction is the absence of the international game board in domestic anti-base protests. Second, the deck is stacked more heavily against foreign anti-base actors because they must contend with both the host government and the strategic preferences of the United States. Third, unlike domestic anti-base actors represented by congressional leaders with direct access to Washington, foreign anti-base actors are thousands of miles away with no direct mechanism to influence U.S. basing policy. There is no reason to assume congressional representatives will actually support local anti-base interests, but the larger point to make is that there is greater access to formal channels of anti-base opposition for domestic movements compared with foreign anti-base movements. Overseas anti-base actors, on the other hand, primarily target

---

[23] This does not mean that broad-based coalitions are not without their own problems, such as factionalism between organizations or across different sectors. Some of this tension is highlighted in the empirical chapters.

[24] Andrew Yeo, "Local National Dynamics and Framing in South Korean Anti-Base Movements," *Kasarinlan* 21, no. 2 (2006): 34–69; and Herbert Docena, "Plenary Panel Four Presentation: How Do We Strengthen the International Network for the Abolition of Foreign Military Bases?" Quito, 2007.

[25] I refer to U.S. bases here, but the same logic may be applied to French or British bases as well.

their own host governments. Finally, with the exception of anti-base protests in Hawaii (or U.S. territories such as Puerto Rico or Guam), the collective action frames adopted by domestic anti-base movements do not rely on the same powerful sovereignty claims present in virtually all overseas anti-base movements.

The Security Consensus as a Political Opportunity Structure

How do anti-base movements "penetrate" the state, particularly on issues concerning national security policy? I highlight two key insights borrowed from previous research in the social movements and transnational relations literature: domestic structure and elite access. First, civil society is more likely to gain access to elites under open domestic structures such as those found in democracies.[26] Second, anti-base movements must gain access to elites if they are to play a direct role in base policy outcomes – certainly no easy feat given the strong capacities of states to control national security policy.

Proponents of the political opportunity model view opportunities and state–society interaction from the perspective of social movement actors. For example, Herbert Kitschelt observes that regime openness and state capacity affect the strategy and overall effectiveness of social movements.[27] From the vantage point of states, however, the domestic structures that translate into political opportunities for social movements function as the same institutional tools that provide states with the autonomy and strong capacity necessary to stave off social movement pressure.

Political scientists coming from the statist tradition point to institutional features of state agencies that make states more or less prone to societal pressure.[28] State autonomy and capacity are underpinned by factors such as stable administrative–military control of territory, loyal and skilled bureaucrats, a large treasury, and strong institutions.[29] Rather than focusing on institutional structures, however, I point to *ideational features* that enable key state actors to remain autonomous in the national security policymaking process. In particular, prevailing perceptions and ideology that underpin the security consensus among

---

[26] Kitschelt, "Political Opportunity Structures and Political Protest," 68. Although social movement theorists tend to see open political structures as favorable to social movement outcomes, this is not always the case. As Matthew Evangelista has demonstrated, transnational actors working under open, decentralized political environments, although able to gain elite access, are actually less effective in implementing policy because of the numerous competing voices in a more open system. See Evangelista, *Unarmed Forces.*

[27] Evangelista, *Unarmed Forces,* 64.

[28] Snyder, *Myths of Empire*; Margaret E. Keck and Kathryn Sikkink, *Activists Beyond Borders: Advocacy Networks in International Politics* (Ithaca, N.Y.: Cornell University Press, 1998); and Theda Skocpol, "Bringing the State Back In: Strategies of Analysis in Current Research," in *Bringing the State Back In,* edited by Peter B. Evans, Dietrich Rueschemeyer, and Theda Skocpol (Cambridge: Cambridge University Press, 1985), 16.

[29] Skocpol, "Bringing the State Back In," 16.

host-government elites prevent societal actors from penetrating the state and finding common allies with sympathetic elites.[30] In addition to institutional features, ideological structures enable the state to remain insulated when making important national security decisions, including those pertaining to the U.S. alliance.

The security consensus framework emphasizes that shared perceptions, beliefs, and ideas that promote the U.S.–host-state alliance lead political elites to reject activist demands, ultimately undermining anti-base movement mobilization. However, a weak security consensus, characterized by elite divisions and ambivalence regarding U.S.–host-state relations, enables activists to exert greater influence on government elites over basing policy decisions. In short, the security consensus operates as a political opportunity, constraining or facilitating movement effectiveness on base policy outcomes.

Those expecting to read more about anti-base movement activists may find themselves sorely disappointed with this overwhelmingly structural account thus far. Where is agency? Although the proposed theoretical framework hinges on the security consensus, I steer away from making any *direct* causal claim between an elite security consensus and policy outcomes.[31] Rather than determining outcomes, the security consensus delineates the boundaries of interaction between state and society. In other words, the consensus influences how political elites interpret and react to anti-base pressure. The core of my argument captures the dynamic relations between movement and government actors within the limits of the security consensus.

Where I argue that social movements do matter, anti-base movements make a difference not only because of favorable opportunity structures (a weak security consensus permitting elite access) but because they employ powerful framing strategies, take advantage of mobilization structures and networks, use effective and creative tactics, and form ties with elite allies. Thus, a weak security consensus does not guarantee that anti-base pressure will translate into real policy changes. Activists must actually *take advantage* of favorable political opportunities. And even though anti-base movements are relatively ineffective under a strong security consensus, the development of movement strategies and government counterstrategies shaped by the consensus produces a riveting account of base politics. The take home point is that structure and agency interact to produce particular outcomes. As I demonstrate with each movement episode, the most exciting story of anti-base movements is woven into the

---

[30] The logic here is reminiscent of Jack Snyder's *Myths of Empire*, where he discusses the ability of narrow interest groups with imperial ambitions to penetrate the state. A strong state is capable of ignoring the pressure of domestic groups with vested interests in promoting imperial expansion. See Snyder, *Myths of Empire*, 40.

[31] On this point, see Goldstein and Keohane, *Ideas and Foreign Policy*, 11; and Yee, "Causal Effects of Ideas on Politics," 71. Both scholars note the "egregious error" made by scholars working on ideas in international relations who purport that a direct causal link exists.

patterns of interaction between government and activists, shaped by the security consensus.

As a final word before proceeding with the specific causal mechanisms of my argument, the link bridging social movement analysis with international relations theory is the concept of political opportunity structure (POS). By conceptualizing elite ideas and perceptions of bilateral alliances as a POS, a framework for studying the impact of social movements in international relations becomes possible. The result is an approach to base politics that differs from current power or regime-based explanations.

The fusion of social movement analysis with international relations theory is not without its own set of problems, however. As I discuss later, any research design that attempts to adequately address issues from both disciplines must maneuver between the level of movement episodes and the level of states.[32] Furthermore, scholars grounded in the social movement literature may argue that my concept of POS, focused solely on the security consensus, is too limiting. Instead, social movement scholars would interpret a national elite consensus as only one aspect of a broader set of POSs within the entire institutional system.[33] Therefore, other "political opportunities," such as local elite relations, public opinion, the stability of political alignments, or a decline in the state's repressive capacity, may also affect base policy outcomes. Finally, from the standpoint of international relations, scholars accustomed to macro-level theorizing may find the security consensus framework banal, focusing too narrowly on one aspect of base politics. Why bother with social movements if power or political-economic arguments explain the majority of base politics?

In the empirical chapters, I take into consideration cross-discipline challenges, exploring base politics from both the level of movement episodes and the level of states. This analytical move inevitably shifts us away from the lofty goal of parsimony, which international relations scholars often prize. By disaggregating to the level of movement episodes, however, I propose a much richer, complex narrative of base politics. At the same time, a "statist" account of the security consensus framework and cross-national comparisons of anti-base movements are still possible. After all, anti-base movement episodes are still embedded within national contexts.

---

[32] The tension between state- and movement-level analysis also stems from the two empirical questions driving my argument – one focused on social movements, the other on the role of the state.

[33] See McAdam, "Political Opportunities," 27. The security consensus functions as a political opportunity structure (POS) at the national level. Although POS scholars tend to examine the entire institutional system (i.e., institutional structures at the local, regional, and national levels) to determine the degree of closure or openness, I part ways with traditional notions of POS by limiting my discussion of open or closed structures to the national elite level. Although this may raise valid criticisms from the social movement crowd, it is the state that acts as the common denominator in the security consensus framework, allowing me to link social movement analysis with the international relations literature.

Specifying the Security Consensus Framework

The following section provides a more nuanced discussion of the theoretical framework, specifying the actors and the causal mechanisms linking movements, host-government response, and policy outcomes granted by the United States and the host government.

Actors

ANTI-BASE MOVEMENTS. For illustrative purposes, I treat anti-base movements as a unitary actor. In the proceeding chapters, I discuss in greater length the tension, friction, and different ideological factions that exist within national anti-base movements. Although different ideological strands between moderate and more radical groups certainly complicate the story, treating anti-base movements as a single unit in my framework allows for greater explanation across cases. In each movement episode, a core group of anti-base activists, often associated with broader, left-leaning ideological movements, are usually identifiable. Although the host government is aware of different factions within anti-base movements, and at times takes advantage of movement tension and factionalism, the state tends to treat and confront anti-base movements as a single unit.

HOST STATE. The receiving or "host state" refers to political or government elites[34] within the foreign policy and national security establishments. As argued earlier, these elites include officials and politicians in both the executive and legislative branches of government responsible for foreign and security policy decisionmaking.[35] The government elites that matter most in base politics will vary in each case, depending on specific domestic institutional arrangements. For instance, in the Philippines, new basing agreements require ratification by the Philippine Senate, thus giving senators significant influence in basing policy decisions. In Japan, executive and bureaucratic agencies such as the Defense Facilities Administration Agency handle base policy decisions.

UNITED STATES. It might strike the reader as somewhat odd that the United States has remained outside of base politics to this point. From a systemic perspective, the United States is indeed the most important player in the politics of overseas U.S. military bases. The openings and closures of most bases around the world are heavily dictated by the strategic needs of the U.S. military. In many cases, the United States initiates basing policy changes as a result of changes in the strategic environment or technological improvements.

---

[34] I will use the terms government and political elites interchangeably.

[35] At a secondary level, host-state elites might also include epistemic communities and other knowledge-based experts in academia, think tanks, or business. Although not formally part of the state, epistemic communities and business elites help identify and address policy interests for government elites. See Jacobs and Page, "Who Influences U.S. Foreign Policy?" 108.

Through careful case selection, the research design I employ allows me to incorporate the role of the United States but without washing out the important dynamics between anti-base movements and the host government. First, I select movement episodes around bases of high strategic value to the United States. Given the importance of the base, we can assume that the United States prefers maintaining the status quo regarding basing policies. Second, I examine episodes of contention that reflect changes to basing policies initiated domestically, either by anti-base movements or the host government. Lastly, it is worth noting that the United States and anti-base movements never interact directly. Legally, the United States cannot negotiate with anti-base movement activists. Thus the host state becomes the central arena for base politics, with the most intense action located at the intersection between state and society.

Although the role of the United States remains "bounded" with these caveats in place, it still exerts its influence on base hosts, often in the form of economic incentives or diplomatic pressure. In particular, a strong security consensus favoring U.S. relations already implies that the United States commands significant leverage over host governments. Although the movement episode narratives focus more closely on the interaction between anti-base movements and host governments, where relevant I discuss the diplomatic pressure and negotiating tactics used by the United States to sway host-nation actors. The United States may alter incentives of both movement and government actors, but this is not always the case.

Conditions of Strong Security Consensus

Figures 1.3a and 1.3b outline the interaction process between the United States, host state, and anti-base movements under different conditions of the security consensus.

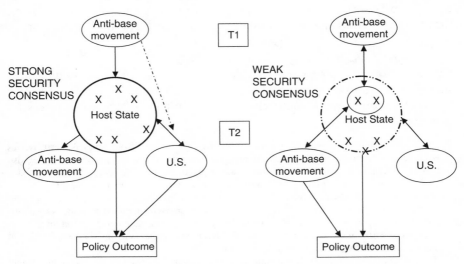

FIGURE 1.3A AND B. Security Consensus as a Political Opportunity Structure.

Figure 1.3a on the left captures movement–government dynamics in the presence of a strong consensus. Although anti-base activists successfully mobilize at T1, the consensus functions as a major constraint for anti-base movements. Unable to penetrate the state (denoted by the solid circle around the host state), activists face stiff resistance from host-government elites favoring strong ties with the United States at T2. The host state marginalizes anti-base movements by co-opting or coercing movements, dragging out negotiations with activists until the movement loses steam, or making minimal concessions to mitigate any potential crisis between the state and civil society. The confrontation between activists and government officials at best leads to token concessions amounting to marginal changes in basing policies and at worst movement defeat and the status quo. In short, the security consensus functions as a barrier against anti-base movement efforts, shaping the patterns of interaction between state and society.

The effectiveness of anti-base movements[36] is significantly reduced without access to key elites (denoted by "Xs" inside the circle). This does not mean, however, that anti-base movements are unable to pressure the state. Figure 1.3a indicates that at T1 anti-base movements put pressure on the host government by creating tensions in host-state–U.S. relations. Paradoxically, anti-base activists are capable of exerting this pressure because elites value strong security ties to the United States.[37] Domestic opposition against bases sends negative signals to the United States. Large-scale protests such as those in Okinawa in 1995 after the rape of a twelve-year-old girl, or in South Korea in 2002, when two schoolgirls were run over by an armored vehicle, eventually reach proportions that if left unchecked have the potential to damage U.S.–host-state alliance relations. Thus, the host government may respond to anti-base movements not necessarily out of domestic political concerns but out of fear that U.S. alliance relations will deteriorate if base protests persist or grow. Sensitive to souring alliance relations, the host state makes at least token concessions to quell anti-base opposition.

Conditions of Weak Security Consensus

Figure 1.3b on the right suggests that the absence of any consensus guiding host-state–U.S. relations provides anti-base activists with the political space necessary to shape discourse or persuade elites on U.S. basing policy issues. Successful

---

[36] I equate movement effectiveness or movement success with base policy outcomes. Admittedly, this is a narrow definition of movement effectiveness or "success." This definition of success may also bias the coding of cases toward movement failure given that movements rarely achieve policy goals in the short run. Although movements may ultimately fail on the policy front, they may achieve success at other levels such as raising issue awareness or shifting public opinion. Moreover, movement "success" is subjective. What movements might define as success (i.e., winning token concessions or delaying base expansion) the state may not. Defining movement success from the vantage point of the state (and hence policy outcomes) rather than social movement actors partially alleviates this problem.

[37] If host-government elites carried ambivalent attitudes toward bilateral U.S. relations, elites would feel significantly less pressure and public embarrassment from widespread anti-U.S. protests.

mobilization at T1, in conjunction with favorable political opportunity structures, enables activists to penetrate the state and form ties with sympathetic elites
(denoted by the "Xs" within the circle).

Although the host government may want to maintain alliance relations with
the United States, the security logic for maintaining U.S. bases for national
defense may not be readily apparent. The host government's response may
therefore be fragmented at T2. Political elites in favor of U.S. bases challenge
or attempt to co-opt social movements. On the other hand, political elites
ambivalent or opposed to bases may encourage or even join anti-base activists,
providing anti-base movements with the leverage needed to influence basing
policy outcomes. Activists influence base policy outcomes by pressuring and
altering the political calculations of elites who, in the absence of significant base
opposition, would otherwise tolerate the status quo on basing issues. Moreover,
in the absence of a strong security consensus, anti-base activists are able to
supply political elites with an alternative foreign policy discourse – one without
U.S. bases – and thus reshape the public debate regarding the U.S. military
presence.

In sum, the degree of security consensus influences the different choices and
strategies of anti-base movement and government actors, which in turn produce
particular policy outcomes. The security consensus functions as a political
opportunity structure constraining or enabling the ability of social movement
actors to penetrate the state and gain elite access. A weak security consensus
provides an open window, enabling anti-base activists to shape outcomes in their
interaction with the host government. It is the combination of a weak security
consensus and the movement strategies employed by anti-base activists, particularly the ability to find support from sympathetic elites, that leads to movement
success at the policy level. Conversely, under a strong security consensus, anti-
base movements have difficulty penetrating the state. Influenced by a strong
security consensus, dominant host-government elites counter anti-base movement pressure by employing strategies that undermine activist efforts.

RESEARCH DESIGN AND METHODS

Measurement and Coding of Variables

Security Consensus
Measuring concepts such as perceptions, beliefs, or ideology is a fuzzy science.
The security consensus, based largely on collective perceptions and beliefs, is no
exception. Although loose quantitative indicators correlated with security
dependence, such as the number of U.S. troops per host-state capita, the number
of U.S. installations, or the cost of sharing the alliance burden, may point toward
a security consensus, the concept is better understood and operationalized by
using qualitative indicators. Table 1.1 presents a simple framework used to
evaluate the strength or weakness of the security consensus among host-
government elites.

TABLE 1.1 *Coding of the Security Consensus*

DEPTH	BREADTH	
	Narrow	Wide
High	Moderate Consensus	Strong Consensus
Low	Weak Consensus	Moderate Consensus

The degree of security consensus among elites can be captured in terms of two dimensions: breadth and depth. "Breadth" refers to the number of elites in the foreign policy and security establishments who share a pro-U.S. security consensus; in other words, how widespread the security consensus is among political elites. Wide breadth implies that virtually all political elites favor strong security relations with the United States and support U.S. basing policy. Conversely, narrow breadth suggests that a few key elites hold onto the security consensus, but it may not be widely shared among the larger foreign policy or security establishments. Narrow breadth is characterized by greater contention among political elites regarding U.S. alliance issues.

"Depth" refers to the security consensus embodied in domestic institutions. High depth implies that the security consensus is deeply embedded within institutions or ideology. Domestic political and ideological constraints prevent political elites from deviating too far from a pro-U.S. security consensus, even if these elites privately prefer loosening security ties to the United States. On the contrary, low depth suggests that the security consensus operates at a more superficial level. Although elites may share a common perception of the U.S. alliance, the consensus rests on more fragile ground if it lacks the norms, institutions, ideologies, or historical legacies that often help solidify collective beliefs about security relations over time.

Table 1.1 indicates that the security consensus is strongest when breadth is wide and depth is high. Conversely, the consensus is weakest when breadth is narrow and depth is low. Naturally, a strong correlation exists between depth and breadth. A higher percentage of elites will favor strong U.S. alliance policies and U.S. bases if the consensus is deeply embedded in institutions and ideology. However, the two dimensions of security consensus are not always congruent. For instance, opposition politicians may challenge U.S.-centered foreign policies advocated by the ruling elite, indicating narrower breadth. At the core, however, ideology and institutions may prevent a pro-U.S. security consensus from completely unraveling, suggesting high depth. Institutional and ideological factors constrain the political choices of oppositional elites, requiring them to acquiesce to the broader foreign policy and national security establishments supportive of the U.S. alliance.[38] This combination of narrow breadth and high depth results in a "moderate" coding of the security consensus.

---

[38] Despite differences on policy issues, oppositional political elites may still accept and value the U.S. alliance (and U.S. bases) as an integral component of its national security strategy.

Likewise, the security consensus is coded as moderate when breadth is wide and depth is low. An example of this scenario may occur when a state previously ambivalent toward U.S. security relations experiences a sharp increase in external threats. Saudi Arabia during the Persian Gulf War provides one such example. After Iraq invaded Kuwait in 1990, Saudi elites previously ambivalent toward the U.S. military presence in the Middle East suddenly perceived U.S. forces in a much more favorable light. At the Saudi government's request, the United States dispatched U.S. troops to protect Saudi Arabia from an Iraqi invasion. However, this widespread consensus favoring a security commitment from the United States was not deeply institutionalized within Saudi domestic institutions.[39]

What pieces of evidence are used to measure dimensions of breadth and depth in determining the relative strength or weakness of the security consensus? To the extent that the security consensus exists as a dominant foreign policy idea guiding state behavior, one will find evidence of an elite security consensus (or lack thereof) embedded in national debates, policy discussions, speeches, and institutional arrangements.[40] I use elite interviews, policy documents, legislative transcripts, government records, and official statements to gauge whether the host government believes U.S. forces are a necessary component of national security.

Wide breadth should be marked by broad support for U.S. troop presence, U.S. bases, and strong host-state–U.S. security relations in elite statements, voting records, or policy documents. Often, wide breadth will also be correlated with high degrees of external threat perceptions. On the dimension of depth, institutionalized agreements such as mutual defense treaties or formalized bilateral security arrangements, as well as domestic institutions that legitimate the U.S. alliance and bases, also point toward a strong (or at least moderate) security consensus. For instance, the creation of the Defense Facilities Administration Agency (DFAA) in Japan to handle U.S. base issues, or provisions in South Korea's National Security Laws tacitly directed against North Korea, help legitimate strong alliance relations and U.S. bases. Asset specificity between military equipment and hardware and the frequency of joint military training exercises may also point to higher dimensions of depth.

On the other hand, coding the security consensus as weak can be justified if government documents and elite statements indicate intense debates among government elites and academic circles regarding the extent of external threat perceptions and the role of U.S. bases for national security. National discourse and debates, elite statements and attitudes, media reports, and elite surveys should point toward major rifts on the issue of the U.S. alliance and bases. Elite statements rejecting U.S. bases, downgrading the importance of the U.S. alliance, or proposing alternative security arrangements reducing U.S. influence

---

[39] This may help explain why Prince Sultan Air Base, operated since 1990 by the U.S. Air Force, was transferred to Saudi control in 2003 in the midst of diplomatic tensions. See Don Van Natta, Jr., "The Struggle for Iraq; Last American Combat Troops Quit Saudi Arabia," *New York Times*, September 22, 2003.

[40] Legro, *Rethinking the World*, 42.

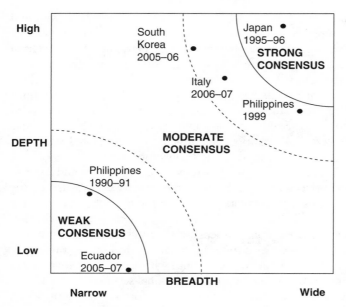

FIGURE I.4. Strength or Weakness of the Security Consensus.

would marshal support for narrow breadth and low depth, and hence a weak security consensus.

Figure 1.4 codes the security consensus for each country evaluated in this book. Although the security consensus is coded as a categorical variable, for the purpose of illustration, breadth and depth are conceptualized continuously in Figure 1.4. This scheme helps clarify the coding of the elite security consensus in countries that most likely fall between the categories of strong and moderate, such as Italy or South Korea. Minor contention regarding the direction of U.S. alliance policies exists within the Italian foreign policy establishment, implying slightly narrower breadth. However, the security consensus is still deeply embedded in institutions, ideology, and historical legacies in these two countries, suggesting high depth. Regarding South Korea, although alternative views calling for greater foreign policy independence exist in Seoul, the institutionalization and embedded nature of the security consensus suggest the presence of at least a moderate, if not strong, security consensus. The security consensus in Japan is coded as "strong." Japanese political elites are largely in favor of strong U.S. alliance relations, with a pro-U.S. consensus deeply embedded in Japanese domestic norms and institutions.[41] On the contrary, the consensus in Ecuador

---

[41] The DPJ's bold 2009 electoral pledge to pursue a more "equal partnership" with the United States has led some to predict a downward shift in the security consensus. Although the dimension of breadth may have narrowed slightly, the depth of the consensus remains very high. Chapter 6 provides further insight on this point.

and the Philippines (1991) is coded as weak. The security consensus was neither particularly deep (especially in Ecuador) nor wide in these two countries during the time of major anti-base protests. From the late 1990s, however, the Philippines has been characterized by a strengthened elite security consensus. Chinese aggression in the South China Sea in the mid-1990s, and political-economic constraints plaguing the Philippines' military modernization program, helped rally the majority of Philippine elites to support strengthened security ties to the United States by the late 1990s.

Base Policy Outcomes

A *range* of base policy outcomes are possible. The spectrum ranges from the maintenance of the status quo on one end to the complete removal of U.S. forces on the other. In the case of base expansion, blocking the expansion of U.S. bases would amount to major movement victory.[42] Partial or token concessions are also possible. This includes minor revisions to the Status of Forces Agreement (SOFA), the closure of outdated or strategically unimportant facilities, or changes in training or operational procedures that reduce externalities in nearby base communities. Here, anti-base movements may obtain tactical concessions from the host state or the United States, but their overall impact on policy outcomes is marginal.

Unit of Analysis: Movement Episodes

Fusing social movement analysis with international relations theory creates a bit of ambiguity, if not tension, in the choice of a proper unit of analysis. For international relations scholars, the use of states as the primary unit of analysis is the default choice.[43] Likewise, the concept of security consensus privileges states by focusing on the perception of national elites. From a social movement perspective, however, the choice of states as the primary unit of analysis is problematic. A study of anti-base movements requires shifting our primary focus from the national level to the subnational level by examining episodes, loosely defined as "bounded sequences of continuous interaction."[44]

---

[42] This raises the issue of whether base opening/expansion or base closure is "easier" for anti-base movements to challenge. In this book, the two cases of anti-base movement success involve base closure, and two cases of anti-base movement failure involve base expansion. No clear consensus seems to exist, however, among activists on this point. On the one hand, shutting down an existing base provides a more powerful collective action frame, especially if the base already presents readily available grievances. On the other hand, a greater variety of strategies and tactics can be devised to prevent the expansion of a new base.

[43] Kenneth Waltz, *Theory of International Politics* (Reading, Mass.: Addison-Wesley, 1979); and J. David Singer, "The Level-of-Analysis Problem in International Relations," *World Politics* 14, no. 1 (1961): 77–92.

[44] An episode can range from something simple such as a two-week hunger strike by students demanding a minority studies program to "major cycles of contention, revolution, and civil wars." See Charles Tilly and Sidney G. Tarrow, *Contentious Politics* (Boulder, Colo.: Paradigm Publishers, 2007), 36.

Throughout the book, I use anti-base movement episodes to examine the relationship between movement dynamics, their impact on U.S.–host-state relations, and base policy outcomes. Using a more precise definition, a movement episode is understood as "a period of emergent, sustained, contentious interaction between at least two collective actors."[45] The use of movement episodes as a unit of analysis offers several analytical advantages. First, examining movement episodes targeting specific policy demands (i.e., base closure, SOFA revisions, the ending of live bombing exercises) enables me to track specific mechanisms linking anti-base movements, the security consensus, and base policy outcomes. Second, studying movement episodes raises the possibility of increasing the number of observations in a single country across time. These episodes and the corresponding policy outcome stemming from movements may then be used to extrapolate generalizations about movement dynamics and alliance relations in specific countries. Third, an analysis of movement episodes allows us to examine possible intervening variables internal to movements that may affect base policy outcomes.

The use of episodes as the unit of analysis does not discredit the important role of the state, nor should it prevent us from making comparisons about base politics across countries in addition to movement episodes. Anti-base movement strategy and effectiveness are affected by bilateral security relations and the existence (or absence) of an elite security consensus at the national level. As argued earlier, movement episodes are nested within the context of a particular state. Thus comparisons regarding the security consensus in different states and its impact on state–societal interaction and subsequent movement outcomes are possible.

Case Selection

To convince skeptics that social movements really matter, I try to select "hard tests" for anti-base movements. Anti-base movements are expected to have the least impact on policy outcomes when bases are strategically important to the United States and the host state. Movement episodes must therefore include mobilization against bases of high strategic value. Next, I limit my case selection to episodes of high movement strength and mobilization. Inherent in this choice is the assumption that the host government ignores minor civil disturbances, small-scale protests, and other "noise." I therefore assume that anti-base mobilization of low movement strength has little impact on base policy decisions. In short, movement episodes involving bases of high strategic value and high movement strength (i.e., major mobilization episodes) constitute theoretically "interesting" cases. The research design follows Mill's "method of difference":

---

[45] Doug McAdam, "Legacies of Anti-Americanism: A Sociological Perspective," in *Anti-Americanisms in World Politics*, edited by Peter J. Katzenstein and Robert O. Keohane (Ithaca, N.Y.: Cornell University Press, 2007), 253. Also see McAdam, Tarrow, and Tilly, *Dynamics of Contention*, 24.

only the level of security consensus varies across cases, whereas the strategic value of the base(s) and protest magnitude are "controlled."[46]

Preview of the Empirical Cases

I use anti-base movement episodes in five different countries – Philippines, Japan, Ecuador, Italy, and South Korea – to test my argument. Two central questions guide our discussion in the proceeding chapters: (1) Why were anti-base movements in the Philippines and Ecuador more successful in shutting down bases, whereas anti-base movements in Okinawa, Italy, and South Korea were relatively unsuccessful? (2) Why and how did host-state elites in Japan, Italy, and South Korea respond differently in balancing between domestic pressure and international alliance commitments compared with elites in the Philippines and Ecuador? In each case, I first determine the degree of elite security consensus at the onset of a movement episode using a variety of evidence cited earlier. I then trace the sequence of events, highlighting the interaction between movement and government actors to test whether the security consensus variable leads to the outcomes hypothesized in the previous section.

Anti-base movements were most effective under conditions of weak security consensus. In the Philippines and Ecuador, elite statements, policy documents, interview records, and parliamentary transcripts highlight the divisions among government officials and policymakers regarding the role of U.S. bases. Key elites influential in the politics of bases rejected the idea that a U.S. military presence was necessary to maintain national security. Unlike countries characterized by a strong or moderate security consensus, no dominant national security discourse dictated U.S.–host-state relations in the Philippines in the early 1990s or Ecuador in the past decade. Thus a significant number of Philippine and Ecuadorian political elites were receptive to anti-base sentiments. In both countries, activists formulated a strategy that targeted elites. This resulted in much more interaction and coalition building between anti-base movement activists and domestic political elites, giving activists the leverage needed to influence base policy outcomes.

On the contrary, in Japan, Italy, and South Korea, a dominant national security discourse and pro-U.S. security consensus permeated the security and foreign policy establishments. The inability to penetrate elite ranks became a major obstacle for Okinawan, Italian, and South Korean anti-base movements in their struggles against U.S. bases. To their credit, anti-base movements pressured the government, occasionally winning "partial concessions." For the most

---

[46] Case selection for this study required, to some extent, selecting on the dependent variable. Although some social scientists might find this selection process troubling, case selection was partially motivated by the need for variation of the independent and dependent variables to strengthen the robustness of the theory. See Gary King, Robert O. Keohane, and Sidney Verba, *Designing Social Inquiry: Scientific Inference in Qualitative Research* (Princeton, N.J.: Princeton University Press, 1994), 129.

part, however, the government tended to ignore activists' core demands. Government officials were aware that domestic pressure and anti-base mobilization operated cyclically. Token concessions usually quelled anti-base activity until the next mobilization cycle, triggered by an accident, crime, death, or some other unforeseen external event. Observing the interaction between anti-base movements and government forces unfold in these three movement episodes demonstrates that the host government responded strategically to anti-base groups in an effort to co-opt, weaken, and demobilize anti-base movements.

Interestingly, in these three cases, the state allowed significant space for pressure groups to oppose U.S. bases, attested by the successful mobilization of anti-base coalition groups from various sectors. Activists even formed ties with minority party government elites. Occasionally, the state gave partial concessions to movement demands. But even though the state entertained anti-base movements to a certain degree, using both muscle and tact, the state ultimately overpowered any mobilization effort when U.S. alliance relations were put in jeopardy by massive anti-U.S. base demonstrations.

Under a Weak Security Consensus

Philippine Anti-Base Movements, 1990–1991

> September 16, 1991, may well be the day when we in this Senate found the soul, the true spirit of this nation because we mustered the courage and the will to declare the end of foreign military presence in the Philippines. . . . Therefore, I vote *No* to this Treaty, and if it were only possible, I would vote 203 million times *No*.[1]

With a resounding "No," Senate President Jovito Salonga cast the final vote against the Treaty of Friendship, Cooperation, and Security between the Republic of the Philippines (R.P.) and the United States. The final tally totaled 12–11 against the Treaty, effectively ending over ninety years of U.S. military presence in the Philippines. Salonga's vote was perhaps less suspenseful than the 12–11 margin would suggest since the Philippine Senate only needed eight out of twenty-three "No" votes to reject the Treaty.[2] Nevertheless, the rejection of the Treaty and U.S. bases in the Philippines was a monumental day for Filipinos. The decision was all the more astonishing given that a traditionally conservative institution such as the Senate ultimately snubbed its nose against its primary international benefactor. Asking how an economically deprived, politically unstable country held its own against a world superpower, Roland Simbulan, a longtime Philippine activist and scholar, and advisor to Senator Wigberto Tañada during the R.P.-U.S. base negotiations, replied, "The real moving spirit behind the twelve Senators was the broad and unified people's movement outside the Senate. . . . [T]he Anti-Treaty Movement was forged with the broadest unity possible among organized forces and individuals. In the end, it was the power of the people that ended the most visible symbols of our colonial legacy and the Cold War in the Philippines."[3]

---

[1] Speech given before voting on the Senate Resolution of Non-Concurrence to the proposed bases treaty, September 16, 1991, in Senate Legislative Publications Staff, *The Bases of Their Decisions: How the Senators Voted on the Treaty of Friendship between the Government of the Republic of the Philippines and the Government of the United States of America* (Manila: Senate of the Philippines, 1991), 242–43.

[2] The Senate required a two-thirds majority to pass the new bases treaty.

[3] Roland Simbulan, "September 16, 1991: The Day the Senate said 'No!' to Uncle Sam – An Insider's Account," NFPC Library Archives, September 11, 2002. Also found at http://www.yonip.com/main/articles/september_16.html (last accessed January 10, 2007).

One cannot attribute the rejection of the R.P.-U.S. Treaty of Friendship, Cooperation, and Security and the subsequent closure of Subic Bay Naval Station, strategically the most important base in the Philippines, to a single explanation. Numerous interacting factors most likely led to the closure of U.S. bases. Immediate factors highlighting the importance of agency focus on the negotiations between U.S. and Philippine officials. Base critics argued that a "lopsided treaty," coupled with the "arrogant negotiating behavior" of the U.S. delegation headed by Richard Armitage, would never pass through the Senate.[4] The revised 1987 Philippine Constitution also factored into the closure of Subic Bay Naval Station in 1991. Article 15, Section 25 of the revised Constitution required both Senate ratification and the passage of a national referendum on any new base treaty. This institutional change shifted decision power from the executive to the legislative branch, providing Philippine senators and civil society greater leverage in the base policymaking process. Others argue that structural factors, such as the end of the Cold War or economic recession in the United States, reduced Washington's political will to continue operating bases with declining strategic value, thus leading to base closures. Finally, unforeseeable events, or "acts of god" such as the explosion of Mount Pinatubo and the destruction of Clark Air Base, affected the decision calculus of elites and the outcome of Subic Bay.

Although Simbulan's preceding quotation regarding the role of anti-base movements should be placed within the context of other proximate and distal factors explaining base closures, I concur with Simbulan that social movements played a pivotal role in the Senate's fateful decision in September 1991. The burden of proof, however, rests on those who contend that civil society and anti-base movements mattered in the Philippines. What was the relationship between anti-base coalition movements and the senators of the Eighth Congress, who were given veto power over the new negotiated bases treaty? Why were Philippine elites divided over the issue of U.S. bases and the future of R.P.-U.S. relations, with the president leading the pro-base faction and the Senate leading the anti-base faction, and how did this affect their response to anti-base movements? How were anti-base activists, agents considered peripheral to state security policymaking, able to oust U.S. bases? Finally, how did the relationship between the state and civil society interact with alliance politics to produce particular responses and outcomes that would alter the future direction of R.P.-U.S. relations?

I argue that a weak security consensus enabled anti-base movements to penetrate the state by taking advantage of divisions among Philippine elites over the fate of U.S. bases. In the absence of any strong security consensus, anti-base activists and nationalist politicians provided an alternative national security discourse that distinguished their position from the traditional pro-U.S.

---

[4] For debates between base critics and proponents, see Jovito R. Salonga, *The Senate That Said No: A Four-Year Record of the First Post-EDSA Senate* (Quezon City: University of the Philippines Press, 1995); and Senate Legislative Publications Staff, *The Bases of Their Decisions.*

line previously embraced by the Philippine government. Thus, the weak security consensus functioned as a political opportunity, enabling activists to form ties with sympathetic elites. This in turn provided activists the leverage necessary to influence base policy outcomes – most significantly, the closure of Subic Bay Naval Station.

This chapter begins with a brief background on U.S. bases and the rise of anti-base coalition movements in the Philippines. The next section describes Philippine national security and the nature of R.P.-U.S. security relations between 1988 and 1991 from the perspective of host-government political elites. Evidence based on government policy documents, Senate legislative transcripts, public opinion surveys, and military data all suggest a lack of consensus among Philippine government elites regarding Philippine national security, and specifically strategic thinking toward its alliance partnership with the United States. This position is substantiated by the Philippine security literature as well as interviews with former and current Philippine policymakers and scholars. The following section focuses on the interaction between anti-base movements and the state. Here I describe the tactics and strategies anti-base activists employed and the response to anti-base movements from both pro- and anti-base government factions. In particular, I focus on the relationship between activists and anti-base senators to trace the mechanisms linking the weak security consensus to movement strategies, government reactions, and policy outcomes.

U.S. MILITARY BASES IN THE PHILIPPINES

Contrary to the expectations of Filipino revolutionaries, Spain's defeat in the Battle of Manila in May 1898 and its ultimate defeat in the Spanish-American War did not lead to Philippine independence. Having excluded Filipino representation during negotiations at the Treaty of Paris, Spain merely transferred (at the price of twenty million dollars) its colonial power to the United States.[5] The United States also acquired Spanish military posts, including Subic Bay, and established several new military facilities during and after the Philippine-American War from 1899 to 1901.

After gaining its independence in 1946, the Philippines signed the 1947 R.P.-U.S. Military Bases Agreement (MBA) with the United States, which gave the United States rent-free "certain lands of the public domain" for a period of ninety-nine years. The MBA provided the United States with twenty-three

---

[5] Rosario Cortes Mendoza, Celestina Puyal Boncan, and Ricardo Trota Jose, *The Filipino Saga: History as Social Change* (Quezon City: New Day Publishers, 2001), 235. For other historical overviews of U.S.-Philippine relations, see Frank H. Golay, *Face of Empire: United States-Philippine Relations, 1898–1946* (Madison: University of Wisconsin–Madison Center for Southeast Asian Studies, 1998); Stanley Karnow, *In Our Image: America's Empire in the Philippines* (New York: Foreign Policy Association, 1989); and Patricio Abinales and Donna J. Amoroso, *State and Society in the Philippines* (Lanham, Md.: Rowman and Littlefield, 2005).

facilities, covering approximately 250,000 hectares.[6] However, between 1947 and 1991, the MBA underwent at least forty amendments, which returned base land to the Philippines and provided the Philippine government greater control over U.S. bases.[7] Most notably, the 1966 Ramos-Rusk Agreement signed on September 16, 1966, changed the terms of the base limit from ninety-nine to twenty-five years. Thus the MBA was set to expire on September 16, 1991. Later, the 1979 Romulo-Murphy Exchange of Notes transferred nominal control of U.S. bases to the Philippine government. The United States also agreed to provide $500 million of security assistance to the Philippines between 1979 and 1984. Both sides agreed to review the MBA every five years until its termination.

The revised Philippine Constitution in February 1987 gave the Philippine Senate considerable influence over the retention of U.S. bases after 1991. Under Section 25, Article 18, the revised Constitution stated,

After the expiration in 1991 of the Agreement between the Republic of the Philippines and the United States of America concerning Military Bases, foreign military bases, troops or facilities shall not be allowed in the Philippines except under a treaty duly concurred by the Senate and, when the Congress so requires, ratified by a majority of the votes cast by the people in a national referendum.[8]

Function of Subic and Clark Bases

Subic Bay Naval Station in Zambales Province and Clark Air Base in Angeles City were the two largest U.S. installations in the Philippines. In 1986, Subic and Clark bases hosted 7,000 and 8,500 U.S. military personnel, respectively.[9] The number of U.S. military personnel, civilians, and dependents on both bases totaled 38,550.[10] Both bases provided logistical support, staging areas, fuel and porting, repair facilities, training facilities, military communications, ammunition and supply depots, and rest and recreation. Subic Bay was the largest overseas Navy installation in the Pacific, and served as the primary port, training facility, and logistics hub for the U.S. Seventh Fleet, which operated in the Pacific

---

[6] Roland G. Simbulan, *A Guide to Nuclear Philippines: A Guide to the US Military Bases, Nuclear Weapons, and What the Filipino People Are Doing About These* (Manila: IBON Databank Philippines, 1989), 23.

[7] Ibid., 23. Also see Foreign Service Institute, Department of Foreign Affairs, *Primer on the R.P-U.S. Military Bases Agreement* (Manila: FSI, 1989). Changes in basing status during this period reflect the ability of pro-U.S. presidents such as Ramon Magsaysay or Ferdinand Marcos to take advantage of nationalist sentiment to leverage concessions from the United States. Both Magsaysay and Marcos used concessions to increase their domestic political legitimacy. As Alexander Cooley writes, "Marcos would maintain a tough, pro-Philippine sovereignty domestically, but could do so while maintaining unwavering U.S. support that he leveraged for base-related payments. In turn, these substantial quid pro quo payments allowed him to provide patronage for his military supporters and political base." See Cooley, *Base Politics*, Chap. 3.

[8] Constitution of the Republic of the Philippines, Section 25, Article 18.

[9] Simbulan, *Guide to Nuclear Philippines*, 11.

[10] Ibid., 11.

and Indian Oceans.[11] Cubic Point on Subic Bay also functioned as the land base for the Seventh Fleet's strike force, Task Force 77. Meanwhile, Clark Air Base served as the headquarters of the 13th Air Force, the tactical arm of the U.S. Air Force in the Western Pacific and Indian Ocean. Clark also acted as a staging point for strategic airlifts into the Indian Ocean. From a strategic perspective, bases in the Philippines were used to secure air and sea lanes, balance the Soviet military presence in Cam Ranh Bay, Vietnam, and provide regional defense for Southeast Asia.[12]

Strategic Value of Subic Bay Naval Station

Realists skeptical of anti-base movements argue that the end of the Cold War and reduced threat perceptions ultimately led to base closures in the Philippines. Thus, any analysis of anti-base movement impact in the Philippines must address the context of regional strategic change. Certainly, the strategic environment shifted with the disappearance of the Soviet threat. Despite looming questions regarding the future strategic utility of Subic Bay among U.S. military planners, however, the evidence presented here suggests that the closure of Subic Bay was far from inevitable.

First, throughout all seven rounds of the Philippine American Cooperation Talks (PACT) between 1990 and 1991, the U.S. panel firmly insisted on a ten-year renewal agreement. This insistence suggests that Washington had no intention of shutting down Subic Bay in the immediate future.[13] Second, Subic Bay's strategic value and assets, and the enormous opportunity and financial costs in finding a replacement facility, placed unacceptable demands on the United States to phase out Subic Bay under the preferred terms of the Philippine government.[14] The naval supply depot at Subic Bay served as a logistics hub for all naval forces between Hawaii and the Persian Gulf. Furthermore, Subic was one of only two deep-water ports in the entire Pacific and Indian Oceans large enough to support aircraft carrier and air wing support facilities.[15] In a prepared report on the

---

[11] United States Information Service, *In Our Mutual Interest: U.S. Military Facilities in the Philippines* (Manila: United States Information Service, 1991).

[12] United States Information Service, *Background on the Bases: American Military Facilities in the Philippines* (Manila: United States Information Service, 1988).

[13] See Document 5.10, "Letter of special negotiator Richard Armitage, Washington DC, to Sec. Raul Manglapus, Manila, on the US compensation package proposal," April 27, 1991, and Document 6.8, "Paper written by a member of the U.S. Panel, detailing the requirement of the U.S. side to bring the talks to closure, transmitted by fax to the Ministry of Finance," May 9, 1991, in Maria Castro-Guevara, ed., *The Bases Talks Reader: Key Documents of the 1990–91 Philippine-American Cooperation Talks* (Manila: Anvil, 1997), 209–19; 299–301. In Round VI of the PACT, however, the United States was willing to accept a nine-plus-one-year phased reduction period. The Philippines, on the other hand, continued to insist on a seven-year period.

[14] Desmond Ball, *U.S. Bases in the Philippines: Issues and Implications* (Canberra: Strategic and Defence Studies Centre, 1988), 11.

[15] U.S. House of Representatives, Committee on Armed Services, *Military Installations and Facilities Subcommittee: Hearings on Military Construction, H.R. 1208* (Washington, D.C.: U.S.

status of overseas basing in the Asia-Pacific region, Deputy Assistant Secretary of Defense Carl Ford, Jr., testified in March 1991,

U.S. interest in sustaining a presence in the Philippines remains undiminished. The facilities host the greatest concentration of U.S. logistics, communication, and training facilities in the world. The synergism of these functions and facilities provides the U.S. maximum operational effectiveness, but also an important presence that signifies ... our immediate and potential capabilities in a time of crisis.[16]

Ford did concede the possibility of reductions at Subic, but he insisted that "no single site would be capable of assimilating all the functions that are presently conducted in the Philippines." He continued, "[T]he impact of the loss of Subic would depend upon where and how functions at Subic were dispersed, but at a minimum, annual operating costs would increase ... and Seventh Fleet war-fighting readiness would be reduced by the loss of access to the Philippine training ranges."[17] Shutting down Subic Bay, even after Mount Pinatubo's explosion, "was not the expressed desire of the administration."[18] Third, troop deployment levels in Asia after the Cold War remained around the 100,000 level. Unlike the dramatic decrease in U.S. troop levels in Europe beginning in the late 1980s, the consistent level of U.S. forces in Asia implied less strategic change in the Asia-Pacific region than predicted, even with the collapse of the Soviet Union.[19] In sum, the closure of Subic Bay Naval Station presented a hard test for anti-base movements.

THE RISE OF PHILIPPINE ANTI-BASE MOVEMENTS

Origins of the Anti-Base Movement

The historical roots of the anti-base movement begin with U.S. colonial rule in the Philippines. Although the Philippines declared its "independence" in 1898, the United States did not transfer full government authority to the Filipinos until 1946. Prior to independence, Philippine political elites collaborated with the Americans, but at the same time publicly promoted Philippine autonomy under colonial rule. These conservative nationalists presented a political alternative to armed resistance and revolution.[20] Former revolutionaries, intellectuals, and the urban middle class gradually reentered Philippine politics after the Philippine-American War, organizing the Partido Nacionalista

Government Printing Office, 1992), 816. Hearings held on March 6, March 7, March 13, March 21, April 10, and April 17, 1991.

[16] Ibid., 816.

[17] Ibid., 817.

[18] *Congressional Quarterly*, "Philippine Base Closings, 1991–1992 Legislative Chronology," in *Congress and the Nation* (Washington, D.C.: CQ Press, 1992), 411. Mount Pinatubo's explosion did, however, result in the closure of Clark Air Base.

[19] For example, the potential for conflict continued to exist across the Taiwan Straits and the demilitarized zone between North and South Korea.

[20] Abinales and Amoroso, *State and Society in the Philippines*, 106.

(Nationalist Party) in 1907. Whereas some conservative nationalists privately hoped for Philippine annexation to the United States, the Partido Nacionalista's main goal was the eventual independence of the Philippines.

After independence in 1946, nationalist criticism against American rule transformed into opposition against American neocolonial influence in the Philippines. The Partido Komunista ng Pilipinas (PKP) was the most visible group voicing its criticism against neocolonialism. The call for independence from American influence was also carried by those not necessarily aligned with the ideological left. Most notable were nationalist politicians in the 1950s and 1960s, such as senators Claro Recto, Jose Laurel, Jose Diokno, and Lorenzo Tañada. In the 1950s, Claro Recto was one of the first prominent nationalist politicians to challenge the neocolonial mentality prevalent in Philippine political society.[21] Recto's nationalist call for true independence and the removal of U.S. bases was later taken up by Diokno and Tañada, until the Marcos dictatorship purged them from Philippine politics. Although other elites, including scholars and lawyers, took part in the early years of Philippine anti-base movements, the leadership tended to rest with senators, given their national prominence.

President Ferdinand Marcos declared martial law in 1972, thereby silencing nationalist politicians' calls for the removal of U.S. bases. However, the growth of the Philippine Left during this period helped fuel a growing underground movement calling for the overthrow of the Marcos regime. As Philippine political scientist Miriam Ferrer argues, the Philippine Left "evolved as the most consistent oppositionist to the bases."[22] With U.S. bases viewed as a key pillar propping up the Marcos regime, the removal of bases and imperial foreign influence developed into a major agenda for the Philippine Left. For instance, in their ten-point policy agenda, the National Democratic Front (NDF), the above-ground intellectual movement of the Communist Party of the Philippines (CPP), made it clear that one of their goals was to rid the Philippines of U.S. bases and establish an independent foreign policy.[23] Moreover, the Left argued that U.S. bases were being utilized for counterinsurgency operations and direct and indirect repression against Filipinos.[24]

The involvement of the Left helped bring the anti-base movement to the masses. Nationalists across multiple sectors, including professionals, students,

[21] See the following speeches by Recto: "American Bases and National Freedom and Security," delivered before the Philippine Chamber of Commerce, October 29, 1950, and "The Problem of Our National Physical Survival," delivered on the Senate Floor, May 21, 1958, in *For Philippine Survival: Nationalist Essays by Claro Recto and Renato Constantino* (Manila: Friends of the Filipino People, n.d.).

[22] Miriam Ferrer, "Anti-Bases Coalition," in *Studies on Coalition Experiences*, edited by C. Cala and J. Grageda (Manila: Bookmark, 1994), 5. Also see Miriam Ferrer, "The Dynamics of the Opposition to the US Bases in the Philippines," *Kasarinlan* 7, no. 4 (1992): 62–87.

[23] See National Democratic Front, *Our Vision of a Just and Democratic Society* (Philippines: Gintong Tala, 1987).

[24] Simbulan, *Guide to Nuclear Philippines*, 35.

workers, and farmers, banded together in February 1967 to form the Movement for the Advancement of Nationalism.[25] Anti-base movements also sustained themselves within university campuses. Formed in the 1960s, student organizations such as the Kabataang Makabayan (Nationalist Youth) and the Samahan ng Demokratikong Kabagtaan (Association of Democratic Youth) evoked strong nationalist tendencies. About 350 students from thirty schools around Manila launched an anti-base campaign in January 1979.[26] In accordance with global peace and demilitarization goals, church groups in the Philippines such as the National Council of Churches in the Philippines (NCCP) also grew more vocal against U.S. bases in the early 1980s. In sum, by the 1980s, a growing minority voice against U.S. bases influenced by leftist ideology and nationalism had developed across various sectors in Philippine society.

Development of Anti-Base Coalition Campaigns, 1981–1991

Groups predominantly on the left end of the political spectrum addressed anti-base issues. Rather than focusing exclusively on bases, these groups tended to advocate several issues and platform goals.[27] For instance, in addition to the removal of U.S. bases, coalition groups added to their agenda issues such as democratic reforms and the end of U.S. support for the Marcos regime. The first coalition movement to target U.S. bases almost exclusively was the Nuclear Free Philippines Coalition (NFPC), formed in 1981. As the name suggests, the NFPC's primary goal was the abolishment of nuclear power in the Philippines. The NFPC initially focused on the construction of the Bataan Nuclear Power Plant, but the movement expanded to include the opposition of nuclear weapons and U.S. bases that stored such weapons. As a precursor to the anti-base coalition movement, the NFPC would later devote its entire energy to U.S. bases after the closure of the Bataan Nuclear Power Plant.

Anti-base leaders organized the first formal anti-base coalition movement in February 1983 under the name Anti-Bases Coalition (ABC). Under the guidance of former senator Jose Diokno, the ABC was represented by the political left as well as non-Left nationalists within the professional class who were part of the anti-Marcos campaign. Over the next eight years, the anti-base movement evolved through periods of four different coalition groups: the Campaign for a

---

[25] Ferrer, "Anti-Bases Coalition," 6. Ferrer notes, however, that the anti-base movement was less successful in mobilizing the unorganized working class, whose immediate concerns were economic rather than political. The anti-base movement, foremost a political-ideological struggle, mobilized its working-class base primarily through political blocs.

[26] Ibid., 7.

[27] For a general overview of Philippines civil society and coalition movements, see Marlon Wui and Glenda Lopez, eds., *State–Civil Society Relations in Policy-making* (Quezon City: University of the Philippines Press, 1994); Josephine Dionisio, *Enhanced Documentation on National Peace Coalitions and Citizens' Groups Peace-Building Experiences in the Philippines* (Manila: UNDP, 2005); and Sidney G. Silliman and Lela Garner Noble, eds., *Organizing for Democracy: NGOs, Civil Society, and the Philippine State* (Honolulu: University of Hawaii Press, 1998).

Sovereign Philippines (CSP) in 1986, Kasarinlan in 1988, Anti-Baseng Kilusan (ABAKADA) in 1989, and the Anti-Treaty Movement (ATM) in 1991. Anti-base coalitions were generally led by activists from the national democrat strand of the Left, often supported by prominent national elite figures.[28] Although these coalition groups existed as separate entities at different points in time, the Philippine anti-base coalition movement can be viewed as an evolutionary process, with the start of each campaign coalition acting as a new juncture in the anti-base movement. For example, rather than dissolving completely after a period of inactivity, the ABC acted as a convener for subsequent anti-base campaigns such as the CSP and became a member organization of broader anti-base coalitions such as ABAKADA or the ATM. Thus many of the same key groups and actors tended to appear in each subsequent coalition campaign across time.[29]

Both internal and external reasons account for the formation of five anti-base coalition campaigns in only an eight-year span. Internally, the loose organizational structure of coalitions and lack of institutionalization made it difficult for anti-base movements to sustain themselves over a longer period of time.[30] Pressing external events, such as Ninoy Aquino's assassination in 1983 or the People Power revolution in 1986, also distracted attention away from U.S. base issues. On the other hand, political opportunities following Philippine democratization in 1986, such as the constitutional revisions in 1987 or the renegotiation of U.S. bases under the PACT in 1990–91, served as focal points for anti-base activists to regroup and initiate a fresh round of anti-base campaign activity.[31] Although anti-base coalitions proceeded in a stop-and-go fashion, the movement itself followed an evolutionary trajectory.

The Anti-Treaty Movement, organized in preparation for the PACT, is of particular importance in this chapter. Although not significantly different from previous anti-base campaigns, the timing of the movement prior to the Senate vote on the new base treaty, and the ATM's ability to find allies among political elites opposed to U.S. bases, provided activists the leverage necessary to defeat passage of any new basing agreement. In other words, anti-base activists penetrated the state. Forming ties with anti-base government elites, activists helped establish a new era of Philippine security without U.S. bases.

---

[28] The National Democrats (ND) viewed themselves as the "voice of the marginalized majority" who demand "substantive and radical changes," confronting repressive regimes with more militant action. In contrast, the Social Democrats (SD) viewed themselves as an alternative to the state and the CPP-NPA-NDF faction. They are supported by "the silent and nonideological majority" of Filipinos. See Dionisio, *Enhanced Documentation on National Peace Coalitions and Citizens' Groups Peace-Building Experiences in the Philippines*, 25–26.

[29] Interview with ABC Co-Chair Ma Socorro Diokno, April 10, 2006, UP-Diliman, Quezon City, Philippines.

[30] Ferrer, "Anti-Bases Coalition," 22.

[31] Interview with former Bayan secretary general Lidy Nacpil, April 28, 2006, Quezon City, Philippines.

THE WEAK SECURITY CONSENSUS AND PHILIPPINE POLITICAL ELITES

How did anti-base activists penetrate the state and form ties with sympathetic elites? More broadly, how were social movements, often considered tangential to the security decisionmaking process, able to oust the U.S. military from the Philippines? The success of anti-base movements and the ability of activists to penetrate the state and influence key political elites required movement actors to take advantage of the weak security consensus within the Philippine government. Activists employed mobilization frames and strategies that resonated with sympathetic or divided political leaders, enabling the movement to reshape the public debate on bases. In this section, I marshal evidence supporting my contention that important Philippine political elites were divided on issues of national security.

In measuring the degree of security consensus during the late 1980s and early 1990s, I examine the breadth and depth of the security consensus among Philippine elites. Regarding breadth, the lack of widespread consensus on the direction of U.S.-Philippine relations or the role of U.S. bases was most pronounced in Senate debates on the renewal of the bases treaty. The weak consensus was also reflected in the different preferences held by the pro-base Philippine president, Corazon Aquino, and a core group of senators opposed to a continued U.S. base presence. The narrow breadth of the security consensus beginning in the late 1980s coincides with its declining depth following the overthrow of Marcos in 1986. Underpinned by the U.S.-Philippines Mutual Defense Treaty, ruling elites largely accepted the U.S. security umbrella during the Cold War. Two factors, however, made the basis for a deep-rooted security consensus more tenuous. First, nationalist elites continually challenged Manila's neocolonial dependence on Washington. Although marginalized during the height of the Cold War, the nationalist position gained strong legitimacy in the 1980s. Many of the political and ideological constraints perpetuating pro-U.S. foreign policies were removed with the rise of the People Power movement and the overthrow of the U.S.-backed Marcos regime. Second, in a country historically focused on internal rather than external security, the future role of the U.S. alliance in the post-Marcos era remained unclear. As anti-base senators cited, and a few pro-base elites tacitly agreed, no clear *security* rationale existed for a major U.S. military presence in the Philippines.

Orientation Toward Internal Security

The divergent discourse regarding the future of R.P.-U.S. relations among Philippine elites, and the sudden departure of the U.S. military in 1991, is initially puzzling. Filipinos fought side-by-side with Americans against the Japanese in World War II. Filipinos lived under the U.S. security umbrella during the Cold War. Like other close Asian allies, such as Japan and South Korea, the Philippines signed a mutual defense treaty with the United States in 1951 and hosted a substantial number of U.S. troops and bases. Moreover, internal political stability and national security in the Philippines were always contingent on U.S. support throughout the Cold War. These factors alone would suggest at least a moderate degree of security consensus among Philippine elites.

On the other hand, this finding is less surprising if we place R.P.-U.S. relations under the context of Philippine sovereignty and national security. Unlike South Korea or Japan, the Philippines has historically been concerned with internal, not external, security. In what Renato de Castro labels "the legacy of internal defense," the Armed Forces of the Philippines (AFP) traditionally directed military operations around internal security threats. These included armed insurgencies from the New People's Army (NPA), the armed faction of the Communist Party Philippines,[32] communist rebel groups such as the Hukbalahap, and Muslim separatist groups such as the Moro National Liberation Front (MNLF), Moro Islamic Liberation Front (MILF), and Abu Sayyaf. In the words of one security analyst, "The communist insurgency and Muslim separatist movement in Mindanao have been the principal security preoccupation of the Philippine government for the last three decades."[33]

Under the Marcos regime, the Philippine government only intensified its preoccupation with internal security and domestic stability. Likewise, the AFP expanded its role in counterinsurgency operations to include the administration of martial law.[34] The fall of Marcos and the onset of Philippine democracy in 1986 did not fundamentally alter the Philippines' preoccupation with internal security. Although the CPP-NPA insurgency was on the decline after reaching its peak in 1987, the government continued to direct military resources toward domestic security in the wake of a growing Muslim insurgency and several attempted military coups.[35] Tables 2.1 and 2.2 provide survey data from Social Weather Station (SWS) regarding internal threat perceptions from communist insurgency and Muslim rebel groups between 1986 and 1993. Both survey data indicate that internal threat perceptions were relatively high in the Philippines.

An Underdeveloped National Security Agenda

The U.S. security umbrella also explains the internal focus of Philippine security. Guaranteed protection from outside aggression under the 1951 Mutual Defense Treaty, the Philippine government could afford to allocate its resources toward internal security, while the U.S. alliance guaranteed protection against external threats. However, overreliance on the U.S. and the preoccupation with internal

---

[32] Along with the NDF, this faction is often referred to as CPP-NPA-NDF. See Dominique Caouette, "Persevering Revolutionaries: Armed Struggle in the 21st Century, Exploring the Revolution of the Communist Party of the Philippines," PhD dissertation, Cornell University, 2004.

[33] Charles Morrison, ed., *Asia Pacific Security Outlook 1997* (Honolulu: East–West Center, 1997), 97.

[34] Renato de Castro, "Adjusting to the Post-U.S. Bases Era: The Ordeal of the Philippine Military's Modernization Program," *Armed Forces and Society* 26, no. 1 (1999): 119–38 at 120.

[35] Morrison, *Asia Pacific Security Outlook 1997*, 97; and de Castro, "Adjusting to the Post-U.S. Bases Era," 120.

TABLE 2.1. *Internal Threat Perceptions: Communist Insurgency*

	Oct. 86	Mar. 87[a]	Sept. 88	Feb. 89	July 89[b]	Sept. 89	Sept. 93
Great	68	71	61	64	62	56	75
Small	25	19	17	23	26	20	24
None	1	8	1	12	11	–	–
Maybe/Don't Know	–	2	20	1	1	23	–

Note: Question worded in the survey as follows: "Please tell me how great or small is the danger of the following to the government of President Corazon Aquino: Rebel communists and communist supporters (very great, big, small, very small, none)?"
[a] Tables 2.1 and 2.2 aggregate "very great" and "big" responses into "great" and "small" and "very small" responses into "small."
[b] Survey only conducted in the National Capital Region (Manila).
Source: Social Weather Station, *Social Weather Report Survey, Philippines: 1986–1993.*

TABLE 2.2. *Internal Threat Perceptions: Muslim Rebels*

	Oct. 86	Mar. 87	Sept. 88	Feb. 89	Sept. 89	Sept. 93
Great	65	60	54	63	54	77
Small	28	26	25	16	20	22
None	2	8	18	19	–	–
Maybe/Don't Know	–	5	2	0	24	–

Note: Question worded in the survey as follows: "Please tell me how great or small is the danger of the following to the government of President Corazon Aquino: Muslim rebels (very great, big, small, very small, none)?"
Source: Social Weather Station, *Social Weather Report Survey, Philippines: 1986–1993.*

security did come at the expense of formulating an overarching, comprehensive national security agenda. De Castro notes how four decades of focus on internal security threats undermined the AFP's ability to adequately address potential external security threats after the removal of U.S. bases in 1991. Poorly funded, the AFP weapons arsenal consisted largely of outdated equipment such as UH-1 Huey helicopters and armored vehicles geared toward counterinsurgency.[36] Former Philippine secretary of defense Orlando Mercado, who pushed for AFP modernization while still chair of the Senate Defense Committee, stated:

The Department of National Defense, whose [responsibility is to] chart the policy direction as well as strategic vision [of the armed forces], was historically short on strategic thinking. This resulted from decades of preoccupation with fighting insurgency and separatism. External defense was left to the managers of the 'security umbrella' provided by the Americans. While this made political sense for a cash strapped third world country, it in effect was an abdication of the raison d'etre of a military organization.[37]

[36] de Castro, "Adjusting to the Post-U.S. Bases Era," 121.
[37] Interview via e-mail with former senator and defense secretary Orlando Mercado, April 22, 2006.

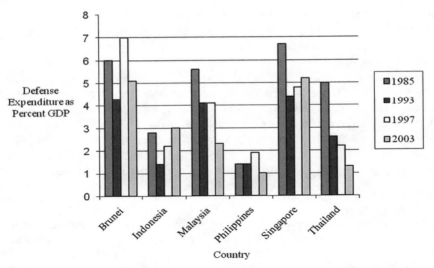

FIGURE 2.1. ASEAN Defense Expenditure as a Percentage of GDP. *Source:* IISS, *The Military Balance.*

In light of Mercado's comments, it is interesting to note that the Department of National Defense (DND) did not regularly publish defense white papers or any other overarching national security strategy agenda. According to political scientist Herman Kraft, the only year the DND conducted any comprehensive systematic study formulating a national security agenda was in the mid-1990s, published in 1998 as a defense policy paper titled "In Defense of the Philippines."[38] Mercado, then still chairman of the Senate Defense Committee, advocated outlining a national security strategy as a means to gather funds for the AFP modernization program. Devising a concrete national security strategy provided the justification necessary for an expanded budget and new equipment requests.[39] However, this suggests that the 1998 defense paper was motivated less by the pressing need for a new overarching security strategy and more by the appropriation of funds for AFP modernization.

The lack of external threat perceptions in the Philippines is confirmed by its low defense spending trends. Figure 2.1 indicates low defense expenditures in the Philippines relative to other Association of Southeast Asian Nations (ASEAN) countries.

Although one might argue that the U.S. security umbrella enabled the Philippines to maintain a low military budget, Figure 2.1 indicates that Philippine defense

[38] Republic of the Philippines, Department of National Defense, *In Defense of the Philippines: 1998 Defense Policy Paper* (Quezon City: DND, 1998). This fact was also substantiated in an interview with former national security advisor Jose Almonte, Manila, Philippines, March 21, 2006. Almonte served as national security advisor under President Fidel Ramos from 1992 to 1998.

[39] Interview with Herman Joseph Kraft, UP-Diliman, Quezon City, Philippines, March 28, 2006.

spending remained low even *after* the U.S. withdrawal in 1991. This suggests that the Philippines continued to place a low priority on purchasing the expensive equipment necessary to maintain a grand strategy oriented toward external security threats.

National security priorities were less clear without the presence of any looming external threat. Therefore, the absence of perceived external threats, and the lack of any clear sense of direction in grand strategy, weakened political support for U.S. bases. In the weeks prior to the Senate vote on the Treaty of Friendship, Cooperation, and Security, numerous senators repeated that no clear security rationale existed for maintaining U.S. bases. The most telling speech was given by Senator Juan Ponce Enrile, former secretary of defense under Marcos:

In considering the draft Treaty, Mr. President, the first thing we must consider is this: Do we have an external enemy against whom we must be defended with the full panoply of U.S. military power? None that we may know of Mr. President. I have been a Secretary of National Defense of this Republic. I have the good fortune to be so for 17 years, and no one can tell me truthfully that today, in the next 10 years, we will have an external enemy for which we must have the security umbrella of the United States of America. No country in the region has any conceivable interest in invading the Philippines.[40]

Even senators who voted to retain U.S. bases questioned the need for bases from a security standpoint. Chairwoman of the Senate Foreign Relations Committee Leticia Ramos-Shahani recalled:

The world situation wasn't so bad. Gorbachev was talking about perestroika. The Soviet Union was collapsing, and thus the U.S. bogeyman disappeared. China had opened up. I visited China, and they welcomed us with open arms. The ideological threat was gone, so why did we need the Seventh Fleet? What threat is there to defend us from? During that time, we were debating what do we really need the bases for?[41]

The absence of perceived external security threats, and the focus on internal security, certainly weakened political support for U.S. bases. This provided activists the political space necessary to enter the debate over U.S. bases and forge ties with government elites. Even among the executive-led pro-base faction,[42] the

---

[40] Republic of the Philippines, *Record of the Senate. Fifth Regular Session*, Vol. 1, No. 24, "Sponsorship speech of Senator Enrile," September 11, 1991, 806.

[41] Interview with former senator Leticia Ramos-Shahani, Makati City, Philippines, March 15, 2006. Of course, several pro-base senators also cited the need for bases given the weak state of Philippine security. Leading the charge was Senator Vicinte Paterno, who stated, "With the power vacuum in the region that is brought about by the abdication by the Soviet Union of superpower status, we may find regional bullies emerging who want to dominate the region.... [T]he Gulf War illustrated the need for a continued defense umbrella of the United States and assistance to build up the Philippine defense capability. ... If U.S. security assistance were to be withdrawn abruptly, I am afraid our country would be a sitting duck for any aggressor." See Republic of the Philippines, *Record of the Senate. Fifth Regular Session*, Vol. 1, No. 7, "Privilege speech of Senator Paterno," August 1, 1991, 246–47.

[42] This included President Aquino, the Department of Foreign Affairs, and the Treaty negotiating panel represented by various cabinet officials.

security rationale for bases appeared ambiguous at best. Although some officials cited security issues as a reason to maintain bases, many of those inside the Aquino administration, including Aquino herself, were more interested in the potential economic benefits reaped by the bases.[43] Until July 1991, the Philippine panel requested a minimum annual compensation of $825 million for a seven-year period.[44] Foreign Secretary Raul Manglapus expressed this sentiment at a meeting sponsored by Senate President Jovito Salonga's summer retreat in what came to be known as the *Pansol Reflections*: "Our optimum position is to eliminate both bases immediately; but the interest of our citizens as has been already clarified here by congressmen, labor leaders, and others, demand[s] that we negotiate something that will take care of the welfare of our citizens."[45] The Philippine government eventually signed the treaty at a much lower cost ($325 million). The lower compensation package certainly did not help ratification of the treaty in the Senate, but it is still important to highlight that economic benefits alone were unable to generate the political will necessary to maintain U.S. bases.

Would the Philippine Senate have voted "yes" to U.S. bases had a strong security consensus existed? The theory I propose suggests such a possibility. One theoretical implication is that the presence of a strong security consensus among government elites – that is, a shared perception and intersubjective understanding of national security embedded in R.P.-U.S. security relations and U.S. bases – would have resulted in the retention of Subic Bay Naval Station regardless of the low economic compensation. Implicit here is the assumption that security trumps economics. In short, the Philippine state lacked a strong security consensus. This lack of consensus among government leaders, contributed by low external threat perceptions and the focus on internal security, produced divergent attitudes regarding U.S. bases and R.P.-U.S. relations among Philippine elites. Anti-base activists were thus able to take advantage of divided elites by supporting anti-base senators and forming ties with political elites sympathetic to their cause.

INTERACTION BETWEEN STATE AND SOCIETY

Although a weak security consensus may have helped shape base policy outcomes, a complete picture is only provided by examining structural elements

---

[43] President Aquino stated, "We have stressed to the American Panel our need for an immediate and sizeable capital infusion to shore up our international reserves, stabilize our currency, improve the investment climate, promote employment, and accelerate economic growth." See Document 4.14, "Press statement of President Corazon Aquino on the results of Pact V, Manila, 16 February 1991," in Castro-Guevara, *Bases Talks Reader*, 168.

[44] Document 4.12, "Letter of Secretary Raul Manglapus, to Special Negotiator Richard Armitage, in reply to his 5 February 1991 Letter on the U.S. Compensation Package of the Philippines, 12 February 1991," in Castro-Guevara, *Bases Talks Reader*, 163–65.

[45] Belinda Aquino, *Reflections on the U.S. Bases in the Philippines*, transcript of the Pansol Reflections Series, Calamba, Laguna, Philippines, August 5, 1990 (Manila: Senate Legislative Publications Staff, 1990), 45.

such as the security consensus in conjunction with agency and the role of anti-base activists. In the Philippines, the causal mechanisms linking the security consensus to movement outcomes were embedded in the relationship between anti-base movements and sympathetic elites. The absence or presence of a security consensus did not produce outcomes per se but rather provided a favorable opportunity structure for movements to penetrate the state and form ties with key elites.[46] Activists, in turn, needed to make the right strategic decisions and tactical choices to successfully promote their anti-base agenda at the policy level. In sum, the combination of a permissive structural environment (the weak security consensus) and the movement strategies of anti-base actors led to the withdrawal of U.S. bases in the Philippines. This section proceeds with an analysis of anti-base mobilization strategies and the interaction between the ATM and the anti-base senators under the context of a weak security consensus.

Anti-Treaty Movement (ATM)

Formed in 1990 in preparation for PACT negotiations and the expiration of the 1947 Mutual Base Agreement (MBA), the ATM held one major advantage over previous anti-base coalition groups: after the MBA's expiration, any new agreement negotiated between Washington and Manila required ratification from the Senate by a two-thirds majority. This provision, stipulated in the 1987 amended Constitution, suddenly enhanced the political clout of senators as the MBA approached its September 16, 1991, expiration date. ATM activists recognized the Senate's pivotal role, understanding that the fate of bases, if not terminated or negotiated favorably by President Aquino's base panel negotiating team, rested with the twenty-three senators. The amended Constitution also called for a national referendum on any new base agreement approved by the Senate. Important constitutional revisions therefore provided Senators, and indirectly civil society, political power in the politics of bases. The lack of security consensus and the ensuing division regarding the role of U.S. bases thus worked to the advantage of the ATM.

Mobilization

The ATM was an extension of the previous coalition group, ABAKADA, which had grown relatively inactive by 1991. As with previous coalitions, the National Democrat (ND) faction of the political left organized and directed the

---

[46] The security consensus (or lack thereof) in the Philippines may have been shaped to some degree by nationalist leaders and activists during the formative period of anti-base movements. In other words, the degree of security consensus may be partially endogenous to anti-base movements. Although this creates an endogeneity problem between social movements and the elite consensus, the issue is less problematic for my argument since I only need to demonstrate whether the security consensus is weak or strong rather than the formation of the security consensus itself. I am more interested in the interaction between activists and elites once I determine the degree of elite security consensus.

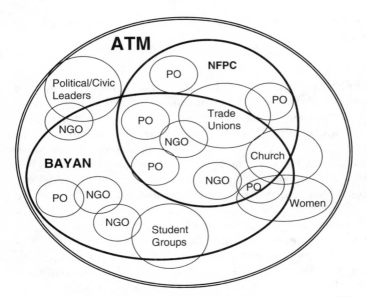

FIGURE 2.2. Membership of the Anti-Treaty Movement Coalition.

coalition.[47] The political bloc Bayan, and coalition groups traditionally involved in anti-base movements such as the NFPC and ABC, spearheaded mobilization efforts. Figure 2.2 diagrams the coalition structure of the ATM and its relationship with Bayan, as well as other groups, sectors, nongovernmental organizations (NGOs), and people's organizations (POs).

Similar to that of previous coalitions, ATM membership consisted of various NGOs, POs, interest groups, and individual political and community leaders. Sectors represented in the coalition included peace, environmental, women's, student, religious, intellectual, and labor groups. Note the degree of overlap among the various groups and organizations, indicating that none of the groups were necessarily mutually exclusive.

Anti-base activists used existing mobilizing structures, such as social networks and institutions, to expand their coalition. Bayan, with its large political network across multiple sectors such as labor and peace groups, directed much of the mobilization work at the grassroots level. Also, groups affiliated with Bayan organized committees and sent representatives to the larger ATM meeting, who in turn directly mobilized their own members. Lidy Nacpil, former general secretary of Bayan, notes that many of the "personalities," the recognizable faces of the movement such as politicians or celebrities, had little to do with the actual mobilization effort. However, their presence as prominent public

---

[47] Despite its ND orientation, the ATM did manage to convince some Social Democrat (SD) factions to work together in blocking the passage of the new negotiated base treaty. See fn. 27 on the SD/ND distinction.

leaders or celebrity status did help gather crowds. This was particularly true for the unorganized masses.[48]

Framing

In addition to mobilization structures, anti-base activists employed cognitive frames that resonated with various sectors of Philippine civil society. Nacpil states, "If for example you mobilize the labor group, you have to frame it in their language and how it affects them."[49] Like other movements, activists faced an uphill battle mobilizing the masses since the heart of the base issue rested on more abstract principles such as sovereignty or respect. Nevertheless, the ATM utilized nationalist and sovereignty rights frames in the larger anti-base debate. These frames were visible in the ATM's community discussion groups and the literature on bases distributed to the public. Nacpil and other movement leaders noted that a clear explanation of the issues through public forums, position statements, and media coverage was essential for mass mobilization.

Paradoxically, ATM conveners narrowed their focus from an anti-base to anti-Treaty position to form the broadest coalition possible. The coalition's name, "Anti-Treaty Movement," was indicative of this conscious shift in strategy. As Nacpil, Diokno, Simbulan, and other key anti-base activists commented, forming the ATM was a strategy that focused on the narrowest target possible; defeating the Treaty equaled a defeat for the bases. Nacpil argued, "To frustrate the extension of the life of the bases, this Treaty [had to] be junked. It didn't matter if others would be [rejecting] it for reasons not as comprehensive as ours. What was important was that we mobilized the broadest opposition to the Treaty to [remove] the bases."[50] By focusing on the Treaty rather than bases, the ATM drew in other groups and individuals who were not necessarily opposed to U.S. bases but opposed to the unequal terms of the Treaty. The "paltry" $203 million annual compensation particularly drew the ire of many Filipinos. By lowballing Filipinos, the U.S. negotiators underestimated the reactions of nationalist elites. Simbulan writes, "The lopsided treaty sealed the unexpected alliance between the Senators who were pro-bases but anti-treaty, and the core group of anti-base Senators."[51] For example, Senator Teofisto Guingona states in his Senate speech of nonconcurrence, "We want friendship with America. We want cooperation. We want trade. But we do not want servitude. We do not want an agreement that debases us as a nation. We do not want terms that degrade our dignity as a people."[52] Senator Rene Saguisag argued, "Saying yes to the Treaty, *in its present form* [italics mine], is, in my view, to condemn the Philippines to another ten years of exploitation under a

---

[48] Interview with Roland Simbulan, March 10, 2006; and interview with Lidy Nacpil, April 28, 2006.

[49] Interview with Lidy Nacpil, April 28, 2006.

[50] Ibid.

[51] Simbulan, "September 16, 1991."

[52] Senate Legislative Publications Staff, *Bases of Their Decisions*, 53.

one-sided, unequal, invidiously discriminatory arrangement."[53] The more progressive media outlets, sympathetic to anti-base movements, printed scathing
editorials criticizing the unequal terms of the Treaty. Nacpil remarks, "One of
the most important decisions made at the time was the shift in framing the issue
to an anti-Treaty movement. Whether you were opposing the Treaty for the right
reasons or not, for the comprehensive reasons or not, if we were divided at that
time we would not have succeeded."[54]

Strategy

The ATM took advantage of the political opportunity provided under conditions of weak security consensus. Activists recognized divisions among
Philippine elites regarding the future role of U.S. bases, particularly within the
Philippine Senate. As part of a two-pronged strategy, activists first targeted
elites. The immediate goal was to block ratification of any new base treaty in
the Senate. Thus significant amounts of time and energy were directed at lobbying senators or providing them with information about the ongoing PACT
negotiations and the implications of a lopsided Treaty favoring the United
States. For instance, the ATM obtained an early draft of the Treaty proposed
by the R.P-U.S. panel and provided this information to senators. Activists also
leaked the unfavorable Treaty terms to the press in the early rounds of the
PACT.[55] Highlighting the lack of respect from "arrogant" American negotiators
and their insultingly low base compensation package, activists publicized the
unfair terms of the Treaty. By feeding senators detailed analyses of the draft and
publicizing the unfair Treaty terms in the media, activists provided fuel for anti-
base senators in their call to remove U.S. bases.

Realizing the large stake senators held in deciding the future of U.S. bases,
ATM activists immediately devised a lobbying strategy toward senators. The
first task was an analysis of the Senate "straw vote." Senate President Jovito
Salonga held two informal surveys, the first on February 21 and the second on
July 30, 1991, to assess where the other senators stood on the bases issue. In the
first straw vote, twelve senators indicated in writing that they were against the
bases without any qualification. The majority of the other senators positioned
themselves ambiguously, stating they wanted to study the draft treaty before
coming to any conclusion.[56] Anti-base activists obtained a record of the informal

[53] Ibid., 173.
[54] Interview with Lidy Nacpil, April 28, 2006.
[55] Interview with Ma Socorro "Cookie" Diokno, April 10, 2006. This information was confirmed
by Roland Simbulan during a panel discussion at the Third World Studies Center Roundtable
"Alliances, Anti-Base Movements and the Politics of US Military Bases: The Philippines Case in
Comparative Perspective," UP-Diliman, Quezon City, May 2, 2006. Reportedly, a Philippine
government official sympathetic to movements had provided this information. Also see Ma
Socorro "Cookie" Diokno, "Analysis of the Bases Talks" and "Outline of Objections to Draft
Agreement on Installations and Military Operating Procedures," internal ATM documents, 1991,
obtained from the personal collection of Corazon Fabros.
[56] Salonga, *Senate That Said No*, 209.

straw vote held by Salonga, and in a document dated March 1, 1991, drafted a strategy and various tactics to influence the Senate vote in September. In the draft, the ATM grouped the senators into five columns based on their stance toward the bases and how committed they were to their stated position. In other words, activists gauged the probability that senators could be swayed by ATM lobbying. The five categories and the respective movement strategies were as follows:[57]

Column 1: **Senators voting no.** Those listed in column 1 need support by the different anti-base groups: their voting positions need to be reinforced. Senators Aquino, Enrile, Estrada, Guingona, Laurel, Mercado, Romulo, Saguisag, Tañada, Ziga, Salonga.

Column 2: **Senators voting no on current terms with option to change vote subject to final terms.** Those listed in column 2 need reinforcement of their voting positions. They need to be furnished more information. They need to be lobbied personally. Senators Alvarez, Lina, Pimentel.

Column 3: **Judgment reserved pending review of final draft.** Those listed in column 3 can be classified into (a) *Pro-bases and least likely to change their vote, regardless of the outcome of the talk and the terms and conditions of the new treaty.* Senators Maceda, Paterno, Shahani, Angara, Gonzales. (b) *Still undecided, and open to the possibility of changing their vote, given more information.* Senators Rasul, Herrera, Tamano. Little or no efforts at all should be expended towards reaching or trying to influence those listed under column 3a and column 4. On the other hand, every effort should be exerted towards influencing those listed under Column 3b.

Column 4: **Tentative Yes, subject to compensation and other terms.** Senator Osmeña.

Column 5: **Yes.** No senators.

Activists then proposed contacting various anti-base groups to "adopt" a bloc of senators to target, and listed various tactics to be used to influence them. For example, activists were encouraged to maintain support for senators who were clearly going to vote "no" by sending letters, postcards, and telegrams of support and congratulations, and by "holding rallies, pickets, and other mass actions of support." Meanwhile, the ATM proposed spending the bulk of its resources and energy on the "wavering" or "swing vote" senators. Activists formed a "Special Lobby Task Force" with three subcommittees: (1) Research; (2) Lobby/Delegation; (3) Writers/Media.[58]

---

[57] The following comes from an internal ATM document, "Senate Straw Vote, 01 March 1991," copy obtained from the personal collection of Corazon Fabros. Documents transferred to UP-Diliman Library Archives.

[58] Ibid.

The ATM's second, broader goal was the mass public campaign to educate Filipinos about the negative impact of U.S. military bases. As mentioned previously, if the base treaty passed through the Senate, it would then have to pass through a national referendum. Thus anti-base groups needed to sway public opinion against U.S. military bases in case the Senate did not reject the treaty. Anti-base movement leaders traveled around different regions of the Philippines, giving presentations or organizing forums to educate the public about U.S. bases and presenting reasons why base removal was in the best interest of Filipinos. Groups opposed to bases, such as the National Council of Churches in the Philippines (NCCP) or NFPC, also produced primers, pamphlets, and other literature to raise awareness about bases. Lastly, mass rallies were held in Manila and around central Luzon. Although the majority of Filipinos were in favor of U.S. bases, large anti-base rallies signaled the presence of a strong, vocal minority opposed to bases.[59] Figure 2.3 recreates the flow chart drawn by ATM activists demonstrating how the two-pronged strategy, Senate lobbying and mass action, was timed and coordinated as a response to specific government activity.

Host-State Response: Anti-base Elites and the Anti-Treaty Movement

The preceding section discussed anti-base movement strategies and tactics aimed at both government officials and the mass public. Did any of this lobbying, media reporting, picketing, or marching have any bearing on actual policy outcomes? If the final Treaty vote rested with the Senate, how much influence did anti-base activists have over the base policymaking process? Can a link be established between ATM pressure and the decisions of key political elites? What was the nature of the relationship between anti-base senators and activists? These questions must be addressed to substantiate the claim that social movements mattered in the closing of Subic Bay Naval Station.

As suggested in the February 21 straw vote, twelve of the senators already held an anti-base stance before any formal ATM lobbying efforts. That a group of senators were already open to anti-base arguments significantly aided the ATM campaign. In addition to having valuable activist resources to apply toward lobbying, ATM activists found potential allies among key government elites with significant power in the base policy process. Nationally respected, with many coming from privileged backgrounds, the formal participation of senators within the anti-base campaign increased the legitimacy, mobilizing capacity, and power of the ATM. In particular, three anti-base senators would

---

[59] In July 1991, perhaps the height of the anti-base debate, 25 percent opposed U.S. bases, whereas 44 percent were in favor of the U.S. presence (Social Weather Station, 1991). Anti-base activists argue, however, that, in addition to numbers, mobilization capacity and the composition of movement activists were just as important. Participating in anti-base campaigns were notable intellectuals, politicians, and lawyers, who carried significant political weight beyond their numbers. As one activist remarked, *who* was protesting was just as important as "how many" (interview with Cora Fabros, March 6, 2006).

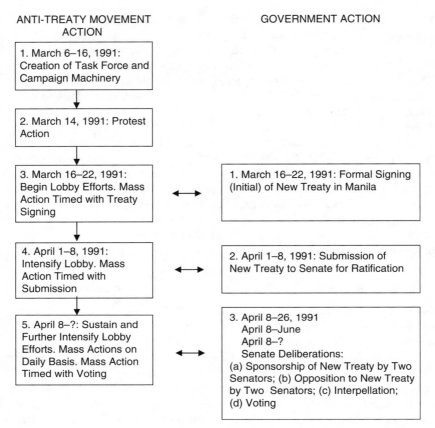

ANTI-TREATY MOVEMENT
ACTION

GOVERNMENT ACTION

1. March 6–16, 1991:
Creation of Task Force and
Campaign Machinery

2. March 14, 1991: Protest
Action

3. March 16–22, 1991:
Begin Lobby Efforts. Mass
Action Timed with Treaty
Signing

1. March 16–22, 1991: Formal Signing
(Initial) of New Treaty in Manila

4. April 1–8, 1991:
Intensify Lobby. Mass
Action Timed with
Submission

2. April 1–8, 1991: Submission of
New Treaty to Senate for Ratification

5. April 8–?: Sustain and
Further Intensify Lobby
Efforts. Mass Actions on
Daily Basis. Mass Action
Timed with Voting

3. April 8–26, 1991
   April 8–June
   April 8–?
   Senate Deliberations:
(a) Sponsorship of New Treaty by Two
Senators; (b) Opposition to New Treaty
by Two Senators; (c) Interpellation;
(d) Voting

FIGURE 2.3. Flowchart of ATM Coordinated Strategy. *Source:* Internal ATM document, "Senate Straw Vote, 01 March 1991." Copy obtained from personal collection of Corazon Fabros.

become crucial players within the ATM: Wigberto "Bobby" Tañada, Joseph Estrada, and Juan Ponce Enrile. Tañada, whose father, Lorenzo Tañada, served as a key organizer in previous anti-base coalitions, was the most active of the three and played a crucial role in updating the ATM with information from the Senate.[60] The addition of Enrile and Estrada into the movement also boosted the image and credibility of the ATM. Their addition invited the possibility of broader support by signaling to both the masses and other political elites that the anti-base movement traveled beyond leftist political rhetoric.[61] As mentioned earlier, former defense secretary Enrile represented the established political

[60] Interview with activist Roland Simbulan, March 10, 2006. Simbulan served as senior political consultant to Senator Tañada in 1991.
[61] Interview with former senator Wigberto Tañada, March 19, 2006.

right. Meanwhile, Senator (and later President) Estrada, a former action movie star, carried widespread popularity among the masses. Regarding the involvement of Enrile and Estrada in the ATM, Senator Rene Saguisag noted, "Since they stood for the right and the masses, the nation more easily accepted our vote. Enrile brought in the right, and Estrada brought in the masses. Some of the anti-base Senators were perceived as Communists so their presence gave us a tremendous boost."[62]

The active participation of Senators Tañada, Enrile, and Estrada also helped ATM activists coordinate their tactical campaign against other senators. The most important battleground for the ATM was not necessarily on the streets but inside Parliament, with all attention focused on the Senate vote on September 16, 1991.[63] As argued earlier, rather than blanket lobbying the senators, ATM activists strategically lobbied political elites based on information from "insiders" like Senator Tañada.

One should note that the collaboration between ATM activists and anti-base senators was not automatically given simply because activists and elites shared similar positions regarding U.S. bases. Activists made a conscious strategic decision to reach out to Philippine elites, even those formerly associated with the Marcos dictatorship. For instance, many activists were initially wary of Senator Enrile's participation in the ATM because of his ties to the Marcos regime. Activists suspicious of Enrile's role during the Marcos era questioned whether the movement should allow his active participation. Etta Rosales, an official with Partido ng Bayan (PnB), states, "It was Bobby Tañada who invited Enrile to the launching [of ABAKADA] and even asked him to sit in front. He ended up wedged between Crispin Beltran and Nathaniel Santiago. The rest didn't want to sit beside him at all. Of course, we had to shake hands with him."[64] Also, some anti-base senators, aware of the ATM's leftist political leanings, were cautious not to tie themselves too closely with groups associated with the extreme left.[65] Nevertheless, the ATM worked hard to reach out to all elites, putting aside former ideological differences.

In addition to the three senators active inside the ATM, several other senators who eventually voted against the Treaty tacitly supported the anti-base movement. For instance, although Senate President Salonga stated that his "no" vote was independent of any anti-base movement pressure, he did welcome anti-base activity from the "legal left" since it strengthened his own position.[66] Activists also note the immense pressure faced by senators, particularly from pro-base groups, the business lobby, and public opinion, which was generally in favor of bases. After reaching its peak in April 1990 with 43 percent of Filipinos

---

[62] Interview with former senator Rene Saguisag, March 22, 2006.
[63] Ferrer, "Anti-Bases Coalition," 20.
[64] Quoted in Ferrer, "Anti-Bases Coalition," 15.
[65] Interview with former Senate president Jovito Salonga, March 4, 2006.
[66] Ibid. Suspicious of more radical groups such as the NDF, Salonga was careful to distinguish between the center-left and extreme left.

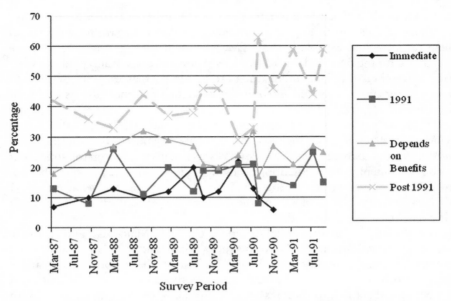

FIGURE 2.4. Public Opinion Indicating Desired Length of Stay for U.S. Bases in Metro Manila, 1987–1991. Question in survey stated: "The existing treaty with regard to the US Bases here in the Philippines will expire in 1991. Which of the following resembles closest your opinion regarding the bases?" Possible responses: (1) Should be removed at the earliest possible time without waiting for 1991; (2) Should be retained until 1991 only, and removed thereafter; (3) Should be retained until 1991 only, and thereafter removed if the benefits offered by the US are not increased; (4) Should be retained beyond 1991 because present setup provides huge benefits to the Philippines from the US. *Source:* Social Weather Station, *Social Weather Report Survey.*

expressing their desire for base closures on or before 1991, anti-base public opinion declined to 25 percent in July 1991.[67] Figure 2.4 presents survey data on the desired length of stay for U.S. bases in the metro Manila area.

Activists feared that senators not firmly committed to an anti-base position would cave in to public opinion or the business lobby. To counter pro-base pressure, anti-base activists made their presence known, making sure the base issue would not go down quietly. Thus, support for anti-base senators, and the constant presence of the ATM in public debates, helped provide moral support and sustain the position of anti-base senators.

[67] Social Weather Station, *Social Weather Report Survey*, 1987–1991. In July 1991, 44 percent of Filipinos were pro-base and 27 percent stated that their decision depended on the benefits. Despite the 44 percent pro-base majority, survey analysts argued that the "depends on benefits" group acted as a "swing vote," which could also tip anti-base numbers toward the majority. See Felipe Miranda, *Filipino Public Opinion on the Issue of American Facilities in the Philippines* (Quezon City: Social Weather Station, 1989), OP-M-7.

Assessing or "proving" anti-base movement effectiveness is difficult consider-ing the prior preferences held by senators. The February and July 1991 straw votes indicate more than eight senators, or the one-third necessary to reject Treaty ratification, were planning to vote against the bases. Thus, even without anti-base movement activity, one might argue that the Senate would have voted "no" to U.S. bases anyway. Many senators agree with this statement. Anti-base activists all staunchly disagree. Adjudicating the "correct" position ex post facto is diffi-cult.[68] Rather than debating whether anti-base movements independently played an effective role, Cookie Diokno suggests another approach to assessing effective-ness by arguing that the relationship between anti-base senators and activists was symbiotic. Noting that the relationship between the masses and senators is a two-way process, she observes, "It was symbiotic. I don't think one could have won without the other. You needed a mass movement . . . even though Senators [held the decisionmaking power]. If they didn't have anyone listening to them, they didn't have an audience, or if they didn't have any group organizing the forums or people . . . would they have gotten anywhere?"[69] In other words, Diokno implies that the presence of a core anti-base group within civil society helped reaffirm senators' anti-base stance. Additionally, Diokno, who analyzed the Treaty terms in detail, provided information to the other senators through Senator Tañada. She argues that senators themselves did not have time to study all the details of the agreements,and thus relied on the ATM's analysis. Simbulan attests to this by noting that portions of the ATM's position paper and anti-base literature were used in the speeches of many of the anti-base senators.[70]

In hindsight, one can argue that the Senate outcome against bases was never really in question, thus rendering anti-base movements epiphenomenal. However, the months preceding September 16, 1991, were filled with uncertainty and suspense. Two pieces of evidence help adjudicate between several senators' claims that Treaty rejection was inevitable and anti-base activists' claims that the out-come was much more contested. First, public opinion polls consistently indicated a pro-base majority in the Philippines, placing enormous pressure on senators to vote in favor of bases. Fighting against majority opinion, the ATM advocated a position that would require senators to vote contrary to the electoral majority.[71] Senator Salonga and other anti-base senators also acknowledged extensive pres-sure from the United States and other Philippine elites. In addition to pressure

---

[68] The anti-base senators I interviewed acknowledged that ATM support was "welcome" and "helpful," but most stated or implied that their own position and vote was based on their own conscience. Although this is true, activists emphasized that without their role and public support, senators would possibly have caved in under pressure to vote in favor of bases. For example, one activist noted his disappointment with Senator Heherson Alvarez (who had an activist back-ground) and Senator Jose Lina; activists assumed both would vote against the base, but on September 16 both senators voted "yes" to the Treaty (interview with ATM activist, March 10, 2006).

[69] Interview with Ma Socorro "Cookie" Diokno, Quezon City, Philippines, April 10, 2006.

[70] Interview with Roland Simbulan, Quezon City, Philippines, May 2, 2006.

[71] Senators are elected at-large in national elections.

from chief U.S. negotiator Richard Armitage, Salonga notes how several U.S. officials, including Congressman Stephen Solarz, Ambassador Frank Wisner, and embassy officials Kenneth Quinn and John Maisto, all made personal appeals to him, and most likely other senators as well.[72] President Aquino and government officials favoring a five-to-seven-year phaseout of Subic Bay also employed pressure tactics by organizing their own pro-base protests and threatening anti-base senators. Alfredo Bengzon, the vice chairman of the Philippine bases negotiating panel, states in his narrative of the PACT process how the president had rallied thousands on September 10, 1991, in Manila on national television to coerce senators into voting in favor of the Treaty.[73] The government bused state employees "complete with packed lunches paid for with government funds" to the Luneta, the site of the pro-base rally. At the rally, "speakers delivered a message to the anti-treaty Senators that would strike fear into the heart of any politician determined to hang on to his position at all costs."[74] Senate President Salonga also wrote in his memoirs, "I received a number of veiled threats in the Senate. I was told that businessmen from my town were going to picket my residence. . . . For a while, I thought that we, the anti-Treaty senators, were engaged in a lonely struggle against our own people."[75]

Second, several senators who stated they were originally anti-base did switch their positions in the final September 16 vote. Whether because of immense pressure from pro-base factions or their own ambiguous preferences, four senators who initially stated they would vote against the bases switched their positions in favor of bases over the course of time.[76] This confirms activist claims that even as late as August 1991, there was no guarantee that eight senators would vote no, hence requiring activists to continue their campaign efforts. Movement claims that senators would have been more tempted to vote in favor of U.S. bases had there been no public support organized by anti-base movements, and no interaction between the ATM and the Philippine Senate, are therefore substantiated. Cookie Diokno comments, "If there were no loud, critical voices against bases, the Treaty may have just passed quietly without much debate. The fact that there was a vocal anti-base faction opened up a real debate on the bases issue."[77]

Conclusion: Security Consensus and State Penetration

That civil societal actors penetrated the state and formed ties with elites on base issues is rather remarkable given that military base decisions are often decided by

---

[72] Salonga, *Senate That Said No*, 214–15.

[73] Alfredo R. A. Bengzon, *A Matter of Honor: The Story of the 1990–1991 RP-US Bases Talks* (Manila: Anvil, 1997), 1.

[74] Ibid., 2–3.

[75] Salonga, *Senate That Said No*, 219.

[76] These four senators were Heherson Alvarez, Ernesto Herrera, Jose Lina, Jr., and Alberto Romulo.

[77] Interview with Ma Socorro "Cookie" Diokno, April 10, 2006.

the executive or bureaucracies such as the foreign affairs or defense agencies. Relatively well insulated from civil society, activists are often unable to penetrate the more conservative foreign affairs and defense establishments, or even institutions such as the Philippine Senate, and therefore find it difficult to influence policy outcomes. In the Philippines, the executive and the foreign affairs department were largely in favor of retaining U.S. bases, particularly Subic Bay Naval Station.[78] However, as argued earlier in this chapter, forming alliances with domestic political elites was possible because of elite divisions under a weak security consensus. Although this may appear banal at first, it is a crucial point that determines whether anti-base movements are capable of penetrating the state and forming ties with key political figures in the bases debate. Too often civil society is marginalized in security policy because political elites, especially those within the foreign policy establishment, reject alternative security discourses contrary to the status quo. This is particularly true in asymmetric alliance patterns, where the weaker power lacks the leverage and political will to propose an alternative path diverging from the interests of the greater power.

Although the Marcos regime helped promote a common security consensus by silencing opposition and dissent through martial law, in the post-Marcos era, no strong security consensus existed regarding U.S.-Philippine relations and the role of U.S. bases. Even some elites favoring U.S. bases admitted that no external threats warranted bases for security reasons. As argued earlier, the debates regarding military bases in the Philippines *Record of the Senate* largely revolved around sovereignty and economic issues, not security incentives stemming from the U.S. military presence. The pro-base Aquino administration and the majority of business elites were in favor of bases because of their implications for trade, investment, and U.S. economic assistance, rather than security. During negotiations with the R.P. negotiating panel, Armitage complained that his counterparts were engaging in "cash-register" diplomacy. Without a strong security consensus, and consequently any security rationale for maintaining U.S. bases, political elites remained divided on the issue. Additionally, nationalist sentiments, pushed forward by middle-class intelligentsia and the organized left, further fragmented elites.[79] The weak security consensus, divided elites, and the presence of strong nationalist sentiments among several Philippine senators provided the political space necessary for ATM activists and political elites to cooperate.

Activists, of course, had to make the correct strategic choices and jump through the window opened by conditions of a weak security consensus. Again, in hindsight, it appears easy to convey the ATM's success story with a sense of historical determinism. On deeper reflection, however, activists could have selected poor strategies and made "wrong" choices that would have

---

[78] Interestingly, defense officials were marginalized from the base debate (interview via e-mail with former senator and defense secretary Orlando Mercado, April 22, 2006).

[79] Walden Bello, "Moment of Decision: The Philippines, the Pacific, and U.S. Bases," in *The Sun Never Sets: Confronting the Network of Foreign U.S. Military Bases*, edited by Joseph Gerson and Bruce Birchard (Boston: South End Press, 1991), 159.

weakened movement effectiveness and their ability to influence base policy outcomes. What if the ATM resisted putting aside ideological differences to join forces with anti-base elites who were not necessarily coming from the political left? What if activists decided to devote more resources to the mass public campaign rather than narrowly targeting senators? What if the ATM failed to capitalize on information from the leaked draft Treaty proposal, or decided not to reframe its agenda as "anti-Treaty"? Raising these counterfactuals forces us to question whether the closure of Subic Bay Naval Station was simply predetermined by the existence of a weak security consensus and the presence of anti-base senators. Instead, the weak security consensus provided an open window for activists to form ties with sympathetic elites and influence outcomes. Movements took advantage of this window by employing proper framing strategies, mobilizing resources, and targeting both elites and masses using various tactics.

In the absence of a strong security consensus, key government elites sympathetic to anti-base sentiments responded to activist efforts by embracing the anti-base movement cause. On the other hand, the pro-base faction in government, led by the executive, promoted various tactics to confront, disrupt, or co-opt anti-base movements via persuasion and pressure tactics. The lack of security consensus among Philippine elites, however, posed obstacles for the president and other pro-base groups in forging any cohesive policy to counter anti-base rhetoric. Granted, in the final week prior to the Senate vote, public opinion had swung clearly in favor of pro-base groups. However, anti-base activists had already penetrated elite ranks long before September 16, and found a core group of senators willing to align themselves with the ATM to promote the anti-base cause. A former embassy official in Manila noted how the anti-base movement "shaped the whole discussion of bases."[80] Government elites held "widely disparate views" on the bases and the future of U.S.-Philippine relations, thus providing activists the opportunity to form ties with sympathetic elites. In a symbiotic relationship between activists and government elites, anti-base movements were able to affect the policy direction of the government in shutting down Subic Bay Naval Station.

---

[80] Interview with former U.S. Embassy official in Manila, September 2, 2005, Washington, D.C.

3

The U.S.-Japan Alliance and Anti-Base Movements in Okinawa, 1995–1996

> To tell you the truth, I'm in an awkward position myself. Were I to pass on the demands of the Okinawan people, it would be for the complete return of Futenma. However, bearing in mind the importance of U.S.-Japan security ... I realize that this is extremely difficult.
>
> – Prime Minister Ryutaro Hashimoto[1]

August 2009 heralded a rare political moment in Japanese politics. Hailed by many Japanese as the "final blow to the island nation's postwar order," the Democratic Party of Japan (DPJ) resoundingly defeated the Liberal Democratic Party (LDP).[2] Washington policymakers had predicted the LDP's downfall months before the elections. However, political reality now sent U.S. officials scrambling for answers regarding the fate of an important Marine air base in Okinawa. In support of Okinawan anti-base demands, the DPJ had publicly campaigned against construction of Marine Corps Air Station (MCAS) Futenma's replacement facility within Okinawa. The media on both sides of the Pacific honed in on the potential looming crisis in the U.S.-Japan alliance and the precarious future of U.S. base realignment plans in Okinawa. Aside from passing references, however, what media reports often failed to mention regarding Futenma's relocation was the rape of a schoolgirl by two U.S. Marines and a Navy seaman fourteen years earlier. The incident triggered widespread anti-base protests, which eventually led to the promise of Futenma's return by the U.S. and Japanese governments.

This chapter returns to this earlier period of island-wide protests and the initial decision to return Futenma Air Base to Okinawans. As a "prequel" to the latest drama unfolding over Futenma (discussed at length in Chapter 6), this chapter focuses on Okinawan anti-base movements from 1995 to 1996 within the context of a strong security consensus. More specifically, this chapter

---

[1] Quoted in Yoichi Funabashi, *Alliance Adrift* (New York: Council on Foreign Relations Press, 1999), 21.
[2] Martin Fackler, "With Bold Stand, Japan Opposition Wins a Landslide," *New York Times*, August 31, 2009.

examines why massive protests, large enough to reverberate in the halls of government in Tokyo, failed to produce significant shifts in basing policy outcomes in the late 1990s. Anti-base protests in Okinawa did initially pressure Washington and Tokyo, leading to government concessions and partial victory for anti-base movements. However, contrary to anti-base movements in the Philippines, the existence of a strong security consensus among Japanese political elites prevented Okinawan anti-base movements from winning substantial long-term gains on basing policy outcomes. In particular, heightened anti-base opposition coincided with a period of alliance tightening between Tokyo and Washington, making it difficult for activists to gain any traction or leverage in their struggle against U.S. bases. Tokyo elites, influenced by a pervading consensus defining the U.S.-Japan alliance as a pillar of Japan's national security strategy, resorted to partial concessions and economic incentives to pacify anti-base sentiment without reneging on Japan's alliance commitments to the United States. The government's use of economic incentives and coercive legal measures undermined anti-base pressure.

Before proceeding, I should clarify where my interpretation of Okinawan anti-base movements is situated relative to other existing accounts and reveal the limited aims of my analysis. Depending on whose point of view and which time frame is considered, Okinawan anti-base movements over the past fifteen years have been assessed as both a success and a failure. Consistent with the other chapters in this book, I define "success" in this chapter in terms of policy outcomes. Although any shift from the status quo may be viewed as a success at the tactical level, as I demonstrate later, concessions predicated on conditional pledges do not constitute a "victory" for anti-base movements.

Further complicating base politics in Japan is the combination of multiple actors, interests, and identities across three different levels of analysis – local, national, and international. Unsurprisingly, based on the level of interaction, different scholars have offered different interpretations of anti-base movements and the politics of bases in Okinawa. I do not attempt to unpack all these complex relationships, and rely on the analyses of numerous other scholars and activists to help clarify Okinawan base politics. Although the tension between different local groups at the micro-level adds a fascinating dynamic to the politics of bases, for the purposes of my argument, more attention will be given to the macro-level (Tokyo and Washington) and meso-level (Tokyo and Okinawa) of interaction. Particularly important are the challenge of anti-base movements and the ability of the central government to balance between international and domestic forces.

U.S. BASES AND THE OKINAWAN RESISTANCE MOVEMENT

Understanding anti-base movements in Okinawa requires examining Okinawa's historical and cultural antecedents in relation to its struggle with mainland Japan. Formerly known as the independent Ryukyu Kingdom, the Ryukyu Islands were annexed by Japan in 1872 and formally incorporated into Japan as Okinawa Prefecture in 1879. The Japanese government pursued a policy of assimilation in Okinawa to civilize what they perceived as a backward group. Although many Okinawan elites supported assimilation with Japan, Japan's growing imperial ambitions and the Pacific war dramatically altered the attitudes and collective memory of Okinawans, and their relationship with the mainland.[3]

Battle of Okinawa and the First Wave

U.S. Marines set foot on Okinawa on April 1, 1945. In preparation for a major battle with the United States, the Japanese military conscripted Okinawan men into the Imperial Army and mobilized women and children to build airfields and defense fortifications. What stands out in the Battle of Okinawa is not the thousands of Okinawan casualties inflicted by American troops but the atrocities committed by Japanese soldiers against Okinawans. Japanese soldiers raped, looted, and extracted rations from the civilian population. The soldiers fortified themselves in the most secure caves as Okinawan civilians were left exposed to the "typhoon of steel." The Japanese military also recruited thousands of women into "comfort stations" as sex slaves. Soldiers executed Okinawans communicating in the Okinawan dialect under the pretense that they were spying on behalf of the Americans. Finally, with defeat imminent, Japanese troops either encouraged or forced residents to commit suicide rather than surrender to the United States. In a matter of months, a third of the entire Okinawan population perished.[4]

The Battle of Okinawa is significant in two respects. First, Okinawa's aversion to war stems directly from the collective memory of the Battle of Okinawa. Thus the battle "punctuates and articulates meanings of protest against war ... and against the existence of U.S. military bases on Okinawa."[5] Second, the battle highlighted the duality of Okinawan identity; although some Okinawans had accepted assimilation with Japan, the brutal treatment of Okinawans by Japanese soldiers stirred resentment and animosity against the mainland. As Julia Yonetani argues, the multiple and contradictory meanings of "Okinawa" and "Japan" have also been replayed in Okinawa's struggle against U.S. bases.[6]

After the war, Japan regained its full independence in 1951 under the terms of the San Francisco Peace Treaty. However, the United States maintained its right to govern Okinawa under the United States Civilian Administration of the Ryukyu Islands (USCAR). In addition to the use of former Japanese bases,

---

[3] Masamichi Inoue, *Okinawa and the U.S. Military: Identity Making in the Age of Globalization* (New York: Columbia University Press, 2007), 56; and Miyume Tanji, *Myth, Protest, and Struggle in Okinawa* (London: Routledge, 2006), 27.

[4] Tanji, *Myth, Protest, and Struggle in Okinawa*, 40.

[5] Ibid., 41.

[6] Julia Yonetani, "Future Asset, but at What Price? The Okinawa Initiative Debate," in *Islands of Discontent: Okinawan Responses to Japanese and American Power*, edited by Laura Hein and Mark Selden (Lanham, Md.: Rowman and Littlefield, 2003).

USCAR expropriated Okinawan land to expand the U.S. military presence. The confiscation of private property for base construction often resulted in local protests against U.S. bases. Thus the "first wave" of the Okinawan struggle was directed against land acquisition by the U.S. military. The first wave culminated in June 1956 with the release of the U.S. House Armed Service Committee's "Price Report." The report justified the permanent leasing of base land as well as further land expropriation. The initial sense of unity in the "all-island struggle," however, proved to be weak and temporary.[7] The broad coalition formed by various groups – political parties, labor unions, teachers' organizations, land-owners, and farmers – eventually fragmented. Okinawans were split between conservative groups who wanted to cooperate with the United States while demanding maximum rent for bases and other groups, such as the Okinawa Teachers Association (OTA) and the Okinawa People's Party (OPP), who sought Okinawa's reversion back to Japan.[8] Although failing to mobilize a cohesive coalition, the "first wave" of the Okinawan struggle did help solidify "the foundations of a new postwar identity and movement against marginalization."[9]

Second Wave

Land disputes with the U.S. military subsided as landowners signed contracts in exchange for large economic benefits. However, the Okinawan reversion movement continued into the 1960s in the "second wave" of the Okinawan struggle. Led by the Okinawa Prefecture Council for Reversion to the Home Country, a coalition headed by members from the OTA, local political parties, and labor unions, the reversion movement raised three specific grievances: crimes and accidents stemming from the U.S. military presence, the suspected deployment of nuclear weapons on U.S. bases, and the use of Okinawan bases to launch B-52 strikes in Vietnam.[10] Okinawans believed that the island's reversion to Japan would resolve these outstanding grievances. In a movement framed as "reversion nationalism," Okinawans united with progressive nationalist groups on main-land Japan opposed to the renewal of the U.S.-Japan security treaty. However, in the mid-1960s, U.S. and pro-U.S. Japanese government officials managed to negotiate legal and political arrangements enabling U.S. bases to remain in Okinawa.[11] This undoubtedly led to criticism against "reversion" as the basis of movement framing. Moreover, the onset of the Vietnam War forced pacifists within the reversion movement to reconsider Okinawa's return to a state that

---

[7] Tanji, *Myth, Protest, and Struggle in Okinawa*, 53.
[8] Ibid., 72–73.
[9] Ibid., 76.
[10] Ibid., 77.
[11] For a detailed discussion of U.S.-Japan negotiations regarding reversion movements, see Robert Eldridge, *The Return of the Amami Islands: The Reversion Movement and U.S.-Japan Relations* (Lanham, Md.: Lexington Books, 2004).

supported U.S. military action in Vietnam. Realizing that reversion would no longer achieve Okinawans' goal of reducing the U.S. military presence, the Council for Reversion attempted to fuse "reversion" with "antiwar" frames.

Third Wave and the Okinawa Prefecture People's Rally

Okinawa reverted back to Japan in 1972. Anti-base protests remained relatively sparse over the next two decades. However, the silence did not remove the tension between Washington and Tokyo's desire to maintain regional order and security and Okinawa's hope for life without U.S. bases.[12] It took the rape of a twelve-year-old girl in September 1995 to rekindle anti-U.S. military sentiment in Okinawa, thus ending the "low period" of Okinawan resistance.[13] On September 4, three U.S. servicemen snatched a twelve-year-old girl while driving their rented vehicle through a residential area in northern Okinawa. Dragging her into the vehicle, they taped her mouth and eyes shut and bound her hands and feet. The men then drove to an isolated beach and raped her.

Reports of the rape did not immediately elicit reactions in Okinawa. Political parties and anti-base groups remained silent, most likely because of the sense of shame attached to the young rape victim.[14] The first groups to break public silence and generate momentum against U.S. bases were women's groups, such as the Okinawan Women Act against Military and Violence (OWAAMV) and the League of Okinawan Women's Groups (*Okifuren*). *Okifuren* voiced their anger in a public statement on September 11. Other Okinawan organizations soon followed *Okifuren*'s lead, incensed over the rape and the U.S. military's refusal to hand over the three suspects. Reminiscent of earlier coalition groups, labor unions, political parties, teachers' unions, peace groups, and environmental groups organized rallies, participated in sit-ins, and formulated public statements against the U.S. military and the U.S.-Japan Status of Forces Agreement (SOFA).[15]

Activists used several collective action frames to mobilize Okinawans. For instance, women's groups became much more visible in the third wave, using the language of rape, dominance, and exploitation to frame their argument against U.S. bases. Like the twelve-year-old rape victim, innocent Okinawans, particularly women and children, were at risk from outside aggression. Frames of injustice highlighting the excessive noise and pollution, and later the destruction of the dugong's natural environment, would also play a powerful role in drawing both Okinawans and mainland Japanese into the anti-base struggle. Despite the diversity of various anti-base actors and their competing claims, the early period of the third wave (1995–96) managed to "reawaken the myth of a united

---

[12] Inoue, *Okinawa and the U.S. Military*, 38.
[13] Tanji, *Myth, Protest, and Struggle in Okinawa*, 106.
[14] Ibid., 152.
[15] Inoue, *Okinawa and the U.S. Military*, 35.

Okinawan Struggle."[16] Thus the mobilization leading up to the October 1995 Okinawa "People's Rally" gave the semblance of an island-wide struggle to those both within and outside Okinawa.

The local and prefectural governments' involvement in the anti-base struggle aided activists tremendously. Reformist political parties and city and village assemblies took part in protests. More importantly, the Okinawa Prefecture governor's direct actions and confrontation with the central government served as a rallying point for Okinawans. On September 20, Governor Masahide Ota met Foreign Minister Yohei Kono and presented a formal appeal to the Japanese government to revise SOFA.[17] As argued later, Ota single-handedly triggered a domestic and diplomatic crisis by refusing to sign the land lease that permitted the U.S. military to maintain bases in Okinawa.

Meanwhile, as Ota confronted Tokyo, anti-base protests in Okinawa continued to grow. On September 25, about 1,000 Okinawans protested in Naha, Okinawa's capital. The following day, 3,000 Okinawans, representing forty-three organizations and civic groups, organized by *Heiwa Undo* (Peace Movement Center), protested in Ginowan.[18] Okinawans also received support from anti-base groups in mainland Japan. Thirty-five local assemblies in seventeen prefectures approved resolutions or produced statements requesting that the Japanese government review the SOFA.[19] The high point of this movement episode took place on October 21, 1995, with 85,000 protestors taking part in the People's Rally. Denouncing the rape, the rally put forth a protest resolution with four demands: (1) imposing strict discipline on American military personnel in an effort to eradicate crime; (2) providing the rape victim immediate and full compensation in addition to an apology; (3) revising the Status of Forces Agreement; and (4) reducing and realigning the number of military bases in Okinawa.[20]

Mass protests in Okinawa and support from local governments and NGOs on the mainland provided Ota additional leverage in negotiations with Tokyo. In an act of protest and defiance, Ota rejected the government's request to sign the land-lease contracts on behalf of Okinawan citizens who were unwilling to grant their land to the U.S. military.[21] Ota stated, "In the past fifty years, Okinawa has always cooperated with the Japanese and U.S. governments, but

---

[16] Tanji, *Myth, Protest, and Struggle in Okinawa*, 16.

[17] *Daily Yomiuri*, "Ota Seeks Revision of Troop Pact," September 20, 1995.

[18] *Yomiuri Shimbun*, "3,000 Rally to Protest in Okinawa," September 27, 1995.

[19] *Yomiuri Shimbun*, "Rape Case Protests Spread Nationwide; Thirty-five Local Assemblies Call for Review of Military Pact," September 28, 1995.

[20] Masahide Ota, *Essays on Okinawa Problems* (Okinawa: Yui Shuppan, 2000).

[21] By law, if landowners and city officials refuse to sign land-lease contracts with the Japanese government for U.S. military use, the governor may legally sign contract renewals on behalf of the landowners. If the prefectural governor also refuses to sign the contracts, the Japanese prime minister may file a lawsuit against the governor.

they did not listen to Okinawan voices. This time, they should listen to us."[22] The conjunction of mass protests and Ota's defiance finally opened Tokyo's ears to Okinawan voices.[23]

Under the leadership of Ota and with support from the prefectural government, Okinawan anti-base activists successfully mobilized citizens to form an island-wide anti-base movement. Mass mobilization and Ota's defiance of Tokyo not only publicized Okinawan base issues in mainland Japan but also attracted its sympathy and support. Anti-base movement demands were directed primarily against the central government rather than the United States. Mass protests signaling increasing antagonism against bases, compounded by Governor Ota's refusal to sign the base lease, threatened to undermine Tokyo's post–Cold War security strategy and efforts to strengthen alliance ties with Washington. Thus, with the crisis reaching a boiling point, U.S. and Japanese officials established the Special Action Committee on Okinawa (SACO) to address Okinawan grievances. The SACO report eventually recommended the return of 21 percent of U.S. military base land, including MCAS Futenma, as well as the implementation of several operational and noise-abatement measures.[24]

Did the December 1996 SACO report recommendations suggest movement success? Although Okinawans achieved successful mobilization and extracted several concessions from Tokyo and Washington, further examination of this episode suggests that movements were less successful in changing the status quo. As Governor Ota remarked, the shuffling of bases within Okinawa merely "shift[ed] our own misery onto others."[25] Many larger demands, such as SOFA revisions, were unmet. The central government's use of compensation politics in later movement episodes also indicated where Tokyo's priorities lay when balancing between domestic and international forces. Undoubtedly, numerous factors, such as fragmentation within the anti-base movement, the marginalization of Okinawa, and the government's use of selective incentives to counter base opposition, may all have curtailed movement effectiveness. However, I argue that one factor in particular, the presence of a strong security consensus, played a heavy role in shaping the host government's response to anti-base opposition. An elite consensus, which elevated the role of the U.S.-Japan alliance, acted as a barrier preventing Okinawan activists from penetrating the state. Thus anti-base movements were unable to effectively push for changes on basing policy issues.

---

[22] Quoted in Inoue, *Okinawa and the U.S. Military*, 38.

[23] Sheila A. Smith, "Challenging National Authority: Okinawa Prefecture and the U.S. Military Bases," in *Local Voices, National Issues: The Impact of Local Initiative in Japanese Policymaking*, edited by Sheila A. Smith (Ann Arbor: University of Michigan Press, 2000), 79.

[24] United States General Accounting Office, *Overseas Presence: Issues Involved in Reducing the Impact of the U.S. Military Presence on Okinawa* (Washington, D.C.: U.S. General Accounting Office, 1998), 26.

[25] Funabashi, *Alliance Adrift*, 152.

SECURITY CONSENSUS

Although it is often assumed that most Japanese elites support the U.S.-Japan alliance, it is worth examining briefly where this consensus comes from and why it persists. That scholars and policymakers have reaffirmed Tokyo's strong alignment toward Washington for the past decade only makes my task easier.[26] With the strength of the alliance rooted in Japan's security norms and postwar domestic institutional arrangements, I marshal evidence from elite statements, policy documents, and public opinion polls confirming the breadth and depth of an elite consensus regarding the U.S.-Japan alliance during the mid- to late 1990s.

Thinking about Consensus

Thinking about Japanese security in terms of "consensus" is not a novel approach. For instance, Richard Samuels traces the trajectory of the Japanese grand strategy by connecting different "ideological dots" that highlight alternating periods of debate and consensus regarding Japanese security policy.[27] The use of consensus as an analytical concept is most appropriate in Japan because security politics is often dictated by the dominant consensus held by powerful political elites. Broadly speaking, the postwar consensus takes into account Japan's comprehensive approach to security, encompassing economic and political dimensions of security. More narrowly, the security consensus reflects Japan's staunch support of the U.S.-Japan alliance in its national defense strategy.

My analysis begins with Japan's defeat in World War II. Physically, mentally, and spiritually broken, Japan's disastrous imperial East Asia Co-Prosperity project ended with the occupation of Japan by foreigners. With Japan at the mercy of the U.S. military, the occupation quashed any lingering hopes of reestablishing it as a military power. The demilitarization of Japan carried out by U.S. forces was a "physical as well as a psychological project."[28] Japan's defeat would eventually pave the way for growing consensus around the Yoshida Doctrine – the emphasis on economic development as a means to national

---

[26] See Richard J. Samuels, *Securing Japan: Tokyo's Grand Strategy and the Future of East Asia* (Ithaca, N.Y.: Cornell University Press, 2007); Peter Katzenstein, *Rethinking Japanese Security: Internal and External Dimensions* (London: Routledge, 2008); Kenneth B. Pyle, *Japan Rising: The Resurgence of Japanese Power and Purpose* (New York: Public Affairs, 2007); Gavan McCormack, *Client State: Japan in American Embrace* (London: Verso, 2007); Thomas U. Berger, *Redefining Japan & the U.S.-Japan Alliance* (New York: Japan Society, 2004); and Mike Mochizuki, *Toward a True Alliance: Restructuring U.S.-Japan Security Relations* (Washington, D.C.: Brookings Institution Press, 1997).

[27] Samuels, *Securing Japan*, Chap.1.

[28] Thomas Berger, "Norms, Identity, and National Security in Germany and Japan," in *The Culture of National Security: Norms and Identity in World Politics*, edited by Peter Katzenstein (New York: Columbia University Press, 1996), 330.

power while relying on the U.S. alliance for national security. The Yoshida consensus effectively institutionalized Japan's postwar "cheap ride" to security under the U.S. security umbrella.[29]

Through 1952, the U.S. military laid the foundations of Japan's political institutions as well as the social and legal norms preventing Japan's military from reemerging as a powerful force.[30] Article 9 of the Japanese Constitution functioned as the cornerstone of Japan's postwar security arrangement. Under Article 9, Japan renounced war as a sovereign right and the use of force as a means to resolve international disputes. Transcending mere legal rhetoric, the Article developed into a norm over time, entrenched in Japan's political culture. Although revisionists today continue to test its limits, normative constraints have thus far made attempts at revising Article 9 extremely difficult.[31]

The Japanese government used institutions, such as the Cabinet Legislative Bureau (CLB), to curb its military ambition. To ensure that military-oriented revisionists would not usurp Article 9, bureaucrats and politicians formed the CLB as a civilian institution interpreting and legitimating Japanese national security. In addition to its function as an advisory body inside the prime minister's secretariat, the CLB interpreted Article 9 and dictated the scope and limitations of the use of Japan's Self-Defense Force (SDF). Over the years, the CLB reinterpreted the Article numerous times to fit Japan's security needs as defined by mainstream elites, giving it an elastic quality.[32]

Reflecting the depth of the security consensus, several other institutional procedures were built to prevent the military from gaining the upper hand on national security policymaking. For instance, the Japanese Defense Agency's (JDA) autonomy and capacity were limited by placing Ministry of Finance (MOF), Ministry of Foreign Affairs (MOFA), and Ministry of International Trade and Industry (MITI) officials within the JDA.[33] To ensure civilian control of the military, Prime Minister Shigeru Yoshida placed the JDA under the jurisdiction of his own office, thwarting any attempts to give the JDA full ministerial status. Yoshida also ordered the CLB to form "internal bureaus" within the JDA. These bureaus were headed by officials without prior military experience.[34]

In sum, Japanese mainstream pragmatists, cultivating institutional and normative constraints, consolidated the postwar security consensus by alienating

---

[29] See Samuels, *Securing Japan*, Chap. 1.

[30] Peter Katzenstein and Nobuo Okuwara, "Japan's National Security: Structures, Norms, and Policies," *International Security* 17, no. 4 (1993): 84–118 at 86; and Berger, "Norms, Identity, and National Security in Germany and Japan," 335.

[31] Katzenstein and Okuwara, "Japan's National Security," 104. For a further discussion of Article 9's revision, see Katzenstein, *Rethinking Japanese Security*, 35; and Samuels, *Securing Japan*, 81.

[32] Katzenstein and Okuwara, "Japan's National Security," 103–4; and Samuels, *Securing Japan*, 45–48.

[33] Samuels, *Securing Japan*, 95.

[34] Ibid., 52.

ultranationalists and pacifying revisionists.[35] The pragmatists' comprehensive approach to security, underscoring economic over military power, was made possible under U.S. protection and the U.S.-Japan security alliance. This comes as no surprise considering that the development of Japan's postwar security norms and institutions was born out of its military defeat in World War II and the political order established by U.S. occupation forces. Although postwar domestic institutions were implanted by the U.S. military, over time Japanese leaders learned to embrace the United States as a key pillar of their country's national defense. These elites cultivated security norms and institutions around the U.S.-Japan security alliance, expanding the breadth and depth of the security consensus.

End of the Cold War

Did the elite security consensus regarding the U.S.-Japan alliance significantly evolve over time? The Cold War's collapse did create an initial degree of uncertainty concerning the future of the U.S.-Japan alliance. Catalyzed by international criticism regarding Japan's tepid response to the Persian Gulf War and the first North Korean nuclear crisis in the early 1990s, Japanese policymakers reexamined their global security role and alliance partnership with the United States. Although some critics predicted a loosening of the U.S.-Japan alliance with the end of the Cold War, a review of defense policies inside Japanese and American policy circles in the mid-1990s foreshadowed a renewed commitment to the alliance heading into the new millennium. In February 1994, Prime Minister Morihiro Hosokawa appointed an advisory group with the intention of revising the National Defense Program Outline (NDPO). The advisory panel advocated a comprehensive security policy while expanding its multilateral role in international affairs.[36] The group report also suggested increasing U.S.-Japanese security cooperation by improving bilateral policy consultations and promoting joint training and operational planning.[37]

In the United States, the Clinton administration conducted its own strategic assessment of East Asia. The 1995 East Asian Strategic Review (EASR) committed 100,000 troops to the region. Intended to provide a stable U.S. presence in Asia, the EASR was partially in response to the first North Korean nuclear crisis and a rising China. The United States also expected Japan to increase its own contribution to the alliance. The EASR restated the importance of Japan as a security partner, declaring, "Our security alliance with Japan is the linchpin of

---

[35] Ibid., 35.
[36] Hisayoshi Ina, "The Japan-U.S. Security Alliance in a New Era of International Relations," in *Japan-U.S. Security Alliance for the 21st Century: Cornerstone of Democracy, Peace and Prosperity for Our Future Generations*, edited by Japan Ministry of Foreign Affairs (Tokyo: Overseas Public Relations Division, Ministry of Foreign Affairs, 1996). Also see Mochizuki, *Toward a True Alliance*, 9.
[37] Mochizuki, *Toward a True Alliance*, 9.

U.S. security policy in Asia."[38] But even prior to the EASR's release, the United States was already seeking ways to strengthen its relationship with Japan. Joseph Nye, then the assistant secretary of defense for international security, initiated a bilateral process encouraging greater Japanese defense cooperation with the United States. The working-level discussions under the Nye initiative influenced Japan's own NDPO revision by reiterating the value of the U.S.-Japan security alliance and suggesting the geographic expansion of Japan's national defense boundaries. Implying the elevated status of the U.S.-Japan Security Treaty, the new NDPO made thirteen specific references to the U.S.-Japan alliance, compared with only two references in the previous defense outline.[39]

It was during this period of alliance affirmation that public outrage over the rape in Okinawa reverberated throughout Japan. Support for the security alliance and U.S. bases in Japan dropped in public opinion polls. The November bilateral summit between President Bill Clinton and Prime Minister Tomiichi Murayama was also postponed. Reactions to the rape had relatively little impact on the larger framework of the U.S.-Japan security alliance. Nevertheless, friction between Tokyo and Washington generated by the rape incident required both governments to address Okinawan base issues.

The consensus regarding U.S.-Japan security relations was manifest in the U.S.-Japan Joint Declaration on Security, forged during the April 16, 1996, summit between Murayama's successor, Prime Minister Ryutaro Hashimoto, and President Clinton. The declaration reaffirmed the importance of the alliance, stating, "The Prime Minister and the President recognize that the Treaty of Mutual Cooperation and Security is the core of the Japan-U.S. alliance, and underlies the mutual confidence that constitutes the foundation for bilateral cooperation on global issues."[40] As MOFA's deputy director general of its North American Affairs Bureau discussed, the Joint Declaration reaffirmed that "the framework for the defense of Japan will continue to rest on the twin pillars of appropriate defense capabilities and the Japan-U.S. security arrangements."[41] The declaration paved the way for strengthened alliance relations in the twenty-first century, concluding:

The three legs of the Japan-U.S. relationship – security, political, and economic – are based on shared values and interests and rest on the mutual confidence embodied in the Treaty of Mutual Cooperation and Security. The Prime Minister and the President reaffirmed their strong determination, on the eve of the twenty-first century, to build on

[38] *Daily Yomiuri*, "The Pentagon's Recipe for Peace in Asia and the Pacific," February 28, 1995.

[39] Ina, "The Japan-U.S. Security Alliance in a New Era of International Relations," 34.

[40] Japan Ministry of Foreign Affairs, "Japan-U.S. Declaration on Joint Security – Alliance for the Twenty-First Century," April 16, 1996. http://www.mofa.go.jp/region/n-america/us/security/security.html (last accessed October 4, 2007).

[41] Hitoshi Tanaka, "Japan-U.S. Alliance for the 21st Century – President Clinton's Visit to Japan," in *Japan-U.S. Security Alliance for the 21st Century: Cornerstone of Democracy, Peace and Prosperity for Our Future Generations*, edited by Japan Ministry of Foreign Affairs (Tokyo: Overseas Public Relations Division, Ministry of Foreign Affairs, 1996), 9.

the successful history of security cooperation and to work hand-in-hand to secure peace and prosperity for future generations.[42]

In addition to strengthened alliance ties, Japan sought to expand the role of its military in national security affairs. The expansion of the military's role was not contradictory to the alliance but rather worked in conjunction with strengthened ties between Washington and Tokyo. For example, prior to the April 1996 summit, Tokyo and Washington signed the Acquisition and Cross-Servicing Agreement (ACSA). The agreement enabled Japan to provide logistical support to the U.S. military in peacekeeping efforts, humanitarian missions, joint exercises, and other U.S. operations during peacetime.[43] In 1997, the United States and Japan produced the "Interim Report on the Review of the Guidelines for U.S.-Japan Defense Cooperation." Produced by the joint government Subcommittee for Defense Cooperation (SDC), the interim report reviewed the new guidelines for cooperation on the basis of Japan's NDPO and the 1996 Hashimoto-Clinton Joint Declaration. The document aimed at improving coordinated responses to an armed attack against Japan.[44] Moreover, the SDC's interim report confirmed the underlying trend of increased security cooperation between the United States and Japan in the mid- to late 1990s. On basic defense postures, both sides would "firmly maintain U.S.-Japan security arrangements" by developing procedures to increase cooperation in bilateral and multilateral operations in areas such as transportation, medical services, information sharing, education, and training. The interim report also permitted the SDF to provide rear-area support to U.S. forces in a military crisis around Japan. Under the threat of imminent attack, Japan and the United States agreed to "intensify intelligence sharing and policy consultations and initiate at an early stage the operation of a bilateral coordination mechanism."[45] In short, the string of bilateral agreements produced in the mid- to late 1990s indicates a certain degree of depth to the security consensus even after the Cold War. Although Japan pushed the limits of Article 9 by seeking to expand its military role in the region, the U.S.-Japan alliance remained deeply embedded in Japan's overall national security framework.

On the dimension of breadth, widespread support for the U.S.-Japan alliance continued in the post–Cold War period. Although Prime Minister Murayama of the Japanese Socialist Party pressed for SOFA revisions, the Japanese government and the bureaucracies, such as the Foreign Affairs Ministry, were reluctant to push the boundaries of the U.S.-Japan alliance. This attitude in the aftermath of the 1995 rape in Okinawa is captured by Yukio Okamoto, the former director

---

[42] Japan Ministry of Foreign Affairs, "Japan-U.S. Declaration on Joint Security – Alliance for the Twenty-First Century," April 16, 1996.

[43] Mochizuki, *Toward a True Alliance*, 15.

[44] Japan Ministry of Foreign Affairs, "Report on the Interim Review of the Guidelines for U.S.-Japan Defense Cooperation," June 17, 1997. http://www.mofa.go.jp/region/n-america/us/security/guideline.html (last accessed October 4, 2007).

[45] Ibid.

of MOFA's National Security Affairs Division, North American Affairs Bureau. Highlighting the strong consensus held by Tokyo elites at the close of the 1996 Hashimoto-Clinton summit, Okamoto stated:

A collective security structure in Asia is still at least twenty years away. Until then, Japan in theory has only two alternatives: we can attempt to provide our own protection, or we can enter into an alliance with another, stronger country. Given the current military concentration in the surrounding regions, protecting ourselves would necessitate a Self-Defense Force several times larger than we have now ... which in turn would require changes to the Constitution. It is unlikely that the Japanese people would accept this alternative. Thus the security alliance with the United States represents the only real alternative.[46]

Attitudes toward the U.S. alliance also remained strong in the National Diet of Japan. For instance, in a study targeting the mid-career generation of Japanese legislators in the House of Representatives, Patrick Boyd and Richard Samuels found that "normal nationalists" – those who advocate tightening the U.S.-Japan alliance and tougher self-defense policies – comprised the single largest group.[47] A 2003 survey evaluating the response of 392 Japanese lower house members also indicated that 40 percent of legislators favored a strengthening of alliance relations, whereas only 21 percent of Diet members disagreed with strengthening the U.S.-Japan alliance.[48]

In sum, elite statements and policy documents reflect a Japanese security discourse favoring close alignment with Washington. The persistence of an elite security consensus partially stemmed from external threats, such as a rising China or North Korean nuclear missiles. More importantly, internal factors, such as Japan's domestic security institutions, norms, and culture, played a significant role in perpetuating a strong consensus throughout the 1990s. The historical legacy of Japan's imperial past and the postwar institutional security arrangements imposed by the United States helped produce norms and domestic structures that prevented Japan from pursuing a military-first security policy.[49] Relying instead on the U.S. security umbrella for external defense, these structures led Japan to formulate a security policy in more comprehensive terms,

---

[46] Yukio Okamoto, "Searching for a Solution to the Okinawan Problem," in *Japan-U.S. Security Alliance for the 21st Century: Cornerstone of Democracy, Peace and Prosperity for Our Future Generations*, edited by Japan Ministry of Foreign Affairs (Tokyo: Overseas Public Relations Division, Ministry of Foreign Affairs, 1996).

[47] At the same time, the authors find that a cumulative majority is ambivalent toward strengthening the U.S.-Japan alliance (29 percent). Ambivalence toward strengthening the U.S.-Japan alliance should not be interpreted, however, as lack of support for the alliance. See Richard Samuels and Patrick Boyd, "Prosperity's Children: Generational Change and Japan's Future Leadership," *Asia Policy* 6 (2008): 15–51. It should be noted that this study was conducted in 2005 and not in the mid-1990s.

[48] See the 2003 *Asahi Shimbun*–Tokyo University Elite Survey (ATES). http://www.j.u-tokyo.ac.jp/~masaki/ats/atpsdata.html. I aggregated responses for "(dis)agree" and "somewhat (dis)agree."

[49] Katzenstein and Okawara, "Japan's National Security," 92.

focusing heavily on economic power.[50] In other words, prevailing norms and institutional arrangements required Japanese policymakers to embed the structure of the U.S.-Japan security alliance into Japan's national security framework, reflecting a high degree of breadth and depth on the security consensus. For these reasons, the security consensus among Japanese political elites has remained strong for over sixty years.

GOVERNMENT RESPONSE TO ANTI-BASE MOVEMENTS

How does the security consensus help explain the interaction between the state and anti-base movements, and the ensuing outcome on base policy issues? Here, I demonstrate how the strong security consensus influenced the government's response toward Okinawan anti-base opposition. More concretely, Tokyo employed strategies undermining anti-base activity, rendering anti-base movements relatively ineffective on the policy front. Activists did extract a few concessions (most notably the promised return of Futenma Air Station) by threatening to unravel Tokyo and Washington's desire for a strengthened alliance. However, as I elaborate later in this chapter and in Chapter 6, these concessions did little to alter the status quo in Okinawa.

From the Rape Incident to the Special Action Committee on Okinawa

As discussed earlier, thousands of Okinawan citizens mobilized to protest against the U.S. military presence in Okinawa following the rape incident in 1995. Anti-base groups demanded revisions to SOFA and a reduction in Okinawa's share of the base burden. What impact did anti-base protests have on basing policy decisions? How did the Japanese and U.S. governments respond to such widespread opposition? In the wake of the 1995 East Asia Strategic Review and strengthening alliance ties between Washington and Tokyo, Japan's initial response to anti-base demands was predictable. Despite bearing the brunt of Okinawan demands and a dip in Japanese support for the U.S. military presence, Tokyo remained firm in its support for the alliance. Although Prime Minister Murayama publicly announced his willingness to open a review for SOFA revisions, the JDA and MOFA quickly asserted that SOFA revisions were a nonissue. Negating Murayama's position, Foreign Minister Kono restated Japan's position that SOFA revisions were off the table. The bureaucracies prevailed. As one Foreign Ministry official commented, MOFA "had no intention of conducting a full-scale review of the status agreement.... The agreement and the Japan-U.S. Security Treaty are two sides of the same coin.... [R]eviewing the framework of the status agreement would have a large impact on Japan's national-security policy."[51]

---

[50] Ibid., 92.

[51] Aurelia George Mulgan, "Managing the U.S. Base Issue in Okinawa: A Test for Japanese Democracy," Working Paper no. 2000/1, Department of International Relations, Australian National University, Canberra, January 2000, 27.

Governor Ota's refusal to sign the land-lease contracts, however, generated concern among Japanese policy circles working to strengthen the alliance and the U.S.-Japanese Security Treaty.[52] Takeshi Ozawa of the Defense Facilities Administration Agency (DFAA) conceded, "The timing of all this is really bad."[53] MOFA officials feared that Okinawa's recalcitrance would jeopardize the security alliance. After an emergency meeting, the prime minister's office dispatched officials from the DFAA to Okinawa to resolve the impasse. Tokyo also sent the DFAA general director to Okinawa in hopes of negotiating directly with Ota. In another national embarrassment, however, Ota rebuffed Tokyo by refusing to meet with the general director.[54]

Over growing public opposition to bases, and the embarrassing row created by Ota, MOFA officials began consulting with Washington to discuss the implementation of criminal procedures under SOFA. Foreign Minister Kono asked Walter Mondale, the U.S. Ambassador to Japan, for further base reductions, hoping that U.S. concessions on military bases and SOFA revisions would placate Okinawan anger.[55] Although the meeting between Mondale and Kono produced an agreement to study further base reductions, activists viewed Tokyo's motives skeptically. An editorial in the *Asahi Shimbun* criticized Tokyo, stating, "Embarrassed by the seriousness of problems arising since the rape of a schoolgirl ... the government, simply eager to avoid inconvenience to the Japan-U.S. military alliance, dithered miserably."[56] Citing Tokyo's past broken promises to Okinawa on base issues, the editorial continued, "Is the Japanese government serious in addressing the cutback issue? The Okinawa prefectural government is very wary of the central government, out of long experience in dealing with [U.S. bases]." A September 20, 1995, editorial in the *Asahi Shimbun* also criticized Tokyo for showing "no sign of being prepared to make a proper response to the pleas of the Okinawan people or to begin to try to ameliorate the situation."[57]

With Ota's actions still threatening diplomatic relations between Tokyo and Washington, the prime minister sent JDA Director Seishiro Eto to Okinawa to seek Okinawan cooperation. The central government also exercised its authority by taking legal action against Ota. Traditionally supporting the executive branch on issues of defense and security policy, the Supreme Court ruled in favor of the Japanese government. The Court argued that the special law created to legalize the acquisition of private land for U.S. military use was constitutional. Adding that Ota's refusal to sign the lease jeopardized the public interest, the Supreme Court ordered Ota to sign the lease contracts.

[52] Of the 2,900 landowners required to sign the land-lease contract, 2,000 refused to sign. Tokyo therefore expected Ota to sign the leases on their behalf.

[53] *Asahi Shimbun*, "Okinawa Says No to Base Leases," September 29, 1995.

[54] *Daily Yomiuri*, "Okinawa Governor Refuses to Meet Defense Official," October 1, 1995.

[55] *Asahi Shimbun*, "Okinawa Bases Cutbacks Asked," October 3, 1995; and *Daily Yomiuri*, "Mondale Vows to Help Cut Bases in Okinawa," October 4, 1995.

[56] *Asahi Shimbun*, "Specific Base Cutback Plan Essential to Placate," October 5, 1995.

[57] *Asahi Shimbun*, "Okinawa Rape Case Spurs Review of Base Accords," September 20, 1995.

Rhetorically at least, Tokyo appeared ready to provide some concessions to Okinawa to break the impasse with Ota and mollify anti-base sentiment. Speaking at a House of Councilors Budget Committee hearing, Prime Minister Murayama stated, "The Japan-U.S. security arrangements are for the security of [all of] Japan, and it is important for the whole nation to share the sentiments of Okinawa residents [over the base issue] who have borne the lingering impacts of their wartime hardships."[58] Tokyo also stated that it would initiate studies to relocate firing ranges from Okinawa to other existing SDF ranges within Japan. Furthermore, the government, led by Murayama's Social Democratic Party, decided to revise its earlier position in a joint communiqué pertaining to the U.S.-Japan Security Treaty by requesting base reductions in Okinawa. Anti-base opposition thus compelled Tokyo to provide at least token concessions to prevent a domestic crisis from boiling over. More importantly, concessions were needed to placate swelling anti-American sentiment in Okinawa that threatened to disrupt positive alliance relations with the United States.[59]

Tokyo and Washington moved quickly to form the Special Action Committee on Okinawa (SACO) in November in response to the rape incident and massive demonstrations. SACO worked to develop solutions that would ensure Japan's security while minimizing the impact of bases on Okinawans. SACO released an interim report on April 15, 1995, two days before the Clinton-Hashimoto summit where the two leaders were expected to produce the Joint Declaration on the U.S.-Japan security alliance. The report recommended that the United States return portions of base land, adjust training and operational procedures, implement noise-reduction initiatives, and improve status of forces agreement procedures.[60] The interim report's release was undoubtedly timed to prevent Okinawan issues from trumping public affirmations of a strengthened U.S.-Japan alliance during the summit. As one Japanese MOFA official commented, "Had we not been able to release anything on Okinawa prior to the summit . . . the summit would probably have been dominated by this one issue. Furthermore, I doubt it would have presented how the future of the Japan-U.S. alliance should be."[61]

In the final report, released in December 1996, SACO requested that the United States return Futenma Air Station and portions of land from other camp sites and training areas. The report also included changes to three operational and five noise-abatement procedures.[62] Through SACO, Tokyo granted

---

[58] *Daily Yomiuri*, "Government to Transfer U.S. Base Functions from Okinawa," October 17, 1995.

[59] Mary Jordan, "Japan to Seek Cutbacks in U.S. Military Bases; Tokyo Responds to Furor Over Okinawa Rape," *Washington Post*, October 20, 1995.

[60] "The Japan-U.S. Special Action Committee (SACO) Interim Report," in Japan Ministry of Foreign Affairs, *Japan-U.S. Security Alliance for the 21st Century: Cornerstone of Democracy, Peace and Prosperity for Our Future Generations* (Tokyo: Overseas Public Relations Division, Ministry of Foreign Affairs, 1996).

[61] Tanaka, "Japan-U.S. Alliance for the 21st Century," 8.

[62] United States General Accounting Office, *Overseas Presence*, 3.

TABLE 3.1. *Base Land Returned under SACO*

Land Return	Proportion Returned	Date	Replacement Facility
MCAS Futenma	All	Between 2001 and 2003	Sea-based facility
Northern training area (9,000 acres)	More than half	March 2003	Remaining northern training area
Aha training area	All	March 1998	Acreage added to northern training area
Gimbaru training area	All	March 1998	Kin Blue Beach training area and Camp Hansen
Sobe communications site	All	March 2001	Camp Hansen
Yomitan auxiliary airfield	All	March 2001	Ie Jima auxiliary airfield
Camp Kuwae	A major portion	March 2008	Camp Zukeran and other facilities
Senaha Communication Station	Nearly all	March 2001	Torti Communication Station
Makiminato service area	Some	Between 1998 and 2000	Remaining Makiminato area
Naha port	All	No date established	Urasce pier area
Housing consolidation on Camps Kuwae and Zukeran		March 2008	Remaining portions of Camps Kuwae and Zukeran

Sources: Military Base Affairs Office, Department of General Affairs, Okinawa Prefectural Government; and U.S. General Accounting Office, *Overseas Presence: Issues Involved in Reducing the Impact of the U.S. Military Presence on Okinawa* (Washington, D.C.: U.S. General Accounting Office, 1998), 26.

several concessions to anti-base movement demands. Table 3.1 presents the specific base-reduction initiatives presented by SACO.

Additionally, the SACO guidelines provided noise-reduction measures around Kadena Air Base and Futenma Air Station. These measures included transferring aircraft such as the KC-130 Hercules or AV-8 Harrier from Futenma to Iwakuni Air Base, installing sound insulation walls at Kadena Air Base, and limiting night flight training at Futenma Air Station.[63]

Paradoxically, anti-base movements were able to gain these concessions, however minimal, because of Washington and Tokyo's commitment to the security alliance. As a thorn in the U.S.-Japan alliance's side, Okinawan anti-base movements threatened to unravel the newly strengthened alliance.

[63] Ibid., 53.

Moreover, although a strong security consensus at the national level prevented activists from forming ties with political elites, they did take advantage of other political opportunities at the subnational level.[64] In particular, access to elites within the prefectural government, most importantly Governor Ota, helped the anti-base movement apply real pressure on Tokyo. Ota's support for the Okinawan anti-base movement raised the diplomatic stakes for Washington and Tokyo. SACO recommendations were offered, in part, to avoid any further diplomatic fallout.

Reduction or Relocation: A "Symbolic" Return

Although the return of 21 percent of military base land is not insignificant, with the exception of Futenma Air Station, the promised returns were largely token concessions.[65] Most of the facilities returned were strategically unimportant, such as the Senaha Communication Station or the Sobe communications site, where base functions could easily be relocated to another facility. A study by the U.S. Government Accountability Office (GAO) assessing the impact of SACO's base reductions on U.S. operational capabilities concluded that ten of the eleven base-return recommendations presented "minimal risks to operations." The GAO report stated, "The services can maintain training opportunities and deployment plans and schedules, because land to be returned is no longer needed or will be returned only after Japan provides adequate replacement facilities on existing bases or adds land by extending other base boundaries."[66] Furthermore, base consolidations were in many ways beneficial to the United States. Through the SACO agreement, Japan agreed to build 2,041 new or reconstructed housing units at Camp Zukeran. Outside the SACO process, Japan agreed to build an additional 1,473 units near Kadena Air Base.[67] As part of Camp Zukeran and Camp Kuwae's consolidation process, the Japanese also agreed to replace the aging hospital at Kuwae with a new medical center in Zukeran at a cost of $300 million.

Base policy changes under the SACO report were relatively minor and did not necessarily reduce the strategic or operational capabilities of the U.S. military. However, as mentioned earlier, the return of Futenma Air Station presented the

---

[64] A more traditional approach to social movement analysis, one that includes the entire institutional system as part of the political opportunity structure (POS), offers a different interpretation of the Japanese case. Presently, the security consensus framework only takes into account POS at the national level. Therefore, the security consensus held by *national-level* elites is coded as strong. However, for the specific movement episode in 1995–96, one could code the security consensus in Japan as "moderate" if POS were expanded to include government institutions and actors at the prefectural and local levels. Under a "semiopen" opportunity structure, anti-base movements formed ties with the sympathetic prefectural government, giving them greater leverage in the policy arena. This helps explain the partial concessions (or "mixed" outcome) represented by the SACO agreement.

[65] For insights from U.S. and Japanese officials on the "symbolic" return of bases, see Funabashi, *Alliance Adrift*, 25, 35, 44.

[66] United States General Accounting Office, *Overseas Presence*, 40.

[67] Ibid., 42.

FIGURE 3.1. Aerial Photo of Marine Corps Air Station Futenma, Ginowan City. *Source:* MCAS Futenma Master Plan.

one major concession offered by the U.S. and Japanese governments. Both officials and activists alike viewed Futenma Air Station's return as the capstone of the SACO report. As one MOFA official noted, "Futenma Air Station has an extremely important function for the security of Japan and the Far East.... It took us about a month...to evoke a response from the U.S. side on Futenma."[68] The GAO's own study of the U.S. military presence in Okinawa dwells on Futenma's strategic importance and the difficulty in finding or constructing an appropriate replacement facility. The GAO stated:

The most significant land deal involves the planned closure and return of Marine Corps Air Station (MCAS) Futenma. The installation is a critical component of the Marine Corps' forward deployment because it is the home base of the 1st Marine Air Wing. The Wing's primary mission is to participate as the air component of the III Marine Expeditionary Force. The wing's Marine Air Group-36 provides tactical fixed and rotary wing aircraft and flies about 70 aircraft, including CH-46 and CH-53 helicopters and KC-130 aerial refueling airplanes. Futenma's primary mission is to maintain and operate facilities and provide services and materials to support Marine aircraft operations.[69]

The return of Futenma, situated squarely in the center of urban growth in Ginowan City, had been requested by Okinawans since the 1980s (see Figure 3.1).

[68] Tanaka, "Japan-U.S. Alliance for the 21st Century," 7.
[69] United States General Accounting Office, *Overseas Presence*, 7.

For Okinawans, Futenma represented all that was wrong with U.S. military bases: noise, pollution, safety hazards, crime, and the unfair burden of bases imposed by the Japanese government on Okinawans.

At first glance, Tokyo and Washington's conditional return of Futenma appeared to be a major victory for anti-base movements. For the United States, Futenma represented a major concession to the Okinawans. Several policy-makers, including Secretary of Defense William Perry, Assistant Secretary of Defense Kurt Campbell, former Assistant Secretary of Defense Richard Armitage, and Senator Mike Mansfield, had pushed for Futenma's return as a means of placating Okinawans and preserving the U.S.-Japan alliance.[70] As then assistant secretary of defense Joseph Nye argued, "Without some relief for Ginowan, another incident could blow things out of proportion and disrupt the alliance."[71]

Under greater scrutiny, however, the return required significant trade-offs for Okinawans. At stake was the *conditional* nature of Futenma's return. Tokyo and Washington stated they would make reasonable efforts to implement the recommendation provided by SACO. However, the report did not function as a bilateral agreement and was therefore nonbinding. USFJ (United States Forces, Japan) officials stated that if "Japan does not provide adequate replacement facilities or complete action needed to implement some recommendations, the United States will not be obligated to implement those particular recommenda-tions."[72] In an interview with *Asahi Shimbun*, Moriteru Arasaki, an activist and leading scholar on Okinawan anti-base movements, questioned the significance of concessions regarding Futenma Air Station. Arasaki stated, "If you look at the contents of the agreement to return the Futenma base you will find several drawbacks. While the U.S. agreed to return the land of the base, its functions are to be transferred to other U.S. bases on Okinawa, such as Kadena Air Base, and on the mainland. This is not the reduction of the U.S. military presence that we are demanding."[73] Teruko Kuwae, secretary general of a women's group opposed to U.S. bases, added, "The return of the land by itself does little to solve the problems. . . . We want to see a reduction of the functions of the bases, not the size of the land."[74] Thus many anti-base activists viewed the SACO agreement as a deal that merely shifted the problems associated with Futenma to different parts of the island rather than promoting any real base reduction. Moreover, the secrecy of SACO negotiations also raised suspicions that the United States was

---

[70] Funabashi, *Alliance Adrift*.

[71] E-mail correspondence with Joseph Nye, April 7, 2010. U.S. and Japanese officials held the *perception* that they had made considerable concessions to anti-base movements. However, little progress was made on Futenma over the next decade, vindicating activists' claims about the "token" nature of Futenma's conditional return. I thank Mike Mochizuki for making this point about perceptions.

[72] United States General Accounting Office, *Overseas Presence*, 18–19.

[73] Mayumi Maruyama, "Okinawa Bluff Pulls Japan Tighter into U.S. Strategy," *Asahi News Service*, April 16, 1996.

[74] Mulgan, "Managing the U.S. Base Issue in Okinawa," 33.

using the Futenma deal to replace the outdated base with a new facility capable of accommodating the MV-22 Osprey tilt-wing aircraft.[75]

Influenced by the pervading security consensus, Tokyo struck a balance between domestic anti-base pressure and its international alliance obligations by working out a deal with the United States on Futenma Air Station. The deal helped pacify anti-base sentiment for the time being. At the same time, the deal negotiated under SACO helped Japan maintain positive alliance ties with the United States. Reflecting on Prime Minister Hashimoto's motive in announcing the return of Futenma, Arasaki stated:

(He) wanted to calm the fierce and persistent protest of Okinawans to smooth the way for redefining the Security Treaty during U.S. President Bill Clinton's visit. Although the return of Futenma base is just cosmetic, it was announced with a big fanfare. Firstly, Tokyo hoped it would sway deliberation by the land expropriation committee of Okinawa prefecture on the central government's request for a six-month emergency use of a land plot occupied by the U.S. military – Sobe communication facility – in Yomitan village. Secondly, it hoped to influence a likely referendum by Okinawans on the whole U.S. bases issue. It appears that yet another purpose was to divide public opinion in Okinawa. The results can be seen in the immediate opposition from residents near the Kadena Air Base to accepting the transfer of Futenma's functions.[76]

Arasaki's words suggesting that Futenma was nothing more than a token concession are echoed by other scholars. Masamichi Inoue writes that the Futenma replacement plan did not arise so much out of "the benevolence of the U.S.-Japan alliance as its cunning manipulation of Okinawa's protest."[77] Inoue, Selden, and Purves state that "Japan had requested America's assistance in providing some symbolic morsel to give to the people of Okinawa, and Washington had complied."[78]

Symbolic concessions in the form of returned base land were merely one aspect of Tokyo's response to anti-base pressure. The central government used the politics of compensation as another strategy to pacify strong anti-base opposition. Taking advantage of Okinawa's economic dependence on Tokyo, the Japanese government applied "soft coercion" to obtain local support for bases.[79] First, the government allocated 7.5 billion yen to each local district hosting U.S. military bases. Second, large endowments were distributed to communities accepting bases slated for relocation within Okinawa. Third, the government offered 100 billion yen over a seven-year period for projects proposed under the Informal Council on Okinawa Municipalities Hosting U.S.

---

[75] Julia Yonetani, "Playing Base Politics in a Global Strategic Theater," *Critical Asian Studies* 33, no. 1 (2001): 70–95 at 72.

[76] Maruyama, "Okinawa Bluff Pulls Japan Tighter into U.S. Strategy."

[77] Inoue, *Okinawa and the U.S. Military*, 128.

[78] Masamichi Inoue, Mark Selden, and John Purves, "Okinawa Citizens, U.S. Bases, and the Dugong," *Ryukyu-Okinawa History and Culture Website.* http://www.niraikanai.wwma.net/pages/archive/dugong.html (last accessed December 12, 2010).

[79] Yonetani, "Playing Base Politics in a Global Strategic Theater," 74.

Bases, an advisory body to the Hashimoto cabinet headed by prime ministerial aide Yukio Okamoko.[80] The Council helped implement Tokyo's preferred policy by circumventing the National Diet and the prefectural assembly. Although the Council endorsed base reductions, it provided a "direct financial pipeline from the cabinet to local municipalities and prefectural business interests," and hence made no genuine effort to reduce Okianwa's share of the base burden.[81]

The central government's response is best summarized by Masamichi Inoue: "Tokyo responded . . . by disclosing the view that global/American interests, rather than strictly national or local concerns, should take precedence."[82] The strong security consensus regarding U.S.-Japan relations acted as an ideological barrier preventing activists from penetrating the state. Although Tokyo and Washington responded to anti-base movements by offering partial concessions and economic incentives, they failed to satisfy the majority of core activist demands on SOFA revisions and base reduction. As one Pentagon official notes, "SACO didn't work because it was a fig leaf solution to a more fundamental problem."[83] From the perspective of anti-base movements, activists were unable to form ties with elites within the central government to promote significant changes on basing issues. In fact, the powerful security consensus privileging strengthened U.S.-Japan relations in the late 1990s meant very few, if any, sympathetic elites were willing to form ties with activists.[84] Unable to gain necessary access to elites to implement policy changes, and severely hampered by the island's economic dependence on Tokyo, activists faced significant challenges. The struggles faced by local residents and activists continued into the following decade, a story I return to in Chapter 6.

CONCLUSION

The prevailing security consensus surrounding Japanese elite strategic thinking presented a formidable obstacle for anti-base activists. Anti-base movements have not completely "failed," winning several tactical concessions over the past decade. However, "victory" remained elusive as Japanese and U.S. officials presented new proposals to maintain a significant U.S. military presence on the island. As Gavan McCormack argues, "[T]he crucial point in the Futenma negotiations has been Japanese government determination to serve U.S. military design."[85] Thus the Japanese government has largely circumvented post-SACO

---

[80] Ibid., 75.

[81] Ibid., 75.

[82] Inoue, *Okinawa and the U.S. Military*, 37.

[83] Interview with John Hill, principal director for East Asia, Office of the Under-Secretary of Defense for Policy, Washington, D.C., May 5, 2010.

[84] This is especially true in Japan, where security and U.S. base policy decisions were conducted almost exclusively by the bureaucracies rather than the Diet.

[85] Gavan McCormack, "The Okinawan Election and Resistance to Japan's Military First Politics," *Japan Focus* no. 688, November 15, 2006. http://www.japanfocus.org/products/details/2275 (last accessed November 27, 2007).

Okinawan protests in Henoko. Through compensation politics, the central government managed to split the anti-base struggle into different local factions. As a result, Futenma Air Base continued to operate even a decade after the final SACO agreement.

Tokyo's response to anti-base protests is driven by a security logic. The central government's strategy of co-optation and legal coercion against anti-base movements is motivated by its desire to maintain a strong U.S.-Japan alliance. The majority of Tokyo elites, particularly those responsible for national defense and foreign policy, contend that the U.S. alliance and U.S. bases serve a critical role in Japan's national security strategy.[86] This consensus is formed by actors' external threat perceptions. But more significantly in Japan, the consensus rests on internal factors such as the norms and domestic institutions that have shaped national security thinking since the end of World War II. Given the strong security consensus among Japanese government elites, Okinawan anti-base activists find it tremendously difficult to sway base policy decisions. McCormack writes that "Japan sees its primary policy imperative as submission to Washington, it has to 'deliver' Okinawa to the Pentagon, and to do that it must somehow ensure the submission of Okinawa's restive local government and civil society."[87] By muddling through the Futenma relocation process, the Japanese government was able to strike a balance between its alliance obligations to the United States and its need to placate domestic anti-base pressure. The SACO agreement was designed to ensure that the United States would retain its strategic effectiveness in Japan and the Asia-Pacific. As I discuss in Chapter 6, the elite security consensus continued to operate in the post-9/11 period, with Okinawan anti-base activists making little progress in pushing beyond the status quo. Only under the prospect of a weakened security consensus after the LDP's ouster in 2009 did the potential for anti-base victory arise.

---

[86] Although Tokyo elites place a high priority on the U.S.-Japan alliance, the Japanese government is also partially responsible for dragging its feet on the Futenma issue. Tokyo does not want to severely undermine its relationship with Washington, but it also wants to avoid a domestic crisis in Okinawa. Thus, although Tokyo and Washington have signed several agreements over the past two decades related to base relocation, implementation and execution on Tokyo's part has been much slower. Interview with Department of Defense official, Washington, D.C., May 5, 2010.

[87] Gavan McCormack, "Abe and Okinawa: Collision Course?" *Japan Focus* no. 914, September 1, 2007. http://www.japanfocus.org/products/details/2512 (last accessed November 27, 2007).

4

Anti-Base Movements in Ecuador and Italy

We'll renew the base on one condition: that they let us put a base in Miami – an Ecuadorian base. . . . [I]f there's no problem having foreign soldiers on a country's soil, surely they'll let us have an Ecuadorian base in the United States.[1]

– Rafael Correa, President of Ecuador

I am about to tell the U.S. Ambassador that the Italian government won't oppose the decision by the previous government and the town council of Vicenza to allow the expansion of the military base. . . . Our attitude in regards to the U.S. is that of friend and ally.[2]

– Romano Prodi, Prime Minister of Italy

The preceding two chapters examined anti-base movement episodes from the Asia-Pacific region. Movement episodes from the Philippines and Okinawa suggest that host-government elite perceptions, ideas, and beliefs regarding the U.S. alliance affect the likelihood of anti-base movement success in winning concessions from governments. Additionally, alliance relations and the degree of security consensus shape government responses to civil societal pressure. This chapter extends the security consensus framework to anti-base movement episodes in other regions. Two cases, the No Bases movement in Manta, Ecuador, and the No Dal Molin movement in Vicenza, Italy, are used to test the robustness of the theoretical argument. In Ecuador, a weak security consensus among political elites, and the ties formed between sympathetic politicians and activists, paralleled the 1991 Anti-Treaty Movement in the Philippines. Conversely, a relatively strong security consensus among Italian government officials raised serious obstacles for anti-base protestors. The Italian case echoes the challenges faced by anti-base movements in Japan/Okinawa. Activists were unable to win

---

[1] Phil Stewart, "Ecuador Wants Military Base in Miami," *Reuters*, March 22, 2007. http://uk. reuters.com/article/reutersEdge/idUKADD25267520071022 (last accessed February 1, 2008).

[2] Stephen Brown, "Italy to Give Green Light to U.S. Air Base Expansion," *Reuters*, January 16, 2007. http://www.reuters.com/article/worldNews/idUSL16239372200701116 (last accessed January 31, 2008).

significant concessions on basing issues when a consensus favoring strong ties with the United States pervaded elite ranks.

ECUADOR

I begin the Ecuador anti-base saga between 1999 and 2007 with a spoiler. In March 2007, President Rafael Correa reaffirmed his election pledge not to renew the Manta base agreement with the United States. In a formal letter addressed to activists attending the International No Bases Conference in Quito, Correa wrote, "I confirm the firm position of the Ecuadorian government to not renew the Agreement (allowing) the use of Manta Base by the United States of America. ... Ecuador joins the social movements that fight for peace, justice, human rights and environmental sustainability."[3] Having rejected the renewal of the Manta agreement even before formal negotiations with the United States, Correa snubbed Washington further by offering the use of Manta's airport facilities to China.

The Ecuadorian government formally presented its nonrenewal decision to the U.S. Embassy in July 2008, thus fulfilling Correa's pledge to remove the U.S. forward operating base in Manta. The important question, however, is whether anti-base movements had any impact on this outcome. Similar questions were confronted in the Philippine case: did the preferences of elites and the voting behavior of the Philippine Senate dictate the eventual closure of Subic Bay Naval Station, thereby making the role of anti-base movements unimportant? The same alternative explanation can be used to evaluate the withdrawal of U.S. forces in Manta: Quito's decision not to renew the Manta base agreement may be explained by President Correa's left-leaning convictions rather than anti-base protests. After all, Ecuadorian anti-base groups had challenged the United States since 1999 but had not achieved "victory" until the rise of a center-left government.[4] How successful were anti-base activists? Did the Ecuadorian government attempt to co-opt or undermine movements using strategies similar to those used by the Japanese government? Or were elites divided or ambivalent in their support for U.S.-related policies as in the Philippines, enabling activists to "penetrate" the state and form ties with sympathetic elites?

The Manta anti-base movement episode follows the latter case. Unlike highly institutionalized bilateral alliances found in U.S. relations with Japan, the substance of U.S.-Ecuador relations has been historically thin. Ecuador did face external threats from neighboring Peru throughout the twentieth century. However, Quito has not relied on the United States for military assistance or

---

[3] Letter from Rafael Correa to participants of the International No Bases Conference, official letter no. DPR-0-07-8, March 6, 2007.

[4] Anti-base activists, who generally associate with the political left, did help elect the center-left Correa into power. Assuming that Correa would have been voted into power even without the support of anti-base groups, however, an elite-driven alternative explanation suggests that base closure hinged on Correa's own personal conviction rather than anti-base pressure.

support, nor has it depended on the United States for protection against external threats. Hence no strong security consensus regarding U.S.-Ecuador relations or the role of U.S. bases ever pervaded the ranks of Ecuadorian political elites. Under conditions of weak security consensus, elites were divided (or perhaps indifferent) in their articulation of foreign or national security policies concerning U.S.-related issues. This lack of strong security consensus among Ecuadorian elites enabled anti-base activists to penetrate the state. Activists supported, lobbied, and encouraged elites to reject the Manta base agreement with the United States. Meanwhile, ties to key government elites responsible for setting base policies boosted the credibility and leverage of anti-base activists.

Background on the Manta Base Agreement

How did the U.S. military end up in Ecuador in the first place? For U.S. Southern Command (SOUTHCOM), Panama had always played an important strategic role. However, the U.S. military's departure in 1999 left Washington scouring the region for replacement sites.[5] In particular, the loss of Howard Air Force Base two years earlier required the United States to find replacement facilities to continue its regional counternarcotics operations. After consultations with the governments of El Salvador, Netherlands Antilles, and Ecuador, the United States chose three locations to function as replacement facilities. In Central America, the United States placed a forward operating location (FOL) in Comalapa, El Salvador. In the Caribbean, two FOLs were established, in Aruba and Curacao.[6] Finally, in the South American Andes, the United States acquired Eloy Alfaro Air Base in Manta, Ecuador. Negotiations with Ecuador began in February 1999.[7] The two sides initially signed an interim agreement in April 1999, later replaced by a ten-year pact signed in November 1999.[8] In addition to Eloy Alfaro Air Base, the agreement authorized the United States to utilize Manta's port and military installations within the surrounding vicinity.

Unlike Subic Bay, the Manta FOL is not a main operating base. Selecting Manta as a comparable case study therefore warrants some brief discussion. The bases examined in the previous chapters were all hard tests for anti-base

---

[5] The United States agreed to withdraw its forces from Panama under the 1977 Panama Canal Treaty.

[6] Office of National Drug Control Policy (ONDCP), "Forward Operating Locations: ONDCP Fact Sheet." http://www.whitehousedrugpolicy.gov/publications/international/factsht/forw_oper_locat. html (last accessed February 3, 2008). It is important to note that these FOLs were built on existing airfields used by the host government.

[7] Activists state that discussions began in January 1999. See Luis Ángel Saavedra, *Operaciones De Avansada O Base Militar Operativa? Un Análisis De La Base De Manta* [Operations of Outpost or Operative Military Base? An Analysis of the Manta Base] (Quito: Fundación Regional de Asesoría en Derechos Humanos, INREDH, 2007), 16.

[8] Center for International Policy, "Just the Facts: A Civilian's Guide to U.S. Defense and Security Assistance to Latin America and the Caribbean" (Washington, D.C.: Center for International Policy, 2003). http://www.ciponline.org/facts/fol.htm (last accessed February 3, 2008).

movements. All three movement episodes revolved around major U.S. military bases of high strategic value. On the contrary, the Manta base is relatively small, hosting on average only 250 military personnel, 65 U.S. civilians, and 180 Ecuadorian contractors.[9] Moreover, as an FOL, the Manta base is used jointly by the Ecuadorian and U.S. Air Forces.

Despite its relatively small size and FOL status, the U.S. military recognized the strategic utility of Manta in the war on drugs. SOUTHCOM used the base for counter-drug surveillance flights over Central and South America. Washington noted that missions involving the Manta FOL in the Eastern Pacific and the Andean mountains significantly contributed to U.S. counter-drug strategic policies in Latin America. SOUTHCOM spokesperson Jose Ruiz stated, "Since 1999, the FOL has conducted more than 3,300 counter-drug missions, totaling over 18,000 flight hours, and has contributed directly or indirectly to the seizure of more than 52,000 kg of illegal drugs with a street value exceeding $2 billion."[10] In a prepared testimony before the House Subcommittee on Criminal Justice, Drug Policy, and Human Resources, Ana Maria Salazar, deputy assistant secretary of defense for drug enforcement policy and support, stressed the importance of the Manta FOL in the war on drugs. She stated, "The Manta FOL is the key to enhancing our source zone and Eastern Pacific counter-drug presence. It is the only FOL that can support counter-drug missions throughout the source zone, providing the necessary reach into southern Peru, Bolivia, and most importantly Colombia, which supplies the largest percentage of cocaine shipped to the United States."[11]

Additionally, sunk costs were invested in the Manta base. The United States spent $63.3 million to upgrade facilities at Eloy Alfaro. Improvements included expanding the runway to increase the load-bearing capacity – necessary for landing an AWACS Airborne Early Warning (AEW) aircraft – constructing additional hangars, and building new dining and maintenance facilities.[12] In short, although the Manta base was strategically less significant than the bases discussed in previous chapters and functionally easier to replace, the FOL was not so insignificant that the United States would give up its claim to Manta without providing some pressure or incentives to Quito.[13]

---

[9] Sam Logan, "U.S. Faces Eviction from Ecuadorian Base," *ISN Security Watch*, January 12, 2007. http://www.isn.ethz.ch/news/sw/archive.cfm?task=cats&Parent=589 (last accessed March 8, 2007).

[10] Ibid.

[11] United States House of Representatives, "Counter-drug Implications of the U.S. Leaving Panama," prepared testimony by Deputy Assistant Secretary of Defense for Drug Enforcement Policy and Support Ana Marie Salazar before the House Committee on Government Reform, Subcommittee on Criminal Justice, Drug Policy, and Human Resources, June 9, 2000.

[12] United States General Accounting Office, *Briefing Report to the Chairman, Caucus of International Narcotics Control, U.S. Senate: Drug Control, International Counterdrug Sites Being Developed* (Washington, D.C.: GAO, 2000), 4. Also see Center for International Policy, "Just the Facts"; and Monte Hayes, "American Airmen Get Warm Welcome in Ecuador Port," *Associated Press*, March 15, 2001.

[13] Interview with FLACSO-Ecuador director Adrian Bonilla, March 9, 2006, Quito, Ecuador.

U.S.-Ecuador Relations

The history of U.S. relations with Ecuador is relatively thin compared with those of countries with deeper U.S. alliance ties, such as Japan, South Korea, or even the Philippines. Unsurprisingly, the weak security consensus among Ecuadorian elites is characterized by narrow breadth and low depth. Ecuador remained a low priority for the United States, and opportunities for interaction between Quito and Washington were fairly limited. Even when confronted by major security threats from neighboring Peru, Ecuador received minimal support from the United States. For instance, the United States maintained neutrality during Ecuador's border crisis with Peru in 1941, rejecting Quito's appeal to dispatch a U.S. warship near Ecuador's shore as a warning to Peru. Likewise, the United States refused Ecuador's request for forty million rounds of ammunition during the ensuing Ecuador-Peru War.[14] While brokering peace negotiations between the two sides, the United States failed to bring a case against Peru's aggression, nor did it raise the issue of Peru's bombing of civilians. The United States certainly sympathized with Ecuador, and in principle opposed territorial expansion through the use of force. However, the United States wanted to quickly resolve the border conflict to focus on the larger concern of building South American support for the Allied war effort.[15]

During World War II, Ecuador permitted the United States to build two military bases on its territory. The United States built an air refueling base in Salinas on the western coast of Ecuador and an air base on the Galapagos Islands as a forward defense against potential Japanese attacks targeting the Panama Canal. After the war, U.S. officials reasoned with Quito that the United States should be able to retain the bases rent-free. After all, the United States had borne all costs in building the bases. Moreover, Ecuador did not have the resources to keep the facilities running. As Secretary of War Robert Patterson and Secretary of the Navy James Forrestal wrote, offering the Galapagos base to the United States "would be a fitting contribution of Ecuador to hemispheric security."[16] The Ecuadorian government thought otherwise. With no financial incentives and public opinion against the Galapagos base, Quito turned down Washington's base proposal in 1946.

During the Cold War, Ecuadorian political elites did not share Washington's preoccupation with the Soviet threat. Instead, Peru continued to remain Ecuador's top security concern. However, the United States stayed outside of the long-standing territorial dispute, remaining on the sidelines during the brief 1995 Alto-Cenepa War between Peru and Ecuador. Even as the Andean region attracted more attention in the 1990s with increasing drug trafficking concerns, Ecuador remained neglected compared with its Andean neighbors Colombia,

---

[14] Ronn F. Pineo, *Ecuador and the United States: Useful Strangers, the United States and the Americas* (Athens: University of Georgia Press, 2007), 115.
[15] Ibid., 114.
[16] Ibid., 128.

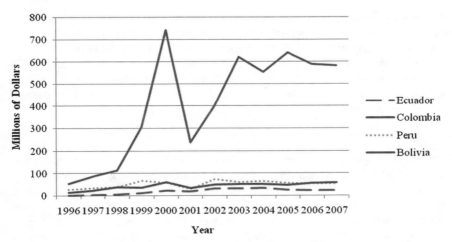

FIGURE 4.1. Military and Police Aid from the United States. *Source:* Center for International Policy. Figures for 2006 and 2007 are estimated and requested amounts, respectively.

Bolivia, and Peru. As Figure 4.1 indicates, of the four countries, Ecuador received the least amount of military and police aid from the United States in the war on drugs.

Having traditionally remained on the fringe of U.S. strategy in Latin America, Quito never developed strong security ties to the United States. Unlike countries such as Japan or Italy, alliance relations were never institutionalized within Ecuador's national security framework. Thus, Ecuadorian political elites never converged on a security policy centered on the U.S. alliance. In sum, the security consensus remained weak (or absent) among political elites. It is true that the asymmetric nature of U.S.-Ecuador relations has often led Quito to adopt a position of compliance and consensual acceptance on foreign policy. However, Ecuadorian security expert Adrian Bonilla adds that Quito does not blindly follow Washington's foreign policy directives, as is often the criticism in Japan where the security consensus remains strong among elites.[17] Given the lack of historical or institutional ties between Ecuador and the United States, Quito was less compelled, or constrained, to follow the policy preferences of Washington.

Mobilization against the Manta Base

Did the anti-base campaign in Ecuador matter? I argue that anti-base movements did make a difference in base policy outcomes. The absence of a strong security consensus provided a favorable political opportunity for anti-base activists. Pro-U.S. political leaders certainly resided in Quito, but government

---

[17] Interview with Adrian Bonilla, March 8, 2007, Quito, Ecuador.

elites as a whole never shared a common understanding or fixed perception of U.S.-Ecuador relations. This enabled activists and political elites sympathetic to the anti-base cause to align with one another on the Manta base issue. Although Ecuadorian anti-base movements first mobilized in 1999 with inauspicious beginnings, by 2005 top government officials were beginning to advocate the nonrenewal of the Manta base agreement. This position was eventually carried by presidential candidate Rafael Correa during his 2006 campaign.

Origins

Unlike other movement episodes, the Manta anti-base movement did not begin as a local NIMBY phenomenon. Rather, the movement emerged at the national level, and only later shifted downward to the local level.[18] Peace and Justice Service of Ecuador (SERPAJ) was the first group to latch onto the Manta base issue. In March 1999, SERPAJ posted an alert to other social groups announcing that Ecuador would grant the United States basing rights in Manta.[19] Despite slow mobilization, activist groups did attempt to protest the U.S. military presence along with a slate of other issues, such as debt relief and privatization. In this vein, the Confederation of Indigenous Nationalities (CONAIE) organized one of the first large-scale demonstrations against the Manta agreement in July 1999. CONAIE had recently won a seat to participate in a formal dialogue with the Ecuadorian government by engaging in two weeks of militant protest.[20] However, the Manta issue was quickly overshadowed by Ecuador's financial crisis and the dollarization of the economy in early 2000.[21]

Although the ten-year agreement signed in November 1999 immediately prompted several peace and human rights organizations to take action, a broader coalition with greater cooperation from local groups did not begin to take shape until 2001. Joining forces with local groups, this formation included

---

[18] Most local communities in Manta were initially pro-base. However, land-displacement issues from decades earlier by the Ecuadorian government did constitute one major grievance for a small group of residents in Manabí Province. See Luis Ángel Saavedra, "The Manta Base: A U.S. Military Fort in Ecuador," *Fellowship* 73, no. 1(2007): 20–21.

[19] Ibid., 15.

[20] As with other anti-base movements, different formations or factions within the movement existed. For instance, although CONAIE publicly declared its opposition to the Manta base, I did not observe a strong CONAIE presence in the Ecuador No Bases Coalition. On this point, Ecuador No Bases Coalition members stated, "CONAIE was invited to participate in the No Bases Ecuador Coalition, and indeed it participated in several coordination meetings. [However], it did not play the main role in the process of resistance in Manta or at the national level. Instead, it incorporated in its discourse the permanent fight against and closure of Manta Base as a matter of sovereignty." E-mail interview with Helga Serrano and Ecuador No Bases Coalition members, August 31, 2007. Nevertheless, CONAIE is listed as a member of the Ecuador No Bases Coalition.

[21] Although their numbers were relatively small, CONAIE and other social and political groups continued to challenge the government in mid- to late 2000. For instance, 3,000 activists held a demonstration in Quito on May 1, 2000. See Ecuador No Bases Coalition, *Base de Manta: Ojos y oidos del Plan Colombia* [Manta Base: The Eyes and Ears of Plan Colombia] (Quito: Ecuador No Bases Coalition, 2007), 24.

organizations such as the Provincial Union of Farmers' Organization of Manabí (UPOCAM), Tohalí Anti-Imperialism Movement, Ecumenical Commission of Human Rights (CEDHU), Andean Program of Human Rights (PADH), International Observance for Peace (OIPAZ), SERPAJ, the Anti-Corruption Network, the Young Men's Christian Association–Ecuador (ACJ–Ecuador), and the Regional Foundation of Consultant's Office in Human Rights (INREDH).

In addition to national protests, anti-base groups invested significant amounts of time mobilizing citizens within Manabí Province. The Tohali Anti-Imperialist Movement, the Land Defense Committee of Portoviejo, and later ACJ–Ecuador were foundational in promoting resistance against the Manta base at the local level.[22] These groups hosted forums, cultural activities, and public debates to raise awareness about base-related issues. In Manta, ACJ and SERPAJ focused on educating local youth and peasants about the dangers associated with U.S. bases.

Human rights groups such as INREDH and the Andean Committee of Services promoted the anti-base cause by lobbying officials, providing communication through its networks, and conducting research on bases and militarization. These groups had compiled enough evidence to present cases of human rights violations on behalf of local residents. Issues of concern included "the right of fishermen to accede to port, the recovery of illegally expropriated land, damages resulting from the sinking and destroying of boats, and the control and access of waterways for military purpose."[23] Anti-base groups were especially concerned about the use of the Manta base as a launching pad to aid Colombia in its fight against rebel insurgents such as the FARC. Activists feared that the U.S. military presence would eventually drag Ecuador into a regionalized military conflict as Colombian rebels traversed Ecuador's borders. By educating Manabí Province residents on the potential dangers of a U.S. military presence, activists hoped to build public opinion against base renewal in 2009.[24] Activists stated that support for the nonrenewal of the Manta agreement increased as more citizens grew aware of the U.S. military presence and militarization through Ecuador's involvement in Plan Colombia.

Transnational Collaboration

One key difference between the Manta anti-base movement and other episodes discussed in previous chapters is the movement's degree of internationalization. Transnational links played a greater role in Ecuador than in other anti-base movements. The movement maintained close ties to groups outside of Ecuador, particularly those working on peace and demilitarization issues. For example, the American Friends Service Committee (AFSC) visited Manta in 2002 to study the political, economic, and cultural impacts of the Manta base. Later, the AFSC,

---

[22] E-mail interview with Helga Serrano and Ecuador No Bases Coalition members, August 31, 2007.
[23] Ecuador No Bases Coalition, *Base de Manta*, 24.
[24] Ibid., 24.

the Regional Foundation of Consultancy in Human Rights, and the Network of the Colombian-Ecuadorian Brotherhood held workshops in Manta to discuss links between the Manta base and Plan Colombia.

In January 2004, Ecuadorian anti-base activists gave a presentation on bases at the World Social Forum (WSF) in Mumbai, India. The following year, the emerging network of global anti-base activists discussed potential locations to host the first international anti-base meeting. Ecuadorian anti-base groups proposed Quito as a possible location. At the request of the network's International Organization Committee (IOC), several Ecuadorian groups with existing ties at the transnational level submitted a proposal on behalf of Ecuadorian activists. Once approved, these groups formally established the Ecuador No Bases Coalition. The AFSC and INREDH acted as the initial coordinators, with ACJ–Ecuador replacing the AFSC in 2006.[25] The Ecuador No Bases Coalition coordinated with the global No Bases network to host a major international conference in Quito in March 2007. The conference concluded with a caravan from Quito to Manta, where 400 international delegates joined thousands of protestors in Manta. The international conference, supported by the mayor's office in Quito and blessed by President Correa, attracted national media attention from all major news sources in Ecuador. In sum, anti-base groups were able to sustain their campaign over a relatively long period, maintain at least a semblance of movement unity, and reach a broad audience through the international conference.

State–Society Interaction

Anti-base protests mattered. However, having powerful leaders backing the anti-base stance may have mattered even more. After all, base politics and the renewal of the Manta agreement were decisions made by political elites. This raises a problem of causal inference, making it difficult to assess the weighted impact of social movements. The absence of any security consensus may simply have led powerful anti-base elites, such as President Correa, to reject U.S. bases based on their own preferences, regardless of social movement pressure. Thus President Correa would have rejected U.S. bases even if activists had never mobilized.

If anti-base movements truly mattered, some doubt should be cast on whether Ecuadorian government officials would have committed to a position of base nonrenewal had an anti-base movement not existed. The answer to base policy outcomes is clearly not monocausal, and certainly not attributed to anti-base movements alone. The crucial question here is whether an actual link existed between state and society, or if anti-base movements were merely cheerleaders on the sideline rooting for politicians to say no to U.S. bases. The security consensus framework helps us think about the connection between anti-base

[25] E-mail interview with Helga Serrano and Ecuador No Bases Coalition members, August 31, 2007. For a complete list of Ecuador No Bases Coalition groups, see Saavedra, *Operaciones De Avansada O Base Militar Operativa?* 49.

movements and government elites. Here I process trace events throughout the Manta base episode to show how activists and sympathetic elites reinforced one another's positions, leading to the removal of U.S. troops.

Legal Action with Sympathetic Elites

As argued earlier, in the formative stages of the anti-base campaign, human rights, religious, and indigenous groups took legal action against the Manta base agreement. That members of the Ecuadorian Armed Forces, National Congress, and Constitutional Court also questioned the Manta agreement added to the credibility of activists' legal challenge.[26] For example, in September 2000, military officials requested that the government review the Manta agreement, arguing that U.S. troops were taking on functions belonging to the Ecuadorian Armed Forces.[27] Several months later, Hugo Moreno, the International Relations Committee chair, also requested that the foreign and defense ministers explain the implications of the U.S. military presence in Manta.[28]

Aside from street demonstrations, in the first stage of the anti-base campaign, several human rights organizations, in conjunction with political parties, decided to challenge the Manta agreement through the Constitutional Court. Activists presented their case before the Constitutional Court on January 15, 2001. Human rights lawyers claimed that the Manta agreement required approval from the National Congress. Activist groups argued that the Manta agreement violated Article 161, Number 2, of Ecuador's Constitution, which authorized the National Congress to approve international treaties and agreements, including those that established political or military alliances.[29] As Representative Gilberto Talahua, chair of the Indigenous Affairs Committee, maintained, "The accord was signed in violation of constitutional norms and without citizen discussion or participation."[30] Moreover, activists claimed that the base served as an outpost for military actions tied to Plan Colombia.[31] Although the Court ruled in favor of the government, anti-base activists had taken the first step in challenging the Manta agreement through formal channels.[32]

---

[26] Saavedra, "Manta Base," 16.

[27] Kintto Lucas, "Ecuador: Indigenous Groups Protest Privatizations, US Army Base," *Inter-Press Service*, September 14, 2000.

[28] Kintto Lucas, "U.S. Base Could Draw Nation into Neighbor's War," *Inter-Press Service*, November 17, 2000.

[29] See the Political Constitution of 1998, Republic of Ecuador. http://pdba.georgetown.edu/Constitutions/Ecuador/ecuador98.html (last accessed February 8, 2008).

[30] Lucas, "U.S. Base Could Draw Nation into Neighbor's War."

[31] The U.S. and Ecuadorian governments denied allegations made by anti-base activists, claiming that the Manta base was limited to counternarcotics and surveillance operations. I do not deny Washington or Quito's official position. However, it is true that Colombian insurgency groups engaged in illicit drug trafficking, making it difficult to separate the war on drugs from counterinsurgency operations.

[32] Pro-base demonstrations supporting the Constitutional Court's ruling also took place in Manta.

The Pro-U.S. Gutierrez Period

With anti-base groups defeated in court, activists turned their attention toward the link between Plan Colombia and the Manta base. Human rights groups began to research and closely monitor social tensions taking place near the Colombia-Ecuador border, fueled by increasing violence and an influx of refugees beginning in late 2000.[33] Acknowledging rising tensions on the borderland, the Ecuadorian government stationed approximately 10,000 troops along the Colombia-Ecuador border. Wanting to steer clear of Colombia's conflict with rebel insurgents, Ecuadorians voiced concern that Manta's surveillance capabilities were being used to monitor FARC activity. Ecuadorians feared that Washington's increasing involvement in Colombia's struggle against insurgents would inadvertently drag Quito into the conflict.[34]

In November 2002, Lucio Gutierrez, who briefly headed the junta government after Jamil Mahuad's ouster in 2000, was voted into power with the backing of indigenous and leftist groups. Much to the consternation of some of his political supporters, however, Gutierrez quickly established a pro-U.S. stance, declaring his intention to be "the best ally of the United States."[35] Under these new political constraints, anti-base groups shifted their strategy and movement frame from immediate base closure to the nonrenewal of the Manta agreement in 2009.

During the Gutierrez period, major protests were less visible. However, anti-base groups organized conferences, such as the International Peace Camp, to reach out to Manabí Province residents. Additionally, civic groups documented base-related incidents around Manta port and the northern border. For example, the Latin American Association of Human Rights (ALDHU) investigated the alleged sinking of fishing boats by U.S. ships. Activists also compiled a series of detailed reports linking the Manta base to surveillance activities in Colombia. These reports were sent to the Ecuadorian National Congress.[36]

More significantly, it was during this period that the Ecuador No Bases Coalition began to coalesce, pooling together groups involved in earlier anti-base initiatives into a broader coalition linked with international anti-base groups.[37] Anti-base groups also redoubled their efforts to educate the Manta population to undermine the city government's support for a continued U.S. military presence. Middle-class citizens had invested in businesses in hopes of profiting from the U.S. military presence and the $70 million renovation and upgrades to the Manta base. However, the economic benefits promised by local pro-base officials never materialized. Unfulfilled promises, coupled with safety

[33] Saavedra, "Manta Base," 25.
[34] "Caught in the Front Line: Manta's FOL Status and ATOA Snub Irk Ecuadoreans," *Latin America Regional Reports: Andean Group*, October 1, 2002.
[35] Kintto Lucas, "Ecuador: Indigenous Angered by Gutierrez's Pledge in D.C.," *Inter-Press Service*, February 12, 2003.
[36] Saavedra, "Manta Base," 26.
[37] Ibid., 27–29.

issues and disruptions in the fishing economy, led to increasing dissatisfaction with the U.S. base presence among Manta residents.[38]

Growing Elite Dissatisfaction

Concerned over growing political instability, the National Congress voted to replace President Gutierrez with his vice president, Alfredo Palacio, in April 2005. Activists contend that Gutierrez's ouster allowed anti-base groups to make public the information compiled by various organizations. Under the Gutierrez administration, Foreign Minister Patricio Zuquilanda refused to engage in dialogue with specific anti-base groups and their representatives, working to undermine and discredit their evidence against the U.S. military presence.[39] Demands to address the sinking of fishing ships and health hazards created by Colombia's fumigation of coca plants were largely ignored by the Gutierrez government.[40] In contrast, key cabinet officials in the Palacio administration hinted that the agreement would not continue beyond 2009. On July 15, 2005, Foreign Minister Antonio Parra commented that he would rather cut his hand off than sign a renewed base agreement.[41] Parra made clear that national sovereignty and nonintervention in internal affairs would guide Ecuadorian foreign policy.[42] Although Parra promised to respect the current base agreement, the new government's emphasis on sovereignty made base renewal less tenable in the future. Parra's words were tested when a U.S. naval ship damaged a fishing boat on May 21, 2005. Indeed, Foreign Minister Parra protested the detainment of the boat's crew and requested compensation for the damaged ship. The Ecuadorian government also refused to bow before U.S. pressure to grant U.S. soldiers immunity from the International Criminal Court, a move that cost the government $7 million in U.S. economic aid.[43]

Foreign Minister Parra was replaced halfway into Palacio's tenure by Francisco Carrión. Carrión's position was even clearer than Parra's on the Manta agreement. Appearing before the International Affairs Committee in the National Congress on February 1, 2006, Carrión stated, "If I were foreign minister in 2009, I would not sign a renewal of the Manta base agreement (with the United States) because I do not consider that it benefits the country's interests."[44] This position was echoed by Deputy Foreign Minister Diego Ribadeneira, who added, "I do not think that the Manta Base [agreement] will

---

[38] Ibid., 39.
[39] Ibid., 41.
[40] Ibid., 41. However, Heinz Moeller, Ecuador's foreign affairs minister under Gustavo Noboa, had requested that the Colombian government halt fumigations in 2001.
[41] "Ecuadoran Minister says Manta Base Agreement Will Not Be Renewed," *BBC Monitoring Worldwide*, July 16, 2005.
[42] Saavedra, "Manta Base," 39.
[43] Ibid., 41.
[44] "Ecuadoran Foreign Minister Opposes Agreement on U.S. Base," *BBC Monitoring Worldwide*, February 11, 2006.

be extended, whoever is foreign minister in 2009."[45] Minister of Defense Marcelo Delgado, speaking as a private citizen, also expressed his disappointment with the current Manta agreement. He argued, "We have received almost nothing in exchange for Manta Base. ... [Ecuador] must receive something in exchange. If we do not have that, there should be no negotiation [for renewal]."[46]

Weak Security Consensus and Movement–Government Ties

The lack of consensus among Ecuadorian elites regarding U.S.-Ecuador security relations is attested by the varying positions of the Gustavo Nobua and Gutierrez governments on the one hand and the Palacio government on the other. Under the Palacio government, activists found key elites sympathetic to their cause. For instance, Foreign Minister Carrión met with Ecuador No Bases Coalition members to discuss his position not to renew the Manta base agreement. Carrion's National Plan of Foreign Policy (PLANEX 2020) was also established with input from various sectors of society, including anti-base groups and other civil societal organizations.[47] In effect, demands from Ecuadorian pacifist groups were satisfied in PLANEX 2020, which stated that "Ecuadorian territory [would] not house foreign troops."[48] As a sign of commitment to PLANEX 2020, the Palacio administration rejected signing an agreement granting U.S. soldiers immunity from criminal jurisdiction while on duty. This decision was announced following a meeting between Minister of Government Mauricio Gandara and members of human rights groups.[49]

More importantly, the connection between social movements and elites became more apparent in the rhetoric of elites. In 1999, the U.S. military presence in Manta was unproblematic. Prior to the Palacio regime, Quito vehemently denied any link between the Manta base and the Colombian insurgency. By 2005, however, policy circles contemplating the future of Manta raised arguments similar to those previously presented only by

---

[45] Ibid. Carrion qualified his comment, however, when reminded of U.S. Ambassador Linda Jewel's optimism about extending the Manta agreement, and the potential friction his position would create with the United States. In response, Carrion asserted his position against base renewal was a personal opinion and not reflective of the Ecuadorian government. He added that the decision ultimately rested with the next government in any case. See "Ecuadoran Foreign Minister against Renewal of Manta Base Agreement," *BBC Monitoring Worldwide*, September 2, 2006.

[46] "Ecuador Defense Minister Slams U.S. Military Base at Manta," *BBC Monitoring Worldwide*, September 11, 2006.

[47] Saavedra, "Manta Base," 43. This was confirmed in an e-mail interview with Helga Serrano and Ecuador No Bases Coalition members, August 31, 2007.

[48] Ministry of Foreign Affairs, Republic of Ecuador, *Plan Nacional de Política Exterior* (PLANEX). http://www.mmrree.gov.ec/mre/documentos/ministerio/planex/planex_esp.htm (last accessed February 15, 2008); and e-mail interview with Helga Serrano and Ecuador No Bases Coalition members, August 31, 2007.

[49] "Ecuador's New Government against Immunity for US Military," *BBC Monitoring Worldwide*, April 23, 2005.

activists – sovereignty and escalation of the Colombian conflict – as reasons not to re-sign the Manta deal.[50]

It was under this shifting political environment that presidential candidate Rafael Correa ran on a platform announcing his pledge of nonrenewal during the 2006 election campaign. The pledge against the U.S. military presence in Ecuador struck a popular chord among numerous constituents.[51] Correa's primary challenger was the conservative Alvaro Noboa, who favored the U.S. military presence in Manta. As Ecuador No Bases Coalition members contend, the 2006 elections enabled the Manta base issue to move beyond activist circles and into mainstream public debates. The fate of the U.S. military presence would rest with the electorate, based on the outcome of the election.

Correa's electoral victory struck a blow against U.S. geopolitical interests. Still, some argued that Correa's position was only a pledge and not policy. Some skeptics argued that Correa's hard-line position on the Manta agreement renewal was nothing more than a bargaining strategy. By beginning with a position of nonrenewal, Correa could leverage additional concessions such as foreign aid or preferential trade agreements.[52] A few activists also expressed uncertainty as to whether Correa would hold onto his electoral pledge. Thus Ecuador No Bases Coalition members continued to lobby and write support letters to keep Correa accountable. Doubt was finally cast aside when Correa reaffirmed his position publicly during the International No Bases Conference held in Quito. The Ecuadorian government also delegated Assistant Secretary of Defense Miguel Carvajal to speak at the No Bases Conference plenary session, where he restated Correa's pledge. In addition to Correa, the Ecuador No Bases Coalition kept in contact with government allies such as the minister of government and police, Fernando Bustamante, and the national security advisor, Gustavo Larrea. In sum, no security consensus existed among Ecuadorian political elites that would guide U.S.-Ecuador relations. Taking advantage of this political opportunity, activists shaped the political debate against the Manta base and gained considerable leverage in their struggle by forming ties with sympathetic elites within the central government.

One might argue that the rise of a leftist president in 2006 may have led to this eventual outcome, rendering anti-base protests epiphenomenal. After all, anti-base groups had challenged the United States since 1999 but had not achieved "victory" until the center-leftist president Raphael Correa had entered power. Much like the Philippine case, however, without strong, organized anti-base opposition, the Manta base issue would have likely maintained a low profile. Instead, anti-base groups challenged the legality of the base agreement in the Constitutional Court, mobilized mass demonstrations, and educated citizens within Manabí Province about the security risks associated with Manta.

[50] "Official Says Ecuador Unlikely to Renew US Air Base Agreement," *BBC Monitoring Latin America*, February 10, 2006.
[51] Logan, "U.S. Faces Eviction from Ecuadorian Base."
[52] Ibid.

Conducting extensive research, human rights organizations constantly fed government officials information pertaining to Manta Base and Plan Colombia. By 2005, major political figures, including Palacio's foreign and defense ministers, hinted they would not re-sign the Manta base agreement with the United States. These sympathetic elites became potential allies in the battle to terminate the Manta base agreement in 2009. Activists had raised the Manta base issue to a level of national importance, attested by the inclusion of base nonrenewal in Rafael Correa's 2006 presidential campaign platform. Through a drawn-out campaign, anti-base movements helped shape a national security discourse against the U.S. military presence, ultimately leading to the closure of the Manta base.

ITALY

As Ecuadorian anti-base activists celebrated victory over the news of the U.S. base closure, halfway around the world Italian anti-base activists struggled to block the expansion of a U.S. air base in Vicenza, Italy. Local resistance against base expansion began brewing in May 2006 when Vicenza city officials publicly revealed base construction plans at Dal Molin airfield. Largely because of anti-base protestors, the Vicenza issue quickly rose to national prominence. On February 17, 2007, the No Dal Molin campaign organized its second major protest against U.S. bases, supported by Far-Left parties within Prime Minister Romano Prodi's ruling coalition government. Four days later, Prodi's frail center-left coalition crumbled over foreign policy issues. Failing to gain Senate majority approval supporting Italy's NATO mission in Afghanistan and the expansion of a U.S. military base, Prodi stepped down as head of government.

How effective was the No Dal Molin campaign in stopping U.S. base expansion? Did anti-base movements pose a real threat to the Italian government and the future of U.S. base plans in northern Italy? How did the Italian government juggle international alliance commitments and domestic political pressure? The Vicenza episode parallels Okinawan anti-base movement episodes in several respects. Although the internal dynamics of the No Dal Molin campaign differ from Okinawan anti-base movements, the cycle of anti-base action and government reaction follows a similar pattern. In the face of anti-base pressure, the Italian government initially dragged its feet on the matter, passing the buck to local city officials. Like Tokyo, Rome resorted to numerous political tactics to keep a lid on domestic opposition, and in particular Far-Left party officials. Activists thus found it much more difficult to form ties with sympathetic elites. As I argued in previous cases, the Italian government's response and the movement's difficulty in penetrating the state ultimately stemmed from U.S. alliance relations and the influence of a strong security consensus among Italian elites. Contrary to that of Ecuador, the historical development of U.S.-Italian relations, and the institutional framework of NATO, helped foster a security "consensus" among elites. What made the Vicenza anti-base movement episode unique from similar cases such as Japan and South Korea (discussed in Chapter 5), however, was the role of coalition politics. Coalition dynamics and a slim parliamentary majority initially provided activists an opportunity to broaden their anti-base agenda. However, Italian coalitional politics acted as a double-edged sword, eventually reinforcing the position of the security consensus.

U.S. Bases in Italy

Although the U.S. military presence in Italy traces back to the postwar occupation, the current system of U.S. bases is more closely associated with Italy's acceptance into NATO.[53] In the south, Naples hosted the headquarters of the Allied Joint Forces Command in Southern Europe and Allied Naval Forces Southern Europe. Installations in Sicily, such as the Sigonella and Comiso bases, took on an increasingly important role in the 1970s as U.S. strategic priorities expanded in the Middle East. In the north, the United States built Camp Ederle in Vicenza, which functioned as the Southern European Task Force headquarters. The United States also established a major air base in Aviano in northeast Italy. These bases were intended to protect Italy from Soviet and Yugoslavian threats across its eastern border.[54]

Most bases were established as NATO facilities with U.S. troops operating under the NATO Status of Forces Agreement. Basing access and jurisdiction of U.S. troops were regulated by the Basic Infrastructure Agreement signed by Rome and Washington in 1954. Rome and Washington signed additional agreements in the mid-1990s placing U.S. bases under Italian command and limiting their use to NATO operations. Although U.S. troops in Italy were under an American commander, Italy still retained sovereignty over U.S. bases.

The 2004 Global Defense Posture Review recommended reducing force levels in Western Europe from 100,000 to 50,000 troops, with most reductions coming from Germany. Despite significant cuts across Europe, troop levels have remained relatively constant in Italy at around 12,000 troops since the mid-1990s.[55] In 2007, 13,076 U.S. military personnel were stationed in Italy, with major bases located in Aviano, Naples, Vicenza, and Sigonella.[56] Sigonella functions as a critical point for air mobility routes.[57] Its strategic location by the

[53] See C. T. Sandars, *America's Overseas Garrisons: The Leasehold Empire* (Oxford: Oxford University Press, 2000), 227–38, for an overview of U.S. bases in Italy.

[54] Carla Monteleone, "The Evolution of the Euro-Atlantic Pluralistic Security Community," *Journal of Transatlantic Studies* 5, no. 1 (2007): 63–85 at 72.

[55] See Tim Kane, *Global Troop Deployment Dataset 1950–2005* (Washington, D.C.: Heritage Foundation, 2005).

[56] For a complete list of installations in Italy, see United States Department of Defense, *Base Structure Report: A Summary of the Department of Defense's Real Property Inventory* (Washington, D.C.: Office of the Deputy Under-Secretary of Defense, 2009), 85–86. An increase in U.S. troop deployments to Afghanistan from 2008 to 2009 drastically reduced the number of forces in late 2008, leaving approximately 7,000 troops stationed in Italy (ibid., 86).

[57] Statement by General James L. Jones, USMC Commander, United States European Command, to the Senate Armed Services Committee, March 1, 2005.

Mediterranean also enables the base to serve as a major naval logistics hub through the Fleet and Industrial Supply Center.[58] In the north, Aviano and Vicenza host the 173rd Airborne Combat Brigade Team (ACBT). Reactivated in 2000, the 173rd ACBT has grown from one to six battalions.[59] Camp Ederle in Vicenza currently hosts two battalions. The remaining four battalions are located in Germany. As part of ongoing plans for U.S. military restructuring in Southern Europe, the Army plans to consolidate the entire 173rd ACBT to Italy.

Anti-Base Mobilization in Vicenza

From Formal to Informal Politics

Limited space at Camp Ederle required the U.S. military to construct a new base facility in Vicenza to accommodate the relocation of 2,000 troops.[60] The United States approached the Berlusconi government in late 2003, inquiring about the use of the Dal Molin airfield in Vicenza.[61] In April 2005, the U.S. ambassador to Italy announced that the Berlusconi government had agreed to set aside part of the airfield for U.S. military use. *Stars and Stripes* reported that negotiations between the U.S. and Italian governments had taken place over the past two years.[62]

The base negotiations were conducted behind closed doors, leaving Vicenza residents in the dark about the Dal Molin project. Rumors and public speculation about base expansion were finally confirmed by the city government on May 25, 2006.[63] A U.S. military representative and a Vicenza city official presented details about the project during a city council meeting. Vicenza citizens criticized the secretive manner in which base negotiations were conducted

[58] Monteleone, "Evolution of the Euro-Atlantic Pluralistic Security Community," 76; and Ron Flanders, "Navy Establishes Fleet and Industrial Supply Center Sigonella, Italy," *Navy NewsStand*, January 28, 2005. http://www.globalsecurity.org/military/library/news/2005/01/mil-050128-nns01.htm (last accessed February 8, 2008).

[59] Paul Iversen, "The Consequences of Bushismo in Vicenza, Italy," March 2005. http://www.peaceandjustice.it/vicenza-dal-molin.php (last accessed January 8, 2008).

[60] Russ Rizzo, "U.S., Italians Reach Agreement for Army to Use Portion of Air Base Near Vicenza," *Stars and Stripes*, April 12, 2005; and interview with Camp Ederle base official, Vicenza, Italy, January 15, 2008.

[61] This date is reported by *Stars and Stripes*. See Rizzo, "U.S., Italians Reach Agreement for Army to Use Portion of Air Base Near Vicenza." Activists claim discussions took place anytime between 1999 and 2004. Dal Molin previously housed NATO command offices. It also hosted a small contingent of Italian Air Force personnel. The land is controlled by the Italian Ministry of Defense (interview with U.S. Consulate official, Milan, Italy, January 18, 2008; and interview with No Dal Molin activist Enzo Ciscato, Vicenza, Italy, January 15, 2008).

[62] Rizzo, "U.S., Italians Reach Agreement for Army to Use Portion of Air Base Near Vicenza."

[63] Activists note that suspicions were aroused because reports about possible base expansion in Italy (but not necessarily Dal Molin) were reported by the media but not by the city. Moreover, upon learning that the U.S military was planning to pay for improved road and traffic conditions in northeast Vicenza, community groups suspected that the U.S. military was making preparations for base construction (interview with No Dal Molin activist Guido Lanaro, January 14, 2008; and interview with No Dal Molin activist Enzo Ciscato, January 15, 2008).

between the U.S., Italian, and Vicenza governments. Echoing grievances by Ecuadorian activists, citizens were notified only after negotiations had been concluded.

Initially focusing on NIMBY issues, local citizens raised several grievances regarding the Dal Molin project. Activists claimed the increase in U.S. soldiers would adversely impact the environment, increase consumption of resources such as water and electricity, congest traffic, and heighten safety risks. Later, activists increasingly focused on antimilitarization frames to broaden their reach. Noting Vicenza's recognition as a UNESCO world heritage site, activists condemned the idea of polluting a historical city with another military base.[64]

In response to the city's announcement in May 2006, residents in Vicenza and surrounding communities coordinated their opposition through several local community councils.[65] Since details of the base expansion were still relatively unknown to the general public, the councils provided information, solicited opinions, and communicated their concerns to city officials. The community councils also used several tactics to try and block base expansion, such as organizing protest marches, voicing opposition at city council meetings, and gathering signatures. Taking advantage of formal channels of politics, opposition community members also held discussions with city officials throughout the summer of 2006. Citizens demanded a thorough study of the base's environmental and economic impacts before passing an agreement. Most importantly, opposition groups requested that the city pass any base decision through a public referendum.

Unfortunately, the path of formal politics led Vicenza citizens to a dead end. On October 26, the Vicenza city council voted in favor of base expansion with twenty-one in favor and seventeen opposed (three abstained).[66] Additionally, the Vicenza city council rejected holding a public referendum. The No Dal Molin campaign thus declared, "In the face of silence, and generic assurances on the political side, (anti-base) committees (began) active protests in October 2006 in front of the mayor's office. Deaf to the various requests of democratic participation of local people, the government had already decided in favor of the base without any type of popular referendum."[67] Having reached the limits of

---

[64] Vicenza is the site of several Palladian buildings and villas. Activists have written to UNESCO requesting Vicenza's removal from the list of world heritage sites. They claim a city occupied by military bases is undeserving of such recognition. See No Dal Molin/Presidio Permanente, *Una rigorosa analisi, dei documenti di progetto, di documenti comunali, di leggi e decreti eseguita da un gruppo di tecnici* [The rigorous analysis of project documents, municipality documents, and decree laws of a group of engineers], 2007. Available at http://www.altravicenza.it/dossier/dalmolin/doc/20070405comitatio1.pdf (last accessed January 28, 2008).

[65] Media and activist reports vary between six and nine such community advisory councils. Councils were organized based on location of residence.

[66] Iversen, "Consequences of Bushismo in Vicenza, Italy."

[67] Stefano Priante and Marta Passarin, *Actions against Wars*, video documentary, April 2007. Available for download at http://www.peaceandjustice.it/vicenza/index.php and http://www.nodalmolin.it/ (last accessed January 26, 2008).

institutional politics, Vicenza citizens now turned toward informal politics by mobilizing a broad campaign against base expansion.

The No Dal Molin Campaign

To draw a broader, national appeal, local activists reached out to antiwar groups, inviting them to support the No Dal Molin campaign. No Dal Molin members also joined the Patto Nazionale di Solidarietà e Mutuo Soccorso (PNSMS) in solidarity with other local Italian movements fighting to protect local resources and territory. Through the PNSMS, anti-base activists networked with other social movements, such as the campaign against the construction of a high-speed railway in Val di Susa or protests against garbage dumps in Grottaglie. No Dal Molin activists stated, "An agreement (has been made) with mutual support for the various movements throughout the country. In this way, local movements protecting local resources were all supporters at the national level."[68] As the No Dal Molin campaign expanded its networks, local activists formed the Presidio Permanente[69] and prepared for their first national protest on December 2. This demonstration attracted approximately 30,000 protestors in Vicenza, signaling the arrival of a major social movement.[70]

On January 16, 2007, Prime Minister Prodi publicly announced his support for the new base at Dal Molin. Anti-base activists immediately reacted to the announcement. Citizens and activists spontaneously marched through the historical center of Vicenza expressing their outrage. Eight thousand citizens held a candlelight vigil. Some protestors burned voter registration cards and party flags to voice their indignation at Prime Minister Prodi, who only months earlier had made an electoral pledge to decrease militarization. Activists then occupied the Vicenza railroad station. The protest march culminated at the Presidio, adjacent to the Dal Molin airfield.

Party Politics and Political Opportunities

Coalition dynamics within Prodi's ruling center-left government initially proved fortuitous for anti-base activists. The slim two-seat Senate majority over the center-right gave fringe parties in Prodi's nine-party coalition a disproportionate amount of power relative to their size. Prodi's announcement to support base expansion in Vicenza, and Italian troops in Afghanistan under NATO, put his frail coalition to the test. Far-Left party members were aghast that Prodi had endorsed a deal negotiated under the pro-Bush Berlusconi government. Members from the Party of Italian Communists (PdCI), Communist Refoundation Party (PRC), and the Green Party all expressed deep reservations about what they perceived as the militarization of Italy's foreign policy. The

---

[68] Ibid.

[69] The Presidio functioned as an assembly or forum. As a physical place, the Presidio was a large white tent serving as the headquarters of the No Dal Molin campaign.

[70] Stefano Osti, *Vicenza's Struggle against Global Militarization*, video documentary, English narration by Aran Nathanson, Vicenza, Italy, December 2007.

three Far-Left parties vowed to oppose the new base, thus opening the door for activists to form ties with members of the ruling government. PRC representative Alfio Nicotra stated, "Romano Prodi's profoundly mistaken decision does not close the Vicenza question, but on the contrary, opens it. . . . This is shown by the way people are mobilizing in Vicenza and by the requests we are getting to hold a national rally, whose goal would be to cut back foreign bases and reduce Italy's military servitude."[71]

Activists took advantage of internal bickering within the center-left coalition. While Prodi's fragile government teetered on the edge of crisis over foreign and defense policy issues, the No Dal Molin campaign made preparations for a second national protest on February 17. The three Far-Left parties gave their support to Vicenza activists. Government representatives from these parties, including several senators and the minister of environment, joined protestors in Vicenza. The demonstration drew approximately 100,000 protestors.[72]

Four days after the protest, Foreign Minister Massimo D'Alema made an appeal to Parliament members to support U.S. base expansion in Vicenza and commit Italian troops to NATO. D'Alema argued that the Vicenza base was essential for maintaining positive relations with the United States, and "to change course would be a hostile act against the United States."[73] Despite his former ties to communists, D'Alema's appeal did not win over the radical left. Two Far-Left senators, Fernando Rossi (PdCI) and Franco Turigliatto (PRC), abstained from voting. To the delight of activists, the government failed to win majority support. Unable to garner the necessary votes from his own coalition, Prodi voluntarily resigned as prime minister. Prodi's fall raised several hopeful questions for activists. If reinstated as prime minister, would Prodi change his stance on the Vicenza issue? Would a new government review the base agreement with the United States?

Successful Mobilization

Italian activists have praised the No Dal Molin campaign as the first major movement specifically targeting U.S. military bases in Italy and as a model for other local movements to follow.[74] Mobilization success goes beyond the size of protests witnessed on December 2 and February 17. Activists repeatedly pointed

---

[71] Tony Barber, "Plans for U.S. Base Split Italian Coalition," *Financial Times*, January 10, 2007, 6.

[72] Activists cite between 100,000 and 120,000 protestors. Police reports cite between 50,000 and 80,000 protestors. See Colleen Barry, "Italians Protest U.S. Base Expansion," *Washington Post*, February 18, 2007.

[73] Ian Fisher, "Italian Premier Resigns after Losing Foreign Policy Vote," *New York Times*, February 22, 2008.

[74] Large protests against U.S. bases took place in the 1980s. However, these protests were aimed at preventing the deployment of cruise missiles stockpiled at U.S. bases rather than military bases themselves. Communities with long-standing anti-base opposition include those in Livorno, Napoli, Aviano, Sigonella, and Sardinia. However, most anti-base groups tend to be relatively small. With the possible exception of movements in Aviano and Sigonella, Italian peace groups have not paid significant attention to these struggles. Thus, as Piero Maestri argues, "Vicenza is

to the diverse social, economic, and political backgrounds of participants, and the transformative effect broad collaboration had on the identity and outlook of Vicenza citizens. Several factors enabled the No Dal Molin campaign to maintain a high degree of cohesiveness up through the February 17 protest.

First, the No Dal Molin campaign maintained its local flavor with a concrete target and goal focused on stopping U.S. base expansion at Dal Molin. Moreover, the movement was organized by local Vicenza citizens with relatively little outside interference, giving the campaign an extra degree of credibility with supporters. An autonomous movement of the citizenry made it more difficult for the government to discredit the legitimacy of the movement.

Second, the blend of younger, radical activists with older, more established "ordinary" citizens had a positive impact on the campaign by appealing to a wider reach of the Vicenza community. Younger activists reported feeling much safer having "ordinary" citizens participate in the movement. Not only did the presence of ordinary citizens and families help moderate the movement's image, but as one local businessman recollects being told by a younger activist, "If it weren't for you guys, I think the police would have cracked down on us."[75] Conversely, the older activists and "ordinary" citizens were encouraged by the passionate resistance of younger activists. An American peace activist in Rome observed how ordinary citizens who had always played by the rules learned it was acceptable to step beyond these boundaries, participating in civil disobedience.[76]

Lastly, the movement successfully turned a local issue into a national movement. Not only did activists network with other local movements and antiwar groups across Italy, but by early 2007 the anti-base movement had the full support of the Far-Left political parties in Prodi's coalition. Support went beyond mere rhetoric. For instance, in Milan, the Refounded Communist Party organized twenty buses to transport activists and party members from Milan to Vicenza for the February 17 demonstration.[77] Moreover, party representatives and government officials joined activists on the streets of Vicenza.

Strong Security Consensus

Anti-base activists reached a point of successful mobilization in Vicenza. Were they effective, however, in shaping base policy outcomes? How did the Prodi government respond to domestic opposition against bases after the embarrassing collapse of his center-left coalition? At the very least, the February 17 protests exacerbated the center-left crisis by exposing popular dissent and elite division in the mainstream media. Rather than wither in ignominious defeat,

---

the first movement in which [peace activists] and the broader public recognize that military bases are an important issue" (interview with Piero Maestri, Milan, Italy, January 17, 2008).

[75] Interview with Enzo Ciscato, Vicenza, Italy, January 16, 2008.

[76] Interview with Stephanie Westbrook, Rome, Italy, January 23, 2008.

[77] Interview with Piero Maestri, Milan, Italy, January 17, 2008.

however, the crisis emboldened Prodi's resolve to keep his coalition alive and push forward with his foreign policy agenda.

Prodi's support for the U.S. alliance and NATO, and more concretely U.S. base expansion, is unsurprising if one accepts the existence of a security consensus among Italian elites. With fragile coalitions and frequent government turnover, one would imagine it difficult for elites to find common consensus on any political agenda. Foreign and security policy, however, is one area where Italian political elites have found common ground. Thus one often finds broad support on key foreign policy issues, including those related to NATO and the U.S. alliance.

Italian Foreign Policy and U.S. Relations

The depth of the elite security consensus is embedded in the historical trajectory of U.S.-Italian relations and the institutionalization of NATO. Rome's favorable attitude toward NATO and the United States initially stemmed from strategic concerns and common threat perceptions after World War II. Italy recognized the necessity of a permanent peacetime alliance to secure its northeast border from Soviet aggression. U.S. forces also played an important role protecting Italian sovereignty from Yugoslavian threats to territorial claims. Meanwhile, vulnerability at sea required Italy to forge an alliance with a major maritime power such as the United States to protect its southern coasts.[78]

In the immediate postwar years, the Truman Doctrine and British troop reductions in the Mediterranean enhanced the United States' role in Italy's postwar security.[79] The Marshall Plan and NATO institutionalized America's protectorate role for Western Europe. As one Italian foreign policy expert noted, Italy's entrance into NATO "assured for the following twenty-five years Italian support to all the initiatives of American foreign policy."[80] The result was "an almost structural inclination" for Italy to rely on the United States for security.[81]

Throughout the Cold War, U.S.-Italian relations were marked by "extraordinary subservience to the United States on security policy."[82] Political elites, or more specifically Christian Democrat leaders, followed "the U.S. lead on crucial foreign policy issues consistently, almost slavishly."[83] Italy's virtual client-state status in the early postwar years naturally stemmed from its total political,

---

[78] Marco Rimanelli, *Italy between Europe and the Mediterranean: Diplomacy and Naval Strategy from Unification to NATO, 1800–2000* (New York: P. Lang, 1997), xxiii.

[79] Ibid., 13.

[80] University of Bologna, Master's in International Relations Students 2005–6, "Italian Foreign Policy," Working Paper for the course on *Analisi della Politica Estera* [Foreign Policy Analysis], July 27, 2006. http://www.foreignpolicy.it/cgi-bin/news/adon.cgi?act=doc&doc=2191&sid=19 (last accessed January 30, 2008).

[81] Leopoldo Nuti, "The Role of the U.S. in Italy's Foreign Policy," *International Spectator* 38, no. 1 (2003): 91–101 at 101.

[82] Douglas Forsyth, "The Peculiarities of Italo-American Relations in Historical Perspective," *Journal of Modern Italian Studies* 3, no. 1 (1998): 1–21 at 1.

[83] Ibid., 2.

military, and economic dependence on the United States. U.S. intervention in Italian politics, in particular massive financial support for the Christian Democrats and other anticommunist parties, contributed to this dependence.

The collapse of the Cold War brought forth a more autonomous foreign policy posture for Italy. Rome and Washington faced disagreements regarding peacekeeping and intervention in Somalia and Bosnia, respectively. Despite occasional squabbles, however, Italy continued to maintain strong relations with the United States. Changes in Italy's domestic political environment at the end of the Cold War were offset by a bipartisan consensus on Italian foreign policy based on images of Italian prestige, peace, and the preservation of a transatlantic balance.[84] Thus, Italy provided naval and air support to the U.S.-led coalition in the Persian Gulf War. Italy also permitted the use of its air bases and provided the third largest contribution of aircraft to NATO's mission in Kosovo in 1999. Maintaining close ties to the United States in the post–Cold War period as a matter of choice rather than necessity suggests the internalization and growing maturity of the Atlantic alliance in the minds of Italian elites.

Security Consensus in the Post-9/11 Era

How have U.S.-Italian relations faired in the post-9/11 era under center-left and center-right governments? A review of Italian foreign policy priorities under the second Berlusconi (2001–6) and Prodi (2006–8) governments is helpful in understanding the breadth of the security consensus and how the consensus influenced government responses and movement outcomes. Despite Berlusconi's unabashedly pro-U.S. position, Italian academics diverge in their assessment of his foreign policy. Some scholars cite Berlusconi's foreign policy agenda as anomalous. Berlusconi broke from traditional Italian foreign policy by heavily tilting his position toward the United States at the expense of the European Community.[85] Others, most notably Osvaldo Croci, have argued that Berlusconi brought continuity to Italian foreign policy by sustaining its two pillars, the Atlantic alliance and the European Union (EU), despite throwing his weight behind the "special relationship" with the United States.[86] Regardless of the "correct" interpretation, Berlusconi was undoubtedly pro-U.S. This was apparent in his selection of the staunchly pro-U.S. Antonio Martino as defense minister and Renato Ruggiero as foreign minister.[87] September 11 and the invasion of Afghanistan also reaffirmed Italy's commitment to NATO when

---

[84]   Jason W. Davidson, "Italy-U.S. Relations since the End of the Cold War: Prestige, Peace, and the Transatlantic Balance," *Bulletin of Italian Politics* 1, no. 2 (2009): 289–308 at 291.

[85]   Although strong Atlantic ties were always a part of "traditional" Italian foreign policy, there was still a balance between the "twin pillars" (interview with former Prodi advisor, January 19, 2008, Bologna, Italy; and interview with Robert Menotti, Rome, Italy, January 22, 2008).

[86]   Osvaldo Croci, "The Second Berlusconi Government and Italian Foreign Policy," *International Spectator* 37, no. 2 (2002): 89–105.

[87]   Ibid., 92.

Italy dispatched 2,700 troops to Afghanistan to participate in "Operation Enduring Freedom."

After Berlusconi's defeat in the April 2006 elections, Americans and Italians alike recognized that a shift to the center-left Prodi would result in a less U.S.-centric foreign policy. On the eve of Prodi's victory, Washington policymakers feared that Prodi's victory would "put American-Italian relations on ice."[88] Fears of a cooling of U.S.-Italy relations under a center-left regime were certainly legitimate. Only a year earlier, Spain's pro-U.S. Jose Maria Anzar fell to the left-leaning Jose Luis Rodriguez Zapatero. Zapatero immediately withdrew Spanish troops from Iraq, damaging U.S.-Spain relations.[89] Moreover, Prodi made clear that his foreign policy priority would center around a more autonomous Europe.[90] Prodi also made the oft-quoted statement during his campaign, "I'm going to tell the United States when it's right and when I think it's wrong."[91] Perhaps most disconcerting for the Bush administration was the inclusion of three Far-Left parties in Prodi's ruling government.

Fears of alliance deterioration never materialized. Prodi managed to sustain positive relations with the United States, even as he distanced himself from Berlusconi's U.S.-centric position.[92] As Charles Kupchan notes, Prodi could have easily exploited anti-Bush sentiment in Italy for political gain. With his coalition crumbling, parting with Washington would have been an expedient way to strengthen his slim parliamentary majority. However, Prodi demonstrated his support for NATO by maintaining Italian troops in Afghanistan. He also maintained respect for the U.S.-Italian alliance by approving U.S. base expansion despite significant domestic opposition from members of his own political coalition and civil society.

Italian political elites value their security partnership with the United States and in general accept NATO and U.S. relations as a major tenet of national security policy. Encompassing the bulk of the left to right political spectrum, the consensus is partially a function of political interests. Domestically, left coalitions may avoid insinuating remarks against the United States to placate more moderate or right-leaning coalition members. Internationally, close ties to the United States may provide longer-term security benefits or boost Italy's international prestige. Thus, although the Italian public overwhelmingly disapproved of the Bush administration's foreign policies, elites at the political center were

---

[88] Charles Kupchan, "America Hopes that the Left Helps Prodi," *Corrierre Della Sera*, February 25, 2007. http://www.cfr.org/publication/12703/america_hopes_that_the_left_helps_prodi.html (last accessed January 1, 2008).

[89] Ibid.

[90] Ettore Greco, "Italy's Grand Plans for EU Foreign Policy Rest on Clay Feet at Home," March 1, 2007. http://www.brookings.edu/articles/2007/spring_europe_greco.aspx (last accessed January 1, 2008); and Ettore Greco, *Italy's European Vocation: The Foreign Policy of the New Prodi Government*, U.S.-Europe Analysis Series (Washington, D.C.: Brookings Institution, 2006), 3.

[91] Council on Foreign Relations Interview Transcript: "Conversation with Romano Prodi," September 20, 2006.

[92] Kupchan, "America Hopes that the Left Helps Prodi."

willing to work with Washington. Political elites understand that maintaining ties to the United States is important to Italy's foreign policy interests. Characteristic of the widespread breadth in the security consensus, even when Italians and Americans disagree on specific policies, Italian elites prefer to keep the basic relationship functioning.[93]

Although interests may inform the security consensus, the tendency by both left and right governments to stay on the path of Italy's "traditional" foreign policy indicates that the consensus travels beyond political interests. Indicating greater depth, as argued earlier, the security consensus among Italian elites evolved as a process reinforced by shared norms and historical institutional legacies.[94] Paralleling the domestic politics of other Cold War allies, the Christian Democrats and their American allies placed a "permanent freeze" on communists during the formative years of the U.S.-Italian alliance.[95] The evolution of postwar domestic politics in Italy has kept left-leaning ideologues on the sideline of foreign policy debates. Like their Japanese counterparts, Italian political elites maintained a shared consensus, reified by processes of norm-sharing and repeated interactions with the United States over time. Through these endogenous processes, elites have internalized the significance of U.S.-Italian relations and their international commitment to NATO.[96] The consensus helps explain how Berlusconi received widespread support from the political right and left in the Chamber of Deputies in the initial decision to send Italian troops to Afghanistan.[97] It also explains why Prodi continued to support NATO and U.S.-related policies implemented by his predecessor and political rival. Prodi, along with Foreign Minister D'Alema, a former communist, and the pro-American Defense Minister Arturo Parisi, were willing to work with the United States, even if they intended to shift their foreign policy back to the traditional balance between NATO and the EU.

For the Italian government, base expansion in Vicenza should have been a nonissue. There was little cost or risk for the Italians in providing Dal Molin airfield to the United States. Part of Dal Molin was already designated as an Italian Ministry of Defense site, and Vicenza already hosted existing U.S. military facilities. Why, then, had bases become so politicized in Italy, and how did

---

[93] This logic applies to other European states. For instance, Germany opposed the U.S. war in Iraq. However, they still permitted the United States to fly out of bases in Germany as a means of keeping basic relations functioning.

[94] What I view as a "security consensus" among Italian elites is understood by Carla Monteleone as part of a "pluralistic security community." See Monteleone, "Evolution of the Euro-Atlantic Pluralistic Security Community."

[95] I thank Matthew Evangelista for pointing this out. For a further discussion on the topic of communist isolation, see Mario Del Pero, "Containing Containment: Rethinking Italy's Experience during the Cold War," *Working Paper* no. 2, April (New York: New York University, International Center for Advanced Studies, 2002).

[96] Monteleone, "Evolution of the Euro-Atlantic Pluralistic Security Community," 71.

[97] Only the three Far-Left parties (Green, PdCI, PRC) opposed the resolution. Croci, "Second Berlusconi Government and Italian Foreign Policy," 92–3.

Prodi respond to anti-base pressure? Although I answer these questions through the framework of the security consensus, in the Italian anti-base case, I argue that the security consensus interacted with other political variables. Coalition and party politics created a complicated but exciting dynamic between state and civil societal actors in the Vicenza movement episode.

Security Consensus, Coalition Politics, and Government Response

Understanding how the Prodi government responded to anti-base pressure requires stepping back to the Berlusconi era. Although Berlusconi agreed to base expansion in Vicenza, he requested that the project be put on hold until after the April 2006 elections.[98] Public opinion polls had already given Prodi's center-left coalition a slight edge over the center-right. Berlusconi feared that wider publicity for U.S. base expansion in front of an anti-Bush electorate would tip the scales further toward Prodi. The United States acquiesced to Berlusconi's suggestion and put the base project temporarily on hold.[99]

Unfortunately for him, Berlusconi lost the election. The base project now landed on Prodi's lap. Naturally, questions arose in Washington whether a coalition that included Far-Left parties would accept U.S. base plans brokered under the Berlusconi government. When Washington contacted Rome, the Italian government reassured the United States that it intended to continue with base plans at Dal Molin but needed time to build support. Prodi was not necessarily opposed to U.S. bases. However, opposition from Far-Left parties within his fragile coalition made it difficult to discuss U.S. base expansion immediately following the election.

Buck Passing

Shortly after Prodi officially came to power in May 2006, the central government passed the Vicenza issue down to the local government. The base expansion project required consultation with local authorities on several technical issues such as building codes, zoning requirements, and safety and environmental regulations. Whether the timing was coincidental or deliberate, some U.S. and Italian officials suggested that the Italian government had "passed the buck" onto local officials to avoid any political fallout at the national level. The Italian government had turned the politically charged issue of U.S. military bases at the national level into a technical matter discussed at the local level. By passing the buck, Prodi found the political space and additional time needed to persuade his Far-Left coalition partners to vote in favor of U.S. and NATO-related policies.

---

[98] Interview with Camp Ederle base official, Vicenza, Italy, January 16, 2008; and interview with Robert Menotti, Rome, Italy, January 22, 2008.

[99] Interview with Robert Menotti, Rome, Italy, January 22, 2008; and interview with U.S. Consulate official, Milan, Italy, January 18, 2008.

It was now the Vicenza city government that bore the brunt of anti-base pressure. As argued earlier, citizens first directed their actions against the city council, demanding the base issue be resolved through a public referendum. Even though city officials rejected activist demands, voting in favor of base expansion, the local government had no legal authority over bilateral basing agreements. As an issue of national defense and foreign policy, base agreements needed bilateral approval between national governments. The local government therefore passed the base issue back to Rome. The ball was once again in Prodi's court, but now in an arena quickly filling with anti-base demonstrators not only from Vicenza but across Italy.

Whether intentionally or not, passing the base issue back and forth between the local and national governments created ambiguity over Prodi's support for base expansion, even if Prodi supported U.S. bases in principle. The pro-base Vicenza Popular Bank president, Gianni Zonin, stated, "I am disappointed (with politicians). I do not like this buck-passing of responsibility between the municipal authority and the government. This confusion must stop: It must be either 'yes' or 'no,' with all due explanations."[100] Some Vicenza residents perceived indecisiveness on Prodi's part. For activists, a reversal, or at least a review of the Dal Molin base project, remained possible. With growing anti-base opposition in late 2006, U.S. officials, too, had grown increasingly nervous with noisy demonstrations and increasing delays on the base expansion project. U.S. Ambassador Ronald Spogli arrived in Vicenza on January 9, 2007, putting direct pressure on Vicenza business and government leaders and indirect pressure on Prodi to accept the base.[101]

Prodi finally provided clarity on January 16, 2007, declaring at a press conference in Bucharest, "I am about to tell the U.S. Ambassador that the Italian government won't oppose the decision by the previous government and the town council of Vicenza to allow the expansion of the military base. ... Our attitude in regards to the U.S. is that of friend and ally."[102] Prodi's acceptance of U.S. bases and NATO's Afghanistan mission signaled both to domestic constituents and international allies that he remained committed to the Atlantic alliance. However, Vicenza activists and Far-Left politicians immediately reacted, suggesting that buck passing the base issue to circumvent domestic political tension had backfired. Demonstrations took place in Vicenza. Activists proceeded with preparations for a major national protest on February 17, 2007. Prodi now faced joint opposition from his Far-Left coalition partners and anti-base activists. Not only had the campaign grown in size; it had also grown more militant.

---

[100] Marisa Fumagalli, "Vicenza Business Leader Backs Camp Ederle Expansion Plan," *Corriere della Sera*, January 15, 2007.

[101] Ibid. This was confirmed by a Camp Ederle base official in an interview conducted on January 16, 2008. To put it bluntly, Spogli threatened to shut down Camp Ederle and relocate the 173rd Airborne to Germany if the United States could not use the Dal Molin airfield.

[102] Stephen Brown, "Italy to Give Green Light to U.S. Air Base Expansion," *Reuters*, January 16, 2007. http://www.reuters.com/article/worldNews/idUSL16239372200701116 (last accessed January 31, 2008).

Prodi's Rebound

Anti-base movements, and more specifically two Far-Left senators, packed a significant punch by rejecting Prodi's foreign policy agenda. The blow knocked Prodi out politically. Unfortunately, Prodi's resignation was self-defeating for the radical-left parties in his coalition. Prodi's knockout had awakened his centrist senses. After conferring with President Giorgio Napolitano, Prodi required that all coalition partners sign a twelve-point program, including "support for our foreign and defense commitments within the context of the UN and our membership of NATO and the EU."[103]

Here we see how coalition politics and the security consensus mutually reinforced one another, creating significant political obstacles for anti-base activists. The three Far-Left parties were genuinely opposed to U.S. bases and to Italian troops in Afghanistan. However, to prevent Berlusconi from returning to power, and to maintain their position within the ruling coalition, the Far-Left parties acquiesced to U.S. base expansion and Italy's Afghanistan mission. A portion of the Far Left's support base, including antiwar and anti-base activists, openly criticized these parties for bending their foreign policy principles.[104] Antiwar activist Piero Maestri argued, "The Italian Communist Party is no longer against the [status quo], but are now ... promoting a foreign and military policy for the [mainstream] system."[105] Fringe parties outside this system challenge the status quo. But once inside the system, they try to maintain their power, working within the mainstream's political boundaries.

Ironically, the slim parliamentary majority that gave Prodi the leverage to "discipline" Far-Left parties so they could remain in power also contributed to his brief political fall. Taking advantage of Prodi's slim majority, center-right politicians abstained from voting in favor of Prodi's foreign policy agenda in an attempt to destabilize the ruling government. Under "normal" circumstances, the majority of center-right politicians would have backed U.S. base expansion and Italy's NATO mission, giving Prodi's foreign policy at least two-thirds majority support. As one U.S. official retorted, "Vicenza should have never been an issue in the first place."[106] Thus some of the blame for turning U.S. bases into a messy affair can be pinned on the center-right. Needless to say, the center-right inadvertently provided anti-base activists a platform to turn a local NIMBY protest into a major national issue.

---

[103] Richard Owen, "Prodi Lays Down Terms for a New Coalition," *The Times (London)*, February 17, 2008.

[104] This has led to yet another split from the various existing communist parties, leading to the formation of Sinistra Critica (the Critical Left Party).

[105] Interview with Piero Maestri, Milan, Italy, January 17, 2008.

[106] Interview with U.S. Consulate official, Milan, Italy, January 18, 2008. The official contends, "It was the center right, our normal allies (within the Italian government), that have allowed this to drag on to embarrass the center-left government. Thus, the (political) right was complacent in supporting the base expansion, maintaining tension on the (base) issue."

Continued Anti-Base Efforts

Although Prodi's return to power on March 1 signaled the beginning of a decline for anti-base activists, strong anti-base opposition persisted. Activists resorted to a wide range of protest activities: tree-planting, roadblocks, festivals, and boycotts targeting both the local and national governments. On June 3, 2007, a group of activists interrupted Prodi during a public forum. Sitting in the audience, activists unexpectedly stood up, hollering and waving No Dal Molin banners. Activist leader Cinzia Bottene then stepped onstage to directly confront Prodi. Putting him on the spot, she exclaimed:

It's a disgrace that the city of Vicenza is not defended by the Italian government. We have even tried to put the matter to a public referendum so that the voices of the people can be heard but they have not even allowed us to do that. I am disappointed because I helped vote them in. We voted them in on the basis of a platform of military spending [reduction] and active democracy. Where are those promises now?[107]

As if in direct response to Bottene, in mid-2007, Prodi appointed EU Parliamentarian Paolo Costa as the government's special envoy for base expansion in Vicenza. Costa acted as an intermediary between all interested parties: Vicenza citizens, the city and national governments, and the U.S military. All problems were now directly relayed to Costa. Costa did help negotiate solutions to several local zoning, traffic, and environmental concerns. He managed to convince the United States to change initial project plans by constructing the new base on the west rather than east side of Dal Molin airfield. Beyond this, however, there was no more substantive dialogue between the No Dal Molin movement and Costa (i.e., the national government). As one minister of defense advisor argued, all citizens who could be persuaded by rational means at this point had already been persuaded. Stopping the project, as activists demanded, was not an option. In a letter written to Defense Minister Parisi, Costa himself conveyed the need to "eliminate elements of local opposition at its roots" by addressing legitimate traffic and environmental concerns and separating these demands from other claims driven by anti-American or antimilitarist sentiments.[108]

Fractures

After the February 17 protest, different factions within the No Dal Molin campaign became more pronounced. Factions had existed even prior to this date, but these cleavages became more acute over time as the campaign broadened to incorporate a wider audience. Divisions ensued over strategy and the targeting of protests. The Presidio, the largest subset of the No Dal Molin campaign, became increasingly vocal against the center-left Prodi government. Presidio activists criticized even Far-Left politicians, who opposed bases

---

[107] Osti, *Vicenza's Struggle against Global Militarization.*

[108] Letter by Special Commissioner Paolo Costa to then defense minister Arturo Parisi, September 17, 2007.

rhetorically but avoided taking action in government. The Presidio maintained its grassroots orientation, claiming no allegiance to political groups, parties, or organizations. According to Presidio members, this group accounted for roughly sixty to seventy percent of activists in the No Dal Molin struggle.[109]

By contrast, a second distinct group, the Coordinamento Comitati (CC), continued to maintain ties with political parties and trade unions, working within the boundaries of formal politics. The CC distanced itself from the Presidio, wanting to avoid confrontation with the center-left government. Accounting for approximately twenty to thirty percent of the movement, the CC continued to place hope in a solution to the Vicenza base issue through institutional and legal means. The smallest faction, Comitato Vicenza Est,[110] also split from the Presidio due to personality issues at the leadership level, specifically with those members in the Presidio who had *disobbedienti* roots.[111]

In mid-2007, the Presidio increased efforts to network with international groups, beginning with other anti-base movements in Europe. The Presidio also added an international team to coordinate with other anti-base groups around the world.[112] Officials in the United States observe that the movement has become less focused on local issues and the specific Vicenza base and instead has evolved into a more general antiwar movement. As one consulate official notes, increased criticism against the national government, and the transnational shift of the campaign, indicate movement weakness as activists now recognize the Dal Molin project as a lost cause. What U.S. officials observe about the evolution of the movement corresponds with activists' descriptions of the shift toward Europe-wide mobilization. It is also true that anti-base activists, particularly those associated with the Presidio, hold little hope that the Italian government will stand up against the United States. Vicenza activists have not given up, however. Instead, they have turned their attention to the United States. By disrupting and delaying the base project, activists hope to "be enough of a pain to the U.S." that the United States eventually gives up on Vicenza as the site for a new base.[113]

The destruction of the Presidio and the election of an anti-base mayor of Vicenza in May 2008 pushed the anti-base movement back into the realm of

---

[109] Interview with Stefan Osti, Vicenza, Italy, January 16, 2008.

[110] Vicenza Est is shorthand for *Comitato di cittadini e lavoratori di Vicenza che chiedono la conversione della Caserna Ederle – base militare USA* [Vicenza citizens and workers committee on the conversion of Camp Ederle]. See their Web site at http://www.comitatovicenzaest.splinder. com/ (last accessed February 1, 2008).

[111] The *disobbedienti* group arose from the militant Tute Bianche social movement, best known for their resistance during the G-8 anti-globalization movement. *Disobbedienti* members engage in direct action and civil disobedience against government authority. Realizing the importance of movement unity, representatives from each of the factions have been holding small group meetings to exchange information and maintain open lines of communication.

[112] Other Presidio committees include coordinating teams for strategy, logistics, communications and media, and women's issues.

[113] Interview with Stephanie Westbrook, Rome, Italy, January 23, 2008.

formal politics. This time the local courts ruled to suspend the transfer of Dal Molin to the U.S. military, only to be overruled by the Council of State, Italy's highest administrative court. The central government has consistently blocked any moves to derail base construction.[114]

Italy's political institutional arrangements ultimately constrained the original foreign and security policy preferences of radical-left actors. In particular, party coalition dynamics had the effect of reinforcing the dominant foreign policy consensus. Anti-base movements, reaching limits bounded by ideational and institutional constraints, were never quite able to penetrate the state. Despite successful mobilization, anti-base activists found it increasingly difficult to win major concessions on U.S. base policies. The February crisis, while exposing several flaws in Italy's political institutional design, also affirmed that the majority of Italian political elites still valued strong ties to the United States. The consensus does not imply that all Italian elites are pro-U.S., or even in favor of a strong Atlantic alliance. It only suggests that certain political and ideological constraints prevent political elites from veering too far off the path of the consensus. Thus, guided by certain foreign policy principles, the central government thwarted activist attempts to block base expansion in Vicenza at each stage of resistance.

CONCLUSION: ECUADOR AND ITALY IN COMPARATIVE PERSPECTIVE

Anti-base movement episodes in Ecuador and Italy increase the robustness of the security consensus framework by applying it to different geographic regions. Admittedly, some skepticism is warranted over the choice of Manta and Vicenza bases, which are not as strategically important as Subic Bay Naval Station or Futenma Air Station. The Ecuador anti-base episode in particular may be criticized as an easy test for anti-base movements. Unlike the case with bases in Japan or the Philippines, the United States made little effort to retain the base, lowering the barriers to success for activists. Despite these shortcomings, however, both cases do suggest that the degree of security consensus affects how governments respond to anti-base pressure, and how they align their position between domestic and international forces. Moreover, the Ecuador and Italy cases demonstrate that the security consensus functions as a political opportunity or barrier for anti-base movements.

In Ecuador, although some political elites pursued pro-U.S. foreign policies, a security consensus favoring strong security ties to the United States was not deeply entrenched among elite ranks. Over the course of its campaign, the Ecuador No Bases Coalition and other anti-base groups transformed a banal base agreement into a major national issue. Although officials in the Mahuad and Gutierrez governments blocked activists' attempts to nullify the base

---

[114] See Stephanie Westbrook, "U.S. Military Interests Reign Supreme in Italy." http://www. peaceandjustice.it/vicenza-cds.php (last accessed October 10, 2008).

agreement, activists did find support from important government figures. Unlike Italy or Japan, where elite support for anti-base movements was limited to "radical" politicians, in Ecuador, respected leaders such as Interior Minister Gustavo Larrea, Foreign Affairs Minister Francisco Carrión during the Palacio government, Congressman Julio Gonzáles of the Pachakutik Party, and Manabí Province governor Vicente Veliz publicly took an anti-base stance even before Correa's ascent to power. Absent any strong security consensus, activists were able to work with sympathetic elites and shift the security discourse on bases to prevent the renewal of the Manta base agreement. Ultimately, President Correa rejected the Manta agreement.

On the other hand, a strong security consensus acted as a barrier against Italian anti-base movements. Although the No Dal Molin campaign achieved success in mobilizing activists and drawing national media attention to their cause, to date the movement has been less successful in its efforts to block the expansion of the U.S. base in Vicenza. In common with other movement episodes where governments exhibited a strong security consensus, the Prodi government resorted to foot-dragging tactics to diffuse domestic pressure. Although initially ambiguous on the Vicenza issue, Prodi eventually demonstrated his political resolve to maintain Italy's international commitments. Even the debates that ensued after Prodi's brief fall reaffirmed the existence of an elite "consensus" and the Italian government's continued support for U.S.-Italian relations. Although the security consensus helped maintain generally positive relations between the United States and Italy, it posed a challenge to anti-base movements and, more generally, to leftist groups interested in pursuing policies contrary to the U.S.-Italian security alliance.

Finally, Ecuador and Italy provide an interesting comparison on the question of regime orientation and realism as alternative explanations to the security consensus framework. One might argue that the leftist turn in Ecuador and the rise of anti-U.S. rhetoric enabled activists to achieve success on base policy outcomes. However, the Vicenza anti-base episode suggests that, even under a center-left government, when a strong security consensus is pervasive among key political elites, elites will find ways to stave off domestic pressure to retain positive alliance ties to the United States. In the Italian case, a relatively strong security consensus made it difficult for anti-base activists to translate their movement demands into policy outcomes. Moreover, the persistence of the security consensus among Italian elites, despite relatively low levels of material threat for Italy in the post–Cold War period, suggests that power-based arguments alone do not explain the persistence of U.S. bases in northern Italy. Nor do realist insights fully explain Rome's willingness to provide the United States with additional bases despite intense domestic opposition. Instead, ideas, in the form of a security consensus, led Italian political leaders to reaffirm the Atlantic alliance and promote U.S. bases above the protests of local residents and activists.

5

South Korean Anti-Base Movements and the Resilience of the Security Consensus

It's a crucial and legitimate government project that has much at stake, namely U.S.-Korea relations.

– ROK Defense Minister Yoon Kwang-ung[1]

On May 4, 2005, 12,000 riot police entered Daechuri[2] village, a small village in Pyeongtaek, South Korea, 50 miles south of Seoul in Kyongi Province. Activists and local residents, refusing to leave their farmland, were making a desperate stand to block the expansion and relocation of United States Forces, Korea (USFK) headquarters to Camp Humphreys. While South Korean soldiers erected barbed wire around the base expansion land outside Camp Humphreys, 2,000 activists battled riot police who stormed Daechuri Elementary School, the make-shift headquarters of the Pan–South Korean Solution Committee Against Base Expansion in Pyeongtaek (KCPT).[3] One hundred and twenty protestors, police, and soldiers were injured, and 524 protestors, mostly students and activists, were taken into custody.[4] Immediately following the violence, the Ministry of National Defense (MND) went on a public relations offensive, highlighting the violent tactics of protestors attacking an unarmed engineering brigade. The government's public relations campaign severely damaged the credibility of South Korean anti-base activists in their struggle to block the expansion of Camp Humphreys. The KCPT never fully recovered from the May 4 clash, and eventually faded away by the end of 2007.

---

[1] ROK defense minister's remarks regarding USFK base relocation to Pyeongtaek in the wake of activist resistance. See Jihyun Kim, "Seoul Forges Ahead in Pyeongtaek," *Korea Herald*, May 5, 2006.

[2] Although the focus of anti-base activism took place in Daechuri village, residents in adjacent Doduri village also took part in the struggle. For simplicity, I will refer to the villages of local resistance in this chapter as Daechuri. Both villages are within Pyeongtaek city's jurisdiction.

[3] Various English translations of the national anti-base group in Pyeongtaek have appeared, but their official Web site refers to the coalition by this name and acronym. I will refer to the national-level coalition group as the KCPT.

[4] *Yonhap News Agency*, "Daechu boongyo toiguh jibhang bandae 524 myeong yeonhaeng" [Daechuri school razed, 524 protestors taken into custody], May 4, 2006. http://news.chosun. com/site/data/html_dir/2006/05/04/2006050470455.html (last accessed June 22, 2007).

This chapter examines South Korean anti-base movements, and specifically the Pyeongtaek episode, under a strong degree of security consensus. Understanding the Pyeongtaek anti-base campaign in South Korea highlights the importance of combining a structural account of base politics through an international relations vantage point with a more nuanced account of agency provided by social movement analysis. South Korean anti-base movements remind us that the security consensus framework is not deterministic. Bilateral alliance structures and the elite political consensus shape the pattern of interaction between movements and government forces. However, movement actors, strategies, and internal coalition dynamics also play an important part in determining basing policy outcomes.

For the security consensus framework to hold in the South Korean case, two questions must be addressed. First, is there sufficient evidence supporting my claim that an elite security consensus favoring the U.S. alliance existed at relatively high levels in the mid-2000s? Second, did the movement's inability to affect base policy outcomes result from the constraining effect of the security consensus? Here, my evidence must demonstrate a credible link between the security consensus, anti-base movements, and political outcomes.

Arguing that an elite consensus exists within South Korea may initially appear counterintuitive. At the mass public level, support for the U.S.-ROK alliance has gradually waned among some South Koreans now demanding greater equality in the alliance partnership. The shift in public opinion has undoubtedly led to a gradual ebbing of a strong consensus even among South Korean political elites. In particular, shifting South Korean attitudes toward the alliance have provided anti-base activists a more permissive environment in which to make demands on base-related issues than in the past.

Despite signs of gradual ebbing, however, this chapter presents evidence demonstrating the resilience of the security consensus surrounding the U.S.-ROK alliance. The security consensus regarding U.S.-ROK relations, a legacy forged during the Cold War anticommunist period, continues to persist among many key South Korean political elites. Unlike the internal orientation of security in the Philippines, South Korea relies on its security partnership with the United States to protect itself from external threats, most notably North Korea. Although experiencing friction in the early half of the 2000s, South Korean political elites on the whole continue to value the alliance.

Consequently, from 2004 to 2006, the resilience of the security consensus presented obstacles for anti-base movements. Ties to influential elites were rare. Efforts to educate and shift public attitudes toward bases were stymied by the more powerful security discourse offered by the South Korean state. In its desire to maintain stable U.S.-ROK alliance relations, the South Korean government responded to anti-base pressure by using strategies of co-optation and coercion, sapping the strength of anti-base movements over time. Activists confronting resistance from government forces, and faced with growing internal problems endemic to South Korean coalition movements more generally, were therefore unable to win any concessions on the base relocation project.

This chapter begins with an overview of U.S. military bases and USFK transformation in South Korea. The next section discusses at length the state of South Korean national security and the U.S.-ROK alliance between 2000 and 2006. Despite alliance transformation, evidence based on existing laws and institutions, government documents, and elite statements suggests a baseline consensus still existed among elites regarding South Korean national security and the U.S.-ROK alliance. This argument is corroborated by the South Korean security literature and interviews with Korean policymakers and scholars. The third section describes anti-base movement mobilization and strategies in Pyeongtaek. The final section uses process-tracing methods to analyze state–society interaction as events unfolded in 2005 and 2006. In this section, I highlight anti-base movement tactics and the South Korean government's counterstrategies used to undermine and destroy anti-base opposition.

USFK BASE RELOCATION AND CONSOLIDATION

Until 2002, the configuration of U.S. bases in South Korea had remained virtually unchanged since the end of the Korean War. However, in light of several outstanding land disputes pertaining to U.S. bases, and the dilapidated state of existing USFK facilities, Washington and Seoul initiated the U.S.–South Korea Land Partnership Plan (LPP) in 2001. The LPP was designed as a cooperative effort between the United States and South Korea to "consolidate U.S. installations, improve combat readiness, enhance public safety, and strengthen the U.S.–South Korean alliance by addressing some of the causes of periodic tension" associated with the U.S. military presence in South Korea.[5] Signed in March 2002, the LPP recommended closing fifteen out of forty-one major installations, thereby consolidating forces onto the twenty-six remaining bases without any reduction in troop numbers.[6]

The LPP quickly grew outdated in light of the changing U.S. global force posture. The United States began to consider different options regarding force deployment in South Korea in line with a general reassessment of its overseas military presence conducted under the 2001 Quadrennial Defense Review and the DOD's Overseas Basing and Requirements Study. The Pentagon's reassessment of the U.S. overseas presence would undoubtedly "diminish the need for and alter the locations of many construction projects" associated with the LPP.[7]

In April 2003, high-ranking U.S. officials and South Korean officials discussed a much more comprehensive base-realignment project to supersede the

[5] United States General Accounting Office, *Defense Infrastructure: Basing Uncertainties Necessitate Reevaluation of U.S. Construction Plans in South Korea* (Washington, D.C.: GAO, 2003), 1.
[6] US CINPAC Virtual Information Center, "Special Press Summary: Land Partnership Plan and Yongsan Relocation," January 31, 2002.
[7] United States General Accounting Office, *Defense Infrastructure*, 3.

LPP.[8] The United States suggested moving its troops away from the demilitarized zone. More importantly, the meeting concluded with a decision to relocate Yongsan Garrison, USFK headquarters in downtown Seoul, to a location approximately 50 miles south of the capital.[9] By July 2004, Seoul and Washington had proposed a new vision for the U.S.-ROK alliance, including a greater role for the South Korean military in securing its own defense. After ten rounds of negotiations under the Future of the Alliance Policy Initiative (FOTA), both sides agreed to withdraw 12,500 U.S. troops by December 2008 from South Korea, relocate Yongsan Garrison out of Seoul, and consolidate the 2nd Infantry Division to Camp Humphreys in Pyeongtaek.[10]

A RESILIENT SECURITY CONSENSUS

The political context of USFK transformation in the mid-2000s, and more specifically base relocation to Pyeongtaek, was embedded in a wider debate concerning the future of the U.S.-ROK alliance. U.S. and South Korean security experts unanimously agreed that the alliance had undergone significant transformation since 2002.[11] The consolidation and realignment of USFK on the Korean Peninsula, the gradual withdrawal of 12,500 troops since 2003, and the planned transfer of wartime operational control, initially by 2012,[12] all attested to the changing nature of the alliance – whether for better or worse. Moreover, many U.S.-ROK alliance experts noted changing South Korean attitudes toward

---

[8] Congressional Budget Office, *Options for Changing the Army's Overseas Basing* (Washington, D.C.: CBO, 2004), 30.

[9] United States General Accounting Office, *Defense Infrastructure*, 13. The decision to relocate Yongsan Garrison dates back to a 1991 memorandum of understanding signed between Seoul and Washington. Unfortunately, a dispute over relocation costs and difficulty in finding an appropriate replacement brought the relocation process to a halt.

[10] U.S. Department of State, "U.S. Troop Relocation Shows Strength of U.S.-Korea Alliance," transcript of U.S. and ROK representatives discussing the Alliance Policy Initiative, July 28, 2004. http://usinfo.org/wf-archive/2004/040728/epf307.htm (last accessed May 10, 2007). The troop withdrawal was decided after the ninth FOTA round. See United States General Accounting Office, *Defense Infrastructure*, 13.

[11] The literature here is far too numerous to cite. However, a few representative works include Kunyoung Park, *A New U.S.-ROK Alliance: A Nine Point Policy Recommendation for a Reflective and Mature Relationship* (Washington, D.C.: Brookings Institution, Center for Northeast Asian Policy Studies, 2005); David I. Steinberg, *Korean Attitudes Toward the United States: Changing Dynamics* (Armonk, N.Y.: M.E. Sharpe, 2004); Mikyoung Kim, "The U.S. Military Transformation and Its Implications for the ROK-U.S. Alliance," *IFANS Review* 13, no. 1 (2005): 15–39; David Straub, "U.S. and ROK Strategic Doctrines and the U.S.-ROK Alliance," *Joint U.S.-Korea Academic Studies* 17 (2007): 165–86; Chaibong Hahm, "South Korea's Progressives and the U.S.-ROK Alliance," *Joint U.S.-Korea Academic Studies* 17 (2007): 187–202; and Sook-jong Lee, *The Transformation of South Korean Politics: Implications for U.S.-Korea Relations*. (Washington, D.C.: Brookings Institution, Center for Northeast Asian Policy Studies, 2005).

[12] Following the sinking of a South Korean naval ship by an alleged North Korean torpedo in March 2010, the U.S. and South Korean governments decided to push back the transfer of wartime operational command to December 2015.

the United States. Most public opinion surveys indicated a negative change in attitudes, particularly among the younger generation.[13] The generational gap and shifting trends in South Korean domestic politics consequently polarized South Korean sentiments toward the United States between progressive and conservative camps.[14] Amid polarizing trends, how could one possibly justify the position that a security consensus existed among South Korean political elites during a period of alliance turmoil?

Here, the dimensions of breadth and depth are useful in determining the strength of the security consensus. The "strong" coding of the security consensus is defined by a high degree of depth and a broad level of breadth. In other words, most South Korean foreign policy elites agree on the broad necessity and value of the U.S.-ROK alliance, despite some disagreement on the implementation of specific alliance policies. Conservative foreign policy ideas and institutions have enabled the pro-U.S. security consensus to persist among elites despite shifting attitudes toward the United States among the mass public.

Radicals, Progressives, and Conservatives

A range of attitudes and perceptions exist regarding USFK and the U.S.-ROK alliance among South Korean bureaucrats, politicians, and academics. However, it is impossible to discuss attitudes regarding U.S.-ROK security relations without including North Korea. In fact, early in his administration, former president Roh Moo-hyun attempted to link North–South policy with U.S.–South Korean relations.[15] Attitudes toward U.S. forces and the trilateral relationship between North Korea, South Korea, and the United States from 2000 to 2006 can be roughly divided into three camps, as seen in Figure 5.1.

Radicals believe that USFK should withdraw from the Korean Peninsula given North Korea's weakened state. To radicals, U.S. forces are seen as a liability rather than an asset by hindering inter-Korea reconciliation. This attitude is best represented by the Democratic Labor Party and a minority faction in the former ruling Uri Party (now the Democratic Party). Differing from radicals, progressives believe that U.S. forces are still necessary in the mid- to long term. However, they believe that changes regarding U.S.-ROK relations should occasionally be initiated by South Korea to offset "unequal" relations. Progressives

---

[13] Eric V. Larson, Norman D. Levin, Seonhae Baik, and Bogdan Savych, *Ambivalent Allies? A Study of South Korean Attitudes Toward the U.S.* (Santa Monica, Calif.: RAND, 2004); and Derek Mitchell, ed., *Strategy and Sentiment: South Korean Views of the United States and the U.S.-ROK Alliance* (Washington, D.C.: CSIS, 2004).

[14] Gi-Wook Shin and Kristine Burke, "North Korea and Contending South Korean Identities: Analysis of the South Korean Media; Policy Implications for the United States," *KEI: Academic Paper Series* 2, no. 4 (2007): 1–12; and Chaibong Hahm, "The Two South Koreas: A House Divided," *Washington Quarterly* 28 (2005): 57–72.

[15] The dispatch of 5,000 ROK troops to Iraq was largely seen as a move to persuade the United States to avoid a hard-line stance toward North Korea and support the South in its sunshine policy with the North.

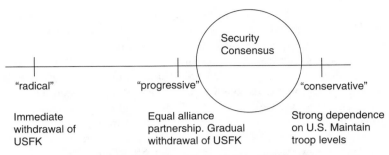

FIGURE 5.1. Security Consensus among Political Elites, 2000–2006.

contend that South Korea's interests are best served by balancing its foreign policy between U.S. alliance interests and North Korean rapprochement. Relations with one should not be sacrificed at the expense of the other. The majority of mainstream progressives subscribe to this view. Moderate conservatives and progressives find common ground in maintaining U.S. forces for a limited period of time. However, conservatives argue that South Korea should react to U.S. policy rather than attempt to initiate changes in the alliance.[16] For conservatives, foreign policy priority is given to the United States over North Korea. The Lee Myung-bak administration and the current ruling Grand National Party favor the conservative view.

The late president Roh's Uri Party achieved some success in moving the alliance toward a more equal partnership. Yet there are limits to what progressive voices can actually achieve on the foreign policy front. In other words, a pro-U.S. security consensus is fairly well embedded in domestic institutions and ideology, suggesting significant depth, even as the breadth of the consensus among elites narrows. South Korea's foreign policy apparatus is still heavily influenced by a conservative line of thinking, and an elite consensus continues to operate on issues pertaining to U.S.–South Korean security relations. Boundaries exist as to how far progressive political leaders can push policies that run counter to Washington.[17] These boundaries are partially a function of the power asymmetries in the alliance relationship, but more immediate is the unacceptability of breaking away from existing norms that guide South Korean national security strategy. Integral to this strategy is the U.S.-ROK alliance. Therefore, despite the diversity in elite attitudes and perceptions regarding national security, progressive and radical political elites find it difficult to implement their preferred foreign policies.

Several studies confirm a significant gap between older and younger generations of Koreans in their attitudes toward the alliance. Some in the progressive and radical camps point to a change in U.S.–South Korean relations as

[16] Interview with Park Kun-young, Catholic University, Seoul, South Korea, May 30, 2006.
[17] Interview with former South Korean National Security Council official, Seoul, South Korea, May 30, 2006.

inevitable. Conservatives in their sixties or older, who experienced the Korean War and were indoctrinated with anticommunist ideology, are being replaced by the younger 386 generation in positions of power.[18] However, because of political and ideological structures embedded in South Korean security politics, high-ranking officials in the foreign policy establishment and radical grassroots activists alike believe that the process of change is much more contested. Despite shifting attitudes and U.S.-ROK alliance transformation toward an equal part-nership, the dissolution of the security consensus is not automatically a given. Yoon Young-kwon, who served as foreign minister during the first half of the Roh administration, states, "As some of the younger National Assembly mem-bers enter [government], they begin to realize through experience that their views are not reflective of the majority of society. The original positions they had when they first entered office often change."[19] As an example, Yoon cites how several government officials and politicians wanted to elevate China as South Korea's new powerful ally while distancing themselves from the United States. However, this group shied away from their original stance after South Korea's public dispute with China over the sovereignty of the ancient kingdom of Goguryeo. Activists' cynicism toward the government also suggests the resil-ience of the security consensus. Activists impatient with the slow pace of change from the "progressive" government expressed their frustration with the previous Kim Dae-jung and Roh administrations. With many 386ers holding positions in the presidential Blue House and the National Assembly under the Roh admin-istration, activists initially expected these officials to promote change, breaking free from what they viewed as psychological dependence on the United States. Once in power, however, these politicians who previously held radical views moderated their positions.[20]

Structural factors place a limit on the speed and extent to which the younger generation can bring about change or inject new progressive ideas into Korean politics. As one South Korean security expert noted, "There are certain realities which cannot be ignored. Even leftist-oriented National Assembly members cannot dare to say that we don't need the alliance with the U.S. because the objective threat of North Korea still exists. As long as these structural factors do not change, there will be limits as to how far progressive politicians can bring change to the alliance."[21] Interestingly, this type of logic applied even to former president Roh's seemingly contradictory foreign policy behavior. Many expected Roh to distance himself from the United States after his infamous campaign pledge not to "kowtow" to the Americans, and to assert Korea's sovereignty in

---

[18] 386 refers to those Koreans who, in the late 1990s and early 2000s, were in their thirties, went to college in the 1980s, and were born in the 1960s. This generation experienced the student democratization movement during the 1980s.

[19] Interview with former foreign affairs and trade minister Yoon Young-kwon, Seoul, South Korea, May 26, 2006.

[20] Interview with several grassroots activists from the KCPT, Pyeongtaek, South Korea, October 19, 2005.

[21] Interview with Park Kun-young, Seoul, South Korea, May 30, 2006.

the alliance relationship. Once in power, however, with the exception of North Korean policy, Roh more or less acquiesced to most of Washington's security and foreign policy demands. These demands ranged from strategic flexibility, to USFK transformation, to the deployment of ROK troops to Iraq.

Political and Ideological Structures

Despite the polarization of South Korean attitudes toward the United States, I argued earlier that political and ideological structures enable the security consensus to persist. These structures prevent elites from diverging too far from the security consensus. However, I do not deny that the security consensus has weakened over time. There was never any doubt about the consensus at the height of North–South tensions during the Cold War. Nor was there any doubt which country South Korea depended on for its national survival. In fact, the national security laws made it illegal to publicly criticize the U.S. military and the U.S.-ROK alliance. However, the fall of communism internationally and the near economic collapse of North Korea in the 1990s loosened the staunch security consensus that had persisted throughout the Cold War. The North–South summit meeting between Kim Dae-jung and Kim Jong-il in June 2000 helped accelerate this decline as hopes of Korean reunification were rekindled in South Korea. GNP Representative Won Hee-ryong reflected on this change, stating, "The things that they say now in public would have been dangerous to say before the Kim Dae-jung Administration. You would have been branded a communist. But the fact that you can say these things now openly in the National Assembly suggests that there has been significant change."[22]

Both progressives and conservatives agree to the principles of the U.S.-ROK alliance. Where they disagree (and at times disagree with the United States), however, is in the policy means used to achieve security. In the past, progressives and conservatives reacted sharply to different policy measures pertaining to the U.S.-ROK alliance. These differences included issues such as the transfer of wartime operational control from the U.S.-ROK joint command to the South Korean military. Whereas progressives welcomed this transfer of authority, conservatives believed the South Korean military would not be prepared to take over operational control by 2012. Conservatives and progressives were also divided on the issue of strategic flexibility, which granted USFK permission to engage in missions outside the Korean Peninsula. In short, progressives wanted a more equal alliance partnership, whereas conservatives were reluctant to see any shifts in the alliance status quo.

Political and ideological structures still remain, however, because the target and source of the security consensus – the external threat of North Korea and the U.S.-ROK alliance, respectively – continue to persist in the minds of powerful elites. Regardless of how benign some South Korean progressives perceive the

---

[22] Interview with National Assembly Foreign Affairs Committee member Won Hee-ryong, Seoul, South Korea, June 19, 2006.

North, foreign policy elites still believe North Korea poses a threat given its nuclear ambitions and unpredictable behavior. South Korea continues to maintain strong defensive measures against the North, even as it pursues rapprochement with Pyongyang.[23] Given the high stakes involved in a North–South conflict, and the uncertain security environment in Northeast Asia, South Korean political elites continue to place a priority on the alliance and U.S. troop presence.

Moreover, internal domestic factors reinforce the security consensus, even in an era of decreased North Korean threat perceptions and changing alliance patterns. For example, the historical legacy of the Korean War and remnants of anticommunist ideology continue to color the perceptions of elite policymakers, particularly those of the older, more conservative generation. Domestic institutions such as the National Security Laws also create a political environment that makes it difficult for foreign policy and security elites to suggest any dramatic shifts away from the existing consensus. Thus political elites agree, at least in principle, that U.S. forces in the mid- to long term are necessary for South Korean security. Other than radicals, very few South Koreans advocate alliance termination, the immediate withdrawal of USFK, or the sudden removal of U.S. bases.

What prevents the security consensus from unraveling completely are various institutional and ideational constraints. As argued earlier, the security consensus takes into account material-based threat perceptions but is also constituted and reinforced by institutions and ideas undergirding the U.S.-ROK alliance. This includes institutional arrangements such as the joint U.S.-ROK military command structure as well as the formation of an "alliance identity" produced over decades of close interaction between alliance partners.[24] These structures help perpetuate the security consensus within elite circles.

The security consensus thus streamlines diverse opinions in the policymaking process. Even with diverging opinions regarding U.S.-ROK relations, the security consensus held by elites, especially in the foreign policy and defense establishments, moderates more extreme views of the alliance. Figure 5.2 indicates South Korean elites' preference for cooperation with the United States in the mid-2000s. In a 2004 study conducted by the East Asia Institute, 79 percent of South Korean opinion leaders preferred cooperating the most with the United States, as opposed to 13 percent for China and 1 percent for Japan. Note the greater preference for cooperation with the United States among elites than among the general public.

Under a strong security consensus, the U.S.-ROK alliance still functions as the linchpin of South Korea's defense, particularly against a nuclear North Korea. South Korea's national security strategy emphasizes this defensive alliance over

---

[23] See Republic of Korea, Ministry of National Defense, *Defense White Paper 2006*.

[24] Jae-Jung Suh, "Bound to Last? The U.S.-Korea Alliance and Analytical Eclecticism," in *Rethinking Security in East Asia: Identity, Power and Efficiency*, edited by Jae-Jung Suh, Allen Carlson, and Peter Katzenstein (Stanford, Calif.: Stanford University Press, 2004).

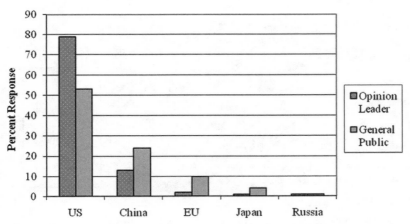

FIGURE 5.2. Country with Which South Korea Should Cooperate the Most.
Sources: EAI, DDFR, CIDE, COMEXI (July 2004). *N* = 724. For analysis, see Nae-young Lee, "Changing South Korean Public Opinion on the U.S. and the ROK-U.S. Alliance," paper prepared for a workshop on "America in Question: Korean Democracy and the Challenge of Non-Proliferation on the Peninsula," Seoul, South Korea, May 10–11, 2005; and Sook-jong Lee, *The Transformation of South Korean Politics: Implications for U.S.-Korea Relations* (Washington, D.C.: Brookings Institution, Center for Northeast Asian Policy Studies, 2005).

other possible scenarios, such as regional security arrangements or increasing bilateral military ties with China. As such, the U.S.-ROK alliance and USFK presence is still viewed by most Koreans as a legitimate source of national security. Figures 5.3 and 5.4 indicate that even the South Korean mass public continued to view U.S. troops and the U.S. security alliance as important during the Pyeongtaek episode, despite 47 percent of Koreans favoring a gradual withdrawal of U.S. forces in 2005.[25]

In sum, a relatively strong pro-U.S. security consensus persisted among South Korean political elites during the mid-2000s. Even as the breadth of the security consensus narrowed over time, conservatives, as well as a significant majority of progressive elites, continued to value security relations with the United States. Of course, government officials in the more progressive Kim Dae-jung and Roh Moo-hyun administrations advocated greater self-reliance on defense issues. However, deeply rooted political and ideological constraints curbed the pace of these reforms and frustrated the agenda of more radical elites demanding

[25] *Joongang Ilbo* national survey conducted August 24–September 10, 2005. *N* = 1200. Only 7 percent favored immediate withdrawal. Although the data refer to public opinion rather than elite perception, I add this to show that a surprisingly large number of South Koreans still admit that U.S. troop presence remains important to South Korean national security, even as attitudes toward U.S. policies have grown more critical.

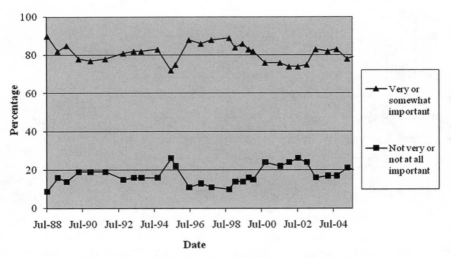

FIGURE 5.3. Importance of USFK for Protecting South Korea's Security, 1988–2005. *Source:* Office of Research, U.S. State Department.

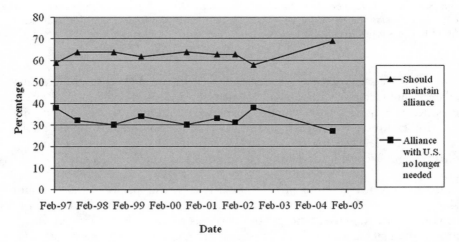

FIGURE 5.4. Should South Korea Maintain the Security Alliance after Reunification, 1997–2004? *Source:* Office of Research, U.S. State Department.

greater concessions from the United States.[26] Key elites dominating the security and foreign policy establishments marginalized voices claiming that U.S. bases functioned as a security liability rather than a common good.

---

[26] These concessions include an increase in alliance burden-sharing, further reductions in U.S. bases, and ceding influence to South Korea on North Korea and other regional issues.

PYEONGTAEK ANTI-BASE MOVEMENT EPISODE

How did an elite security consensus shape the outcome of the Pyeongtaek anti-base movement? Although activists and local residents delayed the base relocation process, the Korean government eventually used force to push ahead with the expansion of Camp Humphreys. As in Japan and Italy, the high security stakes associated with USFK base relocation continued to present challenges for South Korean activists. The South Korean government viewed activists as a public nuisance at best and a group of radicals undermining U.S.-ROK relations and national security at worst. In addition to these structural challenges, KCPT leaders faced problems sustaining mobilization efforts as the movement episode unfolded. Some of these problems were internal to the KCPT, such as increasing tension between moderates and radicals as the government worked to both co-opt and coerce different movement actors. Other problems were outside the control of the KCPT.

Evolution of South Korean Anti-Base Movements

Although outside observers tend to assume that anti-base or anti-American sentiments are a relatively recent phenomenon in South Korea, anti-base movements have deeper roots. Scholars and activists generally agree that the Gwangju Massacre in May 1980 helped propel anti-American sentiment in South Korea.[27] Although anti-American attitudes existed in South Korea even before 1980, the rise of such sentiments did not necessarily lead to an organized, systematic movement against U.S. military bases or USFK. Unification and pro–North Korea groups, particularly those influenced by national liberation (NL) ideology, had always taken an anti-American, anti-imperialist stance, whereas the mass public generally accepted the U.S. military presence. In fact, prior to South Korea's democratic transition in 1987, social and environmental externalities stemming from bases attracted little attention. Moreover, government repression and security concerns severely limited mobilization against bases.[28]

Awareness of social costs and the first signs of a shift in public perception of U.S. bases took shape with the widely publicized brutal rape-murder case of Yoon Geumi in 1992.[29] USFK-related crimes were taken more seriously as civic

---

[27] The United States had no direct role in suppressing mass demonstrations in Gwangju. However, because South Korea's military chain of command was subordinate to USFK, South Koreans often cite that the release of the ROK 20th Division implied U.S. complicity, or at least acquiescence, to Chun Doo Hwan's decision to brutally crack down on protestors. See Kun-young Park, "80 nyun-dae hanguk-ui banmijoo-ui,byun-hwa, jeonmang, geuligo ham-eui" [South Korean Anti-Americanism, Change, Prospects, and Togetherness], presented at Perspectives of Social Science in the 1980s from a 21st Century Perspective, Seoul, South Korea, October 7, 2005.

[28] Park, *A New U.S.-ROK Alliance*, 25.

[29] Youkyoung Ko, "Hanguk-ui banmi-gun-giji undong-gwa dongasia yundae" [Anti-US Military Base Movements and East Asian Solidarity], in *Bipan Sahoehak Daehoe* (8th Meeting), November 4–5, 2005 (Seoul: College of Social Science, Seoul National University, 2005), 297.

groups pushed for revisions to the unequal Status of Forces Agreement (SOFA). Local NIMBY protests had existed prior to this point, but only from the mid-1990s did civic groups at the national level attempt to form a broader coalition movement. In 1997, national civic groups joined forces with local residents across different regions where U.S. bases existed to form the Pan-National Solution Committee to Return U.S. Bases. The movement demanded the reduction and eventual return of U.S. bases in South Korea, as well as the restoration of sovereignty rights, peace, and reunification.[30]

Despite the formation of the Pan-National Committee to Return U.S. Bases, most anti-base movements, led by local NGOs, continued to focus on regional issues. However, in early 1999, Foreign Minister Lee Joung-bin publicly raised the issue of SOFA revisions. Local anti-base coalition movements in Kunsan and Daegu, and NGOs in Seoul such as the National Campaign to Eradicate Crimes by U.S. Troops (USA Crime), viewed Foreign Minister Lee's public statement as an opportunity to open a broader coalition. In addition to base-related issues, SOFA revisions also encompassed other issue areas such as the environment, labor, safety, and women's rights. Thus, anti-base activists and NGO leaders from various sectors established the broad-based coalition People's Action for Reform of the Unjust SOFA (PAR-SOFA) in October 1999 to push Washington and Seoul for substantive SOFA revisions.[31]

In early 2000, protestors staged numerous rallies and public campaigns pressuring the South Korean government to take a resolute stance in negotiations with Washington. Two events in 2000 also triggered large-scale protests and provided fuel not only for SOFA revision movements but other movements related to USFK and U.S. bases. The first event occurred near the Kooni Firing Range in May. An A-10 aircraft dropped its payload early in an emergency procedure, resulting in property damage in the nearby village of Maehyangri. With widespread media coverage, this event eventually triggered a major reaction as national-level civic groups and NGOs joined forces with local residents who had been struggling to shut down the firing range since 1988. The second event was the discovery of USFK personnel dumping formaldehyde into the Han River, again prompting a reaction not only from environmental groups but the general public as well. By alerting the national public about USFK issues and mobilizing massive protests, the Maehyangri anti-base movement and PAR-SOFA pressured South Korean officials to take action on both issues in negotiations with the United States. Both movements subsided with partial concessions granted in Maehyangri and minor revisions to the SOFA in early 2001. Despite a

[30] Ko, "Hanguk-ui banmi-gun-giji undong-gwa dongasia yundae," 298; and Yeo, "Local National Dynamics and Framing in South Korean Anti-Base Movements."

[31] Doo-Hui Oh, "A-jik kkeun-naji ahn-eun SOFA gaejeong undong" [The Unfinished SOFA Revision Movement], in *Nogunri eseo Maehyangri kkaji* [From Nogunri to Maehyangri] (Seoul: Deep Freedom Press, 2001), 202; and Katharine H. S. Moon, "Korean Nationalism, Anti-Americanism, and Democratic Consolidation," in *Korea's Democratization*, edited by Samuel Kim (Cambridge: Cambridge University Press, 2003), 146.

brief, sudden reawaking of the SOFA revision movement in 2002, anti-base movements were unable to extract any further concessions from Seoul or Washington.

Origins of the Pyeongtaek Anti-Base Movement

After Seoul and Washington announced the decision to relocate Yongsan Garrison in 2003 and the 2nd Infantry Division to Pyeongtaek in 2004, activists moved away from SOFA issues and reoriented their struggle against the expansion of Camp Humphreys in Pyeongtaek. The movement was led by the anti-base coalition group Pan-National Solution Committee to Stop the Expansion of U.S. Bases (KCPT). Although the KCPT did not formally launch its campaign until March 2005, the seeds of the Pyeongtaek anti-base movement date from two earlier local coalition groups. A group of local activists formed the Citizens' Coalition Opposing the Relocation of Yongsan Garrison in November 1990 after U.S. and Korean negotiators considered Pyeongtaek as a potential relocation site for Yongsan Garrison in the late 1980s. The coalition group, composed primarily of local NGOs, evolved into the Citizens' Coalition to Regain Our Land from U.S. Bases in 1999, and then the Pyeongtaek Movement to Stop Base Expansion (Pyeongtaek Daechaekui) in 2001 prior to the announcement of the LPP.

In April 2003, the South Korean and U.S. governments formally announced the decision to relocate Yongsan Garrison to Pyeongtaek. The MND also announced its plan to expropriate land surrounding Camp Humphreys for base expansion. Of the designated base expansion land, the MND planned to acquire 240,000 pyeong (about 199 acres) of land from Daechuri village. Thus villagers organized the Paengseong Residents' Action Committee (Paengseong Daechaekui, or Jumin Daechaekui) in July 2003 to prevent the MND from taking over their farmland. After the conclusion of the U.S.-ROK Future of the Alliance Talks (FOTA) in 2004, the MND agreed to grant the United States a total of 3,490,000 pyeong (about 2,897 acres) of land, 2,850,000 pyeong (about 2,366 acres) coming from the Daechuri and Doduri villages.[32] Figure 5.5 indicates the area of expansion, tripling the size of Camp Humphreys from 2005.

The conclusion of FOTA ratcheted up the gravity of the situation. Hence, in May 2004, Father Mun Jung-hyeon, the former PAR-SOFA movement leader, met with leaders of both the local Pyeongtaek anti-base coalition and the anti-base Residents' Action Committee. At that point, Father Mun, along with other prominent NGO leaders, decided that the various anti-base movements in Pyeongtaek needed to unify under one national campaign. In early 2005, Mun and other anti-base leaders organized the KCPT.

---

[32] The figures come from the KCPT, http://antigizi.or.kr/. The MND reports 3,620,000 pyeong (about 3,005 acres) of land being provided to the USFK. See Yoon 2006.

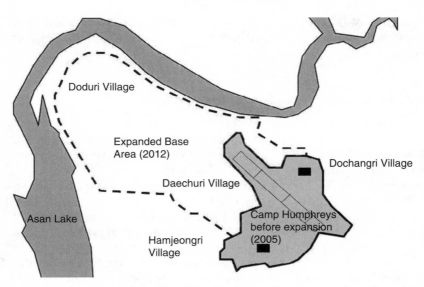

FIGURE 5.5. Camp Humphreys Base Expansion. *Sources: Hankyoreh 21*, KCPT.

Mobilization

Similar to the ATM movement in the Philippines, mobilization structures were already in place through existing anti-base networks formed in previous campaigns such as the Maehyangri and SOFA revision movements.[33] Several leaders who had served on various committees in previous coalition campaigns, such as Father Mun, Yoo Young-jae from Solidarity for Peace and Reunification of Korea (SPARK), or Kim Yong-han from the local chapter of the Democratic Labor Party, were part of the KCPT's executive committee. However, KCPT organizers made a conscious decision to include several representatives from the local Pyeongtaek anti-base coalition and the village-level anti-base Residents' Committee in leadership positions to give local actors a voice in the campaign.[34] The KCPT held its first at-large leaders' meeting with representatives from member groups on March 3, 2005. By July 2005, activists had successfully organized an anti-base coalition campaign linking national-level NGOs, local civic groups, and village residents into one large umbrella coalition. What was originally a local movement in Pyeongtaek had now become a national struggle. Approximately

---

[33] Many of the same organizations and activists from earlier movements reappeared in the Pyeongtaek anti-base struggle. See "2002 nyun yeojoong-saeng bumdaewii chamgadanchae 63% ga pyeontaek bumdaewi chamga" [63 Percent of Civic Groups Involved in the 2002 Hyosoon-Miseon Coalition Group Involved in Pyeongtaek Umbrella Coalition], *Chosun Ilbo*, May 17, 2006. http://www.chosun.com/naitonal/news/200605/200605170036.html (last accessed May 30, 2006).

[34] Minutes of KCPT at-large leaders' meeting no. 1, KCTU conference room, Seoul, South Korea, March 3, 2005.

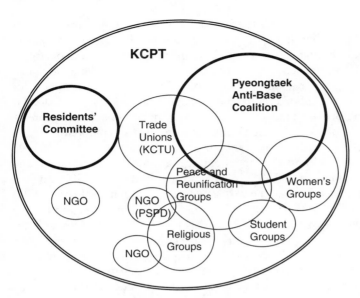

FIGURE 5.6. Membership of People's Task Force to Stop Expansion of Bases in Pyeongtaek (KCPT). *Note:* Overlapping circles represent organizational rather than individual member overlap.

120 organizations from labor, student, women's rights, agriculture, human rights, peace, unification, and religious groups were directly or nominally involved in the campaign.

As is common with other anti-base movements, significant overlap among individual organizations in multiple coalitions makes it difficult to diagram the KCPT's coalition structure. Additionally, many organizations were only nominal members of the KCPT based on their association with other coalition movements supporting the KCPT. The number of civic groups directly and consistently active in the Pyeongtaek anti-base struggle amounted to a few dozen groups. Figure 5.6 outlines the basic organizational pattern of the KCPT.[35]

Mobilizing strategies required maintaining support from local and national NGOs as well as the unmobilized masses. The bulk of the organizing work was conducted by activists residing within or near Pyeongtaek. Organizers also

---

[35] Listing South Korean civic groups involved in anti-base movements is difficult because most organizations are only nominally members through their association with a local or regional coalition group. For instance, all member organizations of the Korean Confederated Trade Union (KCTU) are counted as member organizations of the KCPT, regardless of whether individual organizations are actively involved in the anti-base struggle. On the other hand, individual activists in groups such as the National Campaign for the Eradication of Crime by U.S. Troops or Civil Network for a Peaceful Korea may be extensively involved with anti-base issues. However, because of limited resources, their organization as a whole cannot take part in the actual mobilization, financing, or strategic planning of the movement.

included "local" activists representing national-level civic groups such as PeaceWind or SPARK but living in Daechuri village during the campaign. Representatives from national and regional organizations who were coalitional members of the KCPT attended the members-at-large meetings. These individual representatives were then responsible for mobilizing their local chapters for large events and rallies. Labor unions and student groups, such as the KCTU and Hanchongryon, provided the manpower and warm bodies at larger protests. Communication was largely conducted through the Internet and mass e-mailing.[36]

The KCPT relied primarily on two types of frames: frames of injustice focused on the issue of livelihood and the forced expropriation of farmers' lands, and frames of peace claimed that U.S. base expansion destabilized Korean and Northeast Asian security. Despite the variegated agenda of national-level NGOs under the KCPT, the campaign successfully maintained a semblance of unity by placing the local land expropriation issue as its central focus.[37] Although the KCPT may have been more concerned about peace and sovereignty issues, the plight of elderly farmers forcefully evicted from their homeland was more likely to gain traction with the wider public. Framing the anti-base debate in a manner that highlighted immediate consequences, such as the forced eviction of poor farmers, was much more effective in capturing a wider audience than using abstract frames such as peace and stability in Northeast Asia.[38] Therefore, the support and participation of local residents was essential for the KCPT. It invested significant resources to mobilize and sustain the morale of local residents in the wake of government threats and monetary bribery.

The KCPT used various tactics to mobilize the public. According to PeaceWind activists living in Pyeongtaek, the most effective means of mobilization was a six-week, twenty-city publicity campaign tour around the country. KCPT activists contacted regional NGOs in advance about their visit, particularly labor groups, who had the largest mobilizing capacity. These groups would then contact other local civic groups and NGOs to listen to Father Mun and other KCPT members discuss the Pyeongtaek base relocation issue. In addition to contacting labor groups, the KCPT made special efforts to publicize its events to students, keeping in close contact with student unions.[39] Second, NGOs sponsored both press conferences and public forums, inviting the press, government officials, and

---

[36] Interview with KCPT Steering Committee member, Pyeongtaek, South Korea, November 6, 2005; and interview with Hangchonryon member from Hanshin University, Pyeongtaek, South Korea, November 6, 2005.

[37] In reality, there was always internal dissension regarding tactics, strategy, and even goals of the movement. After violent clashes between police and protestors, differences between grassroots organizations and established NGOs on the base relocation issue became much more pronounced. Grassroots organizations continued to focus on the rights of residents, whereas larger NGOs challenged the legal process, lack of transparency, and strategic motives behind base relocation and other USFK-related issues.

[38] Yeo, "Local National Dynamics and Framing in South Korean Anti-Base Movements."

[39] KCPT internal document, organizational meeting notes, Seoul, South Korea, February 17, 2005, 10:00 A.M.

other activists to discuss pending base-related issues. Third, the KCPT sent out electronic newsletters to all member organizations, as well as individual members who had subscribed to its listserv. Lastly, the KCPT used visual media, art, photo exhibitions, music, and street theater to publicize its cause.

In addition to these mobilizing tactics, the KCPT organized three large rallies to attract media attention and raise public awareness about the negative impact of U.S. base relocation on Pyeongtaek. The rallies, framed as "Grand Peace Marches," were held on July 10, 2005, December 11, 2005, and February 12, 2006, in Pyeongtaek. Gwanghwamun in downtown Seoul also provided a stage for anti-base protestors. In addition to occasional protests near the U.S. Embassy, from August 9 to October 25, 2005, celebrity folk singers Jeong Tae-choon and his wife, Park Eun-ok, performed behind the Kyobo Center as KCPT members handed out leaflets and flyers to the crowd. In January 2006, farmers brought attention to U.S. base issues by driving tractors all around the country bearing signs to stop base expansion at Camp Humphreys.

Despite the KCPT's mobilization efforts and large protest numbers, ranging anywhere from 5,000 to 10,000 protestors, the movement was hampered by several external circumstances and internal constraints. The movement gradually strengthened throughout the summer of 2005, highlighted by a rally with 10,000 protestors outside Camp Humphreys on July 10. The event drew national attention, and the KCPT's momentum was sustained through November. With winter approaching, however, other events, such as the APEC summit in Pusan and the WTO meeting in Hong Kong, "distracted" NGO groups from base issues. They had to devote attention to their own parochial struggles.[40] Activists also attributed the weakened support of labor unions in the anti-base campaign as an obstacle to mobilization. In the midst of financial scandals, and a rift between moderate and conservative labor union members within the KCTU, the labor coalition was unable to devote significant attention to the Pyeongtaek issue.[41] The U.S.–South Korea Free Trade Agreement (FTA) negotiations beginning in May 2006 only distracted labor's attention further away from U.S. base issues.[42]

Strategy

The major difference in strategy between the KCPT in South Korea and more successful movements such as the Anti-Treaty Movement in the Philippines was the lack of coordinated, well-devised strategies directed at the South Korean government. The ATM used a two-pronged strategy aimed at both the mass

[40] Interview with Father Mun Jung-hyeon, Pyeongtaek, South Korea, November 7, 2005; and Bae Hye-jeong, "Interview with KCPT Activist Lee Ho-sung," *Minjung ae Sori*, December 11, 2005.
[41] Interview with Pyeongtaek Democratic Labor Party official and activist Kim Yong-han, Pyeongtaek, South Korea, November 7, 2005.
[42] However, labor activists in the KCPT helped organize a joint rally against U.S. imperialism with the anti-FTA coalition. A short attempt was made to link military bases and the FTA as an anti-U.S. struggle.

public and government elites. Nominally, KCPT activists mentioned targeting the South Korean government, particularly the Blue House, the MND, and the Pyeongtaek city government. However, the bulk of the KCPT's strategy was oriented toward the larger public and "raising the national consciousness of South Koreans" rather than the South Korean government.[43] In an initial KCPT planning meeting in February 2005, organizers listed two primary objectives of the movement: (1) inform and formulate national public opinion; and (2) form strong solidarity with residents to stop the expansion of bases.[44] Explaining why the KCPT focused on society rather than directly targeting the government, Father Mun Jung-Hyeon stated, "I don't try to solve problems with politicians, because I don't expect them to change. Instead we must focus on society. Then we can see change."[45] Mun acknowledged that the KCPT was ultimately trying to push the government to change. However, some activist leaders, such as Mun and Yoo Young-jae, believed influencing public opinion was more effective in pressuring the government to shift policy on security issues than direct government appeals. The KCPT's inaugural declaration illustrated the movement's focus on the mass campaign:

We cannot tolerate the lives of Pyeongtaek residents to be shaken so violently. Nor can we tolerate the serious threat posed by USFK relocation and permanent military dependency. Therefore, we are going to fight with all our strength to block the expansion of U.S. bases in Pyeongtaek. We are going to use a variety of methods, both on and off-line, and through media outlets, to wage a public campaign to inform the mass public about the problems associated with military base expansion and the expanded role of USFK. Through demonstrations at every level, we are going to engage in an intense struggle against our government, which has deliberately ignored its people.[46]

As mentioned earlier, a strategy targeting the mass public required careful framing of the issue. To draw public attention, activists carefully constructed

---

[43] Interview with Father Mun Jung-hyeon, Pyeongtaek, South Korea, November 7, 2005. Some may argue that the institutional arrangements between base issues in the two countries differed because base treaties in the Philippines required Senate ratification. Philippine anti-base activists could therefore affect policy outcomes by directly lobbying government officials. However, the South Korean National Assembly, while not voting directly on base relocation, had the power of the purse to veto the base relocation project. Voting in favor of the budget implies approval of the base expansion plan. Thus, in principle, KCPT activists could have also oriented their strategy toward National Assembly members as in the Philippines. Although the KCPT mobilized too late to affect the December 9, 2004, ratification, NGO groups did attempt to lobby National Assembly members to open a new hearing on the Yongsan base relocation bill. See Republic of Korea, National Assembly Records, Unification and Foreign Affairs Committee, 250th Assembly, 16th Meeting, December 7, 2004.

[44] KCPT internal document, "Organizational Meeting Notes," February 17, 2005.

[45] Interview with Father Mun Jung-hyeon, Pyeongtaek, South Korea, November 7, 2005. Mun notes, however, that there are others within the KCPT Steering Policy Committee who do not necessarily subscribe to this view. These members believe activists should directly pressure the government to promote policy change.

[46] KCPT Inaugural Declaration [translated by author]. Available at the KCPT's Web site, www. antigizi.or.kr/.

their slogans to take into account the local nature of the struggle and the plight of evicted residents. The goal was to attract those who may not necessarily have subscribed to the political views of anti-base activists but agreed with the KCPT on principles of human rights. Support from the Residents' Action Committee was therefore essential.[47] To maintain a locally oriented strategy, activists from national civic groups relocated to Pyeongtaek and occupied houses vacated by residents who had already taken the government's financial compensation. Villagers and activists repainted homes, painted murals evoking images of peace and village life on the outside of walls, and converted abandoned buildings into public spaces, including a library and café. Residing in empty houses was also a tactic used to prevent the government from beginning base construction. The government would not bulldoze houses still occupied by elderly residents and activists. The KCPT activists also participated regularly in the nightly candlelight vigils held in Daechuri, organized festivals, and welcomed visitors to Pyeongtaek and Daechuri village.

To raise national consciousness and influence public opinion on U.S. base issues, the KCPT needed media support. This required activists to refrain from making more radical demands such as the immediate withdrawal of all U.S. bases and troops. Hence the KCPT resorted to more neutral slogans such as "Stop the Expansion of U.S. Bases." The rallies in July and December 2005, and again in February 2006, were used to attract media attention. Progressive Internet media outlets such as *OhMyNews* and *The Village Voice* (*Minjung ae Sori*) devoted extensive coverage to the Pyeongtaek anti-base movement on their Web pages. *Hankyoreh*, a major progressive-leaning daily, also provided frequent, favorable coverage. *Hankyoreh 21*, the weekly magazine produced by the same media company, devoted a section each week to Daechuri residents and the KCPT's campaign. Daechuri residents and KCPT activists appeared in the cover story three times. Acknowledging their struggle, the editors even chose Daechuri residents as "people of the year" for their final 2006 cover story.

THE SECURITY CONSENSUS AND STATE–SOCIETY RELATIONS

The preceding section suggests initial successful mobilization on the part of the KCPT. How, then, did the South Korean government respond to anti-base mobilization? Examining the interaction between KCPT activists and the national government helps explain how the security consensus shaped the state's response to anti-base pressure and reveals why anti-base movements were engaged in what would ultimately become a losing battle. Unlike the ATM movement in the Philippines, the KCPT had few elite "insiders" aiding them in the anti-base campaign. The few elites who were sympathetic to the movement,

---

[47] The loss of resident support in early 2007 was a major blow to the KCPT. It had to reformulate its entire campaign after villagers signed an agreement with the government in January 2007 to relocate by April 2007.

or at least in agreement with the KCPT in opposing the enlargement of Camp Humphreys for USFK transformation, were found in the National Assembly.

Minimal Elite Support

Several representatives within the Democratic Labor Party (DLP) and the ruling Uri Party offered their support to the KCPT and tried to raise the relocation issue within the National Assembly. The two National Assembly members most actively supporting the KCPT's struggle were Uri Party member Lim Jong-in and DLP floor leader and Unification and Foreign Affairs subcommittee member Kwon Young-gil. Representative Lim was by far the most active politician, meeting regularly with residents and activists and organizing public forums bringing together activists and MND officials to promote dialogue.[48] Lim also addressed the base relocation issue and plight of Daechuri residents to other National Assembly members and government officials in hopes of convincing the National Assembly to reopen a hearing regarding the base relocation project to Pyeongtaek. Lim made clear to the public that the entire base relocation process was conducted without the input of Daechuri residents, who were now being forcefully evicted. In addition to Lim, after the May 2006 clash between protestors and police, six Uri Party National Assembly members stepped forward with a public statement calling for the government to hold discussions with both NGOs and Daechuri residents. The Uri Party representatives made three specific demands on the government: (1) to stop using strong-arm tactics against civic groups and residents; (2) to release those students and activists arrested during the May 5 clash; and (3) to withdraw all riot police and military soldiers occupying the expanded base land area, who had been dispatched to Daechuri since early May 2006.[49]

DLP floor leader Kwon Young-gil, who played an active role in the 2000 Maehyangri anti-base movement, also expressed his support for the KCPT and Daechuri residents. In the December 2004 subcommittee meeting concerning Yongsan's relocation, Kwon repeatedly questioned the deputy MOFAT minister over the necessity of such a costly transfer. He criticized the government's lack of transparency in outlining the underlying motives and costs of base relocation negotiated between Seoul and Washington.[50] Kwon and other DLP members also met with Father Mun on several occasions to assess the situation in Pyeongtaek and lend moral support to the KCPT. Members of the DLP were

---

[48] Representative Lim's office sponsored a public forum in October 2005 and an open dialogue between Daechuri residents and MND officials on November 3, 2005.

[49] National Assembly press conference public statement, "Pyeongtaek mi-goon gijee hwak-jang gal-deung hae-gyul-eul eui-han woori-ee ip-jang" [Our View on the Resolution of the Conflict over the Expansion of the Pyeongtaek Base], May 16, 2006. Available from bulletin on Representative Lim's homepage, http://www.wedrea.or.kr (last accessed May 20, 2006). The six representatives were Woo Won-sik, Yoo Seung-hui, Lee In-young, Lim Jong-in, Jung Chung-rae, and Choy Jae-chun.

[50] Republic of Korea, National Assembly Records, Unification and Foreign Affairs Committee, 250th Assembly, 16th Meeting, December 7, 2004, 23.

especially critical of Defense Minister Yoon Kwang-ung, stating that they would call for his resignation in the Assembly. They also reprimanded President Roh and Prime Minister Han for their negligent handling of the base relocation issue.[51]

Yet the handful of National Assembly members sympathetic to the KCPT's cause had very little power to persuade their fellow representatives on the Pyeongtaek issue. The small faction in the Uri Party and the few DLP members calling for a reexamination of the base relocation project in May 2006 were a minority voice in the Assembly. Moreover, the National Assembly as a whole did not carry the same clout in base politics as the Philippine Senate. Most of this power was held in the National Security Council,[52] or bureaucracies such as the MND and the Ministry of Foreign Affairs and Trade (MOFAT), institutions where anti-base activists had few allies and little access.[53] The leverage the bureaucracies held over the National Assembly can be seen again in the December 7, 2004, Unification and Foreign Affairs Subcommittee hearings. In an exchange between Deputy MOFAT Minister Choi Young-jin and Representative Kwon Young-gil, Kwon repeatedly demanded the release of FOTA transcripts to examine the details outlining the motives behind Yongsan Garrison's relocation to Pyeongtaek. However, Deputy Minister Choi sidestepped the issue. Choi claimed that even if documents were declassified, there was no guarantee Assembly members would receive access to the transcripts.[54] Without pushing the issue any further, subcommittee members acquiesced to the MOFAT deputy minister's plea to quickly approve the base relocation bill. The bill passed in a 14–1 vote in favor of base relocation.

The security consensus held among political elites, especially within the foreign policy establishment, made elite access and cooperation difficult for activists. Anti-base movement leaders who were more open to dialogue with government officials also noted this obstacle. KCPT Policy Steering Committee chair Yoo Young-jae stated, "We've talked with several politicians and scholars, and we feel that a big problem is that regarding U.S. power, they [Korean elites] have a fear, or seem defeatist, and are unable to break free from that mentality. That's the biggest problem. On the other hand, the nation as a whole wants to

---

[51] "Lim Jong-in, 'Pyeongtaek-eun migoon jiju-ae maleum-gwa sojaknog-ee sah-woo-neun gyuk'" [In Pyeongtaek, Fighting with the U.S. Landlords], *Chosun Ilbo*, May 14, 2006. http://www.chosun.com/national/news/20605140267.html (last accessed May 20, 2006).

[52] In the early half of President Roh's tenure, the power to make foreign policy decisions rested with the National Security Council rather than MOFAT. Inside the NSC, the more pro-U.S. "alliance faction" prevailed over the "independence faction," advising the president to strengthen the U.S.-ROK alliance through specific policy measures such as the USFK relocation to Pyeongtaek and the expansion of Camp Humphreys. I thank Kim Sung-Han and J. J. Suh for pointing this out.

[53] In the Philippines, anti-base activists had the sympathy of bureaucrats such as Alfredo Bengzon, vice chairman of the Philippine base negotiating panel, and an unnamed DFA official who leaked a draft copy of the Treaty to ATM activists.

[54] Republic of Korea, National Assembly Records, Unification and Foreign Affairs Committee, 250th Assembly, 16th Meeting, December 7, 2004, 25.

move past [that mentality]."⁵⁵ Activist-scholar Jung Wook-shik observes that South Korean political elites either blindly acquiesce to the demands of their patron, or, because of fears of abandonment, dare not pursue policies that counter U.S. policy preferences.⁵⁶ Even within the National Assembly, the voting record of National Assembly members on USFK base relocation indicates how political elites continued to support security policies in line with the security consensus. Voting on December 9, 2004, 145 representatives voted in favor of base relocation, whereas only 27 were opposed.⁵⁷

Government Response

Given the relatively strong degree of security consensus regarding U.S.-ROK security relations, the Roh administration had to walk a fine line in responding to anti-base pressure while also managing its alliance relations with the United States. For South Korea, the agreement signed with the United States approving Yongsan's relocation and the consolidation of the 2nd Infantry Division to Pyeongtaek was an "inevitable process" needed to "strengthen the U.S.–South Korean alliance and deter war from [breaking out] on the Peninsula."⁵⁸ The MND noted that extensive delays in the relocation project caused by activists would result in a breach in diplomatic trust with Washington. Several other security experts referred to the signed 2004 base relocation agreement as a "promise" to the United States, sealed by the National Assembly's ratification.⁵⁹ President Roh also recognized the potential for further deterioration in the alliance if the Korean government failed to fulfill its end of the bargain on base relocation.⁶⁰

At the same time, the South Korean government needed to be careful not to attract negative publicity.⁶¹ Using force could potentially inflame anti-American sentiment and strengthen support for the KCPT. A Pyeongtaek city official working with the MND and USFK on the relocation project stated, "The MND is acting very cautiously regarding forced eviction of residents because the residents are connected to anti-American movements. Evicting residents isn't

⁵⁵ Interview with Yoo Young-jae, Seoul, South Korea, August 22, 2005.
⁵⁶ Jung Wook-shik, *Dongmaeng-ae dut* [Alliance Trap] (Seoul: Samin Press, 2005), 15.
⁵⁷ Republic of Korea, National Assembly Records, Main Assembly, 250th Assembly, 14th Meeting, December 9, 2004, 72. Nineteen members abstained from voting.
⁵⁸ Yoon Kwang-ung. "Pyeongtaek migoon giji eejeon jaegeumtoh opda" [No Reevaluation of Pyeongtaek Base Relocation], special statement prepared by the MND Minister of Defense, May 4, 2006, *MND News Brief*, May 3, 2006. http://mnd.news.go.kr/warp/webapp/news/print_view?id=5ae9967224cc3de6665c2c17 (last accessed May 8, 2006).
⁵⁹ Ibid. Also see comments by KIDA analyst Cha Doo-Hyun in KBS *Simya Toron* transcript, June 8, 2006.
⁶⁰ Interview with General Cha Young-koo, Seoul, South Korea, December 19, 2005. Cha was the director for policy planning in the MND and a key player in the FOTA negotiations with the United States.
⁶¹ This was particularly true for the MND, which was managing the technical aspects behind the base relocation project.

that big of an issue. It happens. But if residents are forced out, the MND is worried that the anti-American voice will become stronger or face negative reaction from the public."[62] How, then, did the South Korean state respond to civil societal pressure while maintaining its alliance obligations to the United States? Influenced by a strong pro-U.S. security consensus, and the belief that the future of the U.S.-ROK alliance rested with base relocation and expansion in Pyeongtaek, the government outmaneuvered the KCPT and Daechuri residents by employing strategies of delay, co-optation, and coercion.

In a twist of irony, the South Korean government ignored and isolated the KCPT by focusing on the local residents. The MND made a sharp distinction between activists and residents, constantly referring to the KCPT as "outside forces" (*woebu saeryuk*) engaged in a political struggle. More than concern for the rights of local residents or the national interest, the MND claimed that the KCPT was more interested in promoting its own political agenda such as USFK withdrawal.[63] In a briefing report, the MND stated, "Last May, external forces [KCPT activists] began residing in Pyeongtaek and joined forces with residents opposed to relocation. But rather than discuss compensation or other livelihood issues, they [KCPT] were opposed to base relocation altogether making dialogue [with residents] difficult."[64] In a follow-up press briefing by Defense Minister Yoon, the MND accused anti-base movements of making unrealistic proposals. Yoon also blamed the KCPT for creating an impasse in negotiations between the MND and local residents.[65] The MND claimed that the KCPT had discouraged residents from taking the government's compensation and instead encouraged them to demand a reevaluation of the entire base relocation project.[66]

After the KCPT's first major protest, in July 2005, the MND decided to hold further discussions with activists and Daechuri residents, hoping residents would sell their land voluntarily if given greater compensation. However, for the remaining residents, the issue was not about compensation but about democratic principles and their livelihood as farmers. With residents and activists refusing to leave, the MND announced it would conclude the eminent domain process in mid-December and acquire the remaining 20 percent of base expansion land.[67] By January 2006, the MND had legally purchased all the land,

[62] Interview with Pyeongtaek city official, Office of ROK-U.S. Relations, Pyeongtaek, South Korea, February 9, 2006.

[63] Yoon Kwang-ung, "Pyeongtaek migoon giji eejeon jaegeumtoh opda."

[64] Yoon Kwang-ung, "Migoon giji eejeon sa-ub gwalyeon" [Related to U.S. Base Relocation], MND Press Briefing, May 3, 2006.

[65] The KCPT and the Residents' Committee were skeptical of the MND's willingness to negotiate. The government claimed it held at least 45 meetings with both pro- and anti-base residents and 150 formal and informal consultations. Activists, however, stated that the government met the anti-base faction only once for any real dialogue. See Yoon, "Migoon giji eejeon sa-ub gwalyeon"; and KBS *Sima Toron* Transcript, June 9, 2006.

[66] Yoon, "Pyeongtaek migoon giji eejeon jaegeumtoh opda."

[67] To the consternation of the KCPT, the court ruling on eminent domain was actually completed a month early on November 23, 2005. See Kim Do-gyun, "Handal ab-dang-gyujin jae-fyul jeol-cha" [Ruling Process Pushed Forward One Month], *Minjung ae Sori*, November 22, 2003.

despite residents and activists still residing in the village. The government certainly had the power to expel residents and activists by this period. The MND, however, decided to wait until spring to forcibly remove KCPT activists and residents. As activists and Pyeongtaek city officials cited, the Korean government was not likely to "throw out grandmothers in the dead of winter."[68] At this stage, the South Korean government was willing to delay base expansion rather than risk a violent confrontation.[69]

In February 2006, USFK relayed to the MND that the South Korean government needed to push ahead with the land acquisition, declaring "time was not unlimited."[70] Originally, USFK had expected the land to be transferred to them by December 31, 2005. However, the MND explained to USFK its situation with anti-base resistance, and agreed to transfer the base land by the end of February. Of particular concern for USFK was congressional funding for base relocation and USFK transformation. At the time, USFK believed that land transfer needed to be completed prior to USFK Commander Burwell Bell's report to Congress on March 7. General Bell was expected to provide an assessment and update on military strategy and operational requirements in a review of the Defense Authorization Request for fiscal year 2007. As one U.S. military official explained, USFK feared the Appropriations Committee would not provide all the funds necessary to push ahead with USFK relocation if General Bell informed Congress that the expansion land had still not been entirely secured.[71] The same USFK official continued that the MND was in a difficult position "trying to find a neutral ground, mediating between its citizens and its security strategy."[72] These statements suggest that the MND was dragging its feet on the base relocation issue. To maintain the alliance and push ahead with the transformation project, USFK expressed to the MND that Seoul needed to follow through and "make good on its part in a timely fashion." At the time, though, USFK understood the situation faced by the MND and was not heavily pressuring Seoul to speed up the land transfer.[73]

However, by April 2006, the MND had shifted from its tactic of delay and foot-dragging to one of resolution and force. At this point, it becomes clear how the security consensus influenced the government's response to anti-base

---

[68] Interview with PeaceWind activist, KCPT headquarters, Pyeongtaek, South Korea, December 12, 2005; and interview with Pyeongtaek city official, Office of ROK-U.S. Relations, Pyeongtaek City Hall, Pyeongtaek, South Korea, February 9, 2005.

[69] Activists hoped to delay the government long enough either for another hearing to be opened regarding base relocation in the National Assembly or for USFK to alter its expansion plans to allow Daechuri residents to keep their land.

[70] Interview with USFK officials, Pyeongtaek, South Korea, February 3, 2006.

[71] Ibid.

[72] Ibid.

[73] By January 2007, however, General Bell was publicly expressing his displeasure with the delay. His remarks prompted Foreign Minister Song Min-Soon to reassure the United States that base relocation would "proceed as agreed." See Jin Dae-Woong, "Seoul Reassures U.S. on Base Relocation," *Korea Herald*, January 11, 2007.

protestors, shaping the ensuing policy outcome. One month earlier, MND workers were sent to Daechuri to dig a trench and erect barbed wire around the expanded base area to prevent residents from continuing their farming. However, MND workers aborted their plan as several hundred protestors set fire to fields and physically took over two of the backhoe tractors used to dig the trenches.[74] Thus, in early April 2006, Defense Minister Yoon stated, "The delay in base relocation is coming close to a point where it may create a diplomatic row with the United States. Therefore, from here on out, we will strengthen our possession over the designated base land."[75] The following day, the MND posted an article on its Web site titled, "Delay in Pyeongtaek Base Relocation May Ignite into a Diplomatic Problem." The article outlined reasons why the process was being delayed and its impact on the national interest.[76] A few days earlier, on April 8, the MND had sent 750 workers accompanied by approximately 5,000 riot police to begin filling in the farmers' rice irrigation system with concrete. The MND blocked the irrigation canals to prevent residents' attempts to continue farming. Protestors fought with riot police and prevented workers from destroying two canals, but workers managed to fill in at least one canal with concrete.[77]

Even after these measures, activists and residents continued to cut through barbed wire and plant rice crops. The concrete the MND used to fill the irrigation canals was also smashed by activists, allowing water to flow again onto the farmland. The MND offered direct negotiations on May 1, but after key leaders such as Kim Jitae of the village Residents' Committee boycotted talks with the MND, Korean officials hinted they would abandon negotiations and secure the land by force. Sensing the gravity of the situation, Prime Minister Han Myeong-sook called an emergency meeting to resolve the stalemate. Han urged the MND and police to look for peaceful means of resolving the dispute and concluded the meeting with an agreement between residents and MND officials to settle the issue through dialogue.[78]

[74] Franklin Fisher, "Camp Humphreys Residents Braced for Conflict," *Stars and Stripes*, April 7, 2006. http://www.estripes.com/article.asp?section=104&article=35432&archive=true (last accessed May 8, 2007).

[75] Chul-eung Park, "Pyeongtaek migoon giji eejeon jiyeon-ddaen whegyo munjae bihwa" [Delay in Pyeongtaek Base Relocation May Spark into a Diplomatic Problem], *MND News Brief*, April 11, 2006. http://mnd.news.go.kr/warp/webapp/news/print_view?id=d8144dfa704233b67b8872 (last accessed May 8, 2006).

[76] Ibid.

[77] Franklin Fisher, "Protestors Stop Workers from Blocking Canals near Humphreys," *Stars and Stripes*, April 9, 2006. http://www.estripes.com/article.asp?section=104&article=35484&archive=true (last accessed June 5, 2007); and "Gookbangboo, ahb-dojeok kyungcha-lryuk dongwon-hae sooro gotgot pagoi" [MND Mobilizes Overwhelming Police Force, Canals Destroyed in Several Places], *KCPT/Village Voice*, April 7, 2006. http://www.antigizi.or.kr/zboard/view.php?id=news&page=1&sn1=&divpage=1&sn=off&ss=on&sc=on&select_arrange=headnum&desc=asc&no=137 (last accessed June 7, 2007).

[78] Dae-woong Jin, "Seoul May Halt Dialogue with Farmers over U.S. Base," *Korea Herald*, May 2, 2006.

After agreeing to dialogue, however, the MND instead went on the offensive and launched a national media campaign on May 3. The MND announced it would dispatch thousands of riot police and ROK soldiers into Daechuri village. Fearing potential public backlash by sending ROK troops (accompanied by riot police) to establish a barbed wire perimeter around the base expansion area, the MND preempted the KCPT in the national media. In a special press conference, Minister Yoon explained the current situation of the base relocation project, the reasons why riot police needed to be dispatched, and the exact nature of work ROK soldiers would be undertaking in Daechuri. Minister Yoon made clear that soldiers would be unarmed. ROK soldiers' duties were limited to erecting barbed wire around the perimeter of the expanded base land. In his briefing to the nation, Yoon outlined the history of the Yongsan relocation project and the purpose of base expansion. He then described how the MND consulted the residents numerous times about the importance and inevitability of the base relocation project. The MND was portrayed as reasonable and willing to continue dialogue with residents. In contrast, the government framed the KCPT as irresponsible radicals bent on inciting residents for their own political purposes. The MND added that the delay in base relocation caused by KCPT "outsiders" was costing South Korean taxpayers millions of dollars.

Preparing the nation for potential violence, on May 4 the MND, in a show of force, sent 2,800 engineering and infantry troops to dig trenches and set up 29 kilometers of barbed wire 2 meters in depth to prevent activists from entering the expanded base land. These troops were accompanied by 12,000 riot police. As soldiers and riot police entered Daechuri before dawn on May 4, KCPT activists in Daechuri quickly alerted their members by e-mail and telephone, mobilizing about 1,000 activists, mostly students, labor union members, farmers, and peace activists.[79] About 200 students linked arms and lay flat inside Daechuri Elementary School, the makeshift headquarters of the KCPT. As morning approached, riot police physically removed hundreds of activists and students barricading themselves inside KCPT headquarters and bulldozed the building. As soldiers were setting up the barbed wire fence, several activists managed to break through the perimeter and began beating unprotected soldiers with bamboo poles. About 120 police, soldiers, and protestors were injured and 524 students and activists were detained in the two-day fiasco.[80] Of those detained, no Daechuri residents were taken into custody. The MND used this information to support their claim that the conflict stemmed from the "outside forces" of the KCPT rather than local residents.

---

[79] Yoon-hyeong Kil, "Yeong won hi dole kilsoo eobs eulee: jak jeon meong yeo myeong ui hwang sae ul" [The Point of No Return: Operation "Hwangs-ae-ul at Dawn"], *Hankyoreh* 21, May 16, 2005, 14.

[80] Joo-hee Lee, "Cheong Wa Dae Says No More Delays to Pyeongtaek Base Plan," *Korea Herald*, May 6, 2006; and *Yonhap News Agency*, "Pyeongtaek migun giji haeng-jeong daejibhaeng daechi naheuljjae" [Fourth Day of Pyeongtaek Anti-Base Protest], *Chosun Ilbo*, May 7, 2006.

The violence in Pyeongtaek, instigated primarily by student activists who were not necessarily KCPT members, was a devastating blow to the anti-base movement. The MND and conservative mainstream media capitalized on the violence, claiming how activists had beaten unprotected soldiers who were merely engaged in manual labor.[81] Consequently, the general public held anti-base and anti-American activists responsible for the violence in Pyeongtaek. Public opinion polls released by the prime minister's office indicated that 81.4 percent of Koreans were against the protestors' use of violence and 65.8 percent opposed NGO and civic group involvement in the relocation issue.[82] Moreover, rifts within the anti-base movement began to widen as more moderate civic groups and NGOs began to distance themselves from the radical core of the KCPT.[83]

With its remaining resources, the KCPT attempted to mobilize one last major stand. The coalition group organized a candlelight vigil in Seoul on May 13 and a protest in Pyeongtaek on May 14 to denounce the stationing of 8,000 riot police in Daechuri and the violence "sanctioned" by government forces the previous week. In another display of power and resolve, the government sent 18,000 riot police to Daechuri. To prevent any activists from entering Daechuri, the government blocked off all roads into the village, establishing four different checkpoints. With the exception of Daechuri residents, government officials, and mainstream media, nobody was allowed to enter the village. As one resident lamented, the entire village had been put under de facto martial law.[84] Unable to enter the village, the 5,000 activists who came in support of the KCPT and Daechuri residents ended up protesting either at the train station or in a village adjacent to Daechuri. Aside from a few scuffles, the protest in general remained peaceful. The government managed to subdue the KCPT, both physically and mentally, and cut it off from any of the national support the activists desperately sought.

After the May 4–5 incident, the office of the Blue House and prime minister stepped forward in response to the violent clashes and the delay in the relocation process. The Blue House issued a statement after the clash, reaffirming its support for USFK base relocation and expansion. Noting that the eviction of residents was inevitable, the Blue House stated, "Hereafter, the base relocation project must progress without any more setbacks to avoid further losses to the

---

[81] Seok-woo Lee, "2m jookbong gong-gyeok. Goon-sok youngji choso buswu" [Attack with 2m Bamboo Sticks . . . Destroys Soldiers' Quarters], *Chosun Ilbo*, May 6, 2006. http://news.chosun. com/site/data/html_dir/2006/05/06/2006050670021.html (last access June 29, 2007).

[82] Dae-woong Jin, "Government Warns against Protests," *Korea Herald*, May 12, 2006.

[83] PSPD Press Conference, "Pyeongtaek migun giji hawk jang eul dulleossan gal deunge daehan simin sahoe-ui ibjang gwa je eon" [Civil Society's Position on the Conflict Regarding U.S. Base Expansion in Pyeongtaek], Seoul Press Center, 7th floor, May 10, 2006. http://www. peoplepower21.org/article/article_view.php?article_id=16661.

[84] Not even public transportation was allowed to enter the village. I walked 8 km and, to the bewilderment of activists, through all four checkpoints to enter the village that day. Ironically, the peace activist "guarding" the entrance to the village also requested identification, and it was not until I contacted Father Mun that I was given clearance into the village.

national interest."[85] Presidential spokesman Jung Tae-ho also made similar statements, again citing the delay's diplomatic and economic costs and the importance of base relocation for the U.S.-ROK alliance.[86]

Fearing another clash between police and protestors, Prime Minister Han Myeong-sook, herself a former activist, issued a much anticipated public statement in a live national broadcast. In her televised speech, she expressed regret and sadness for the previous weeks' violence and sympathy and concern for residents forced to relocate. Her message implored activists to use restraint and to express differences in opinions in a legitimate and peaceful manner. However, taking the same position as the MND and Blue House, Prime Minister Han reiterated the importance of the base relocation project in maintaining positive bilateral relations with the United States. Prime Minister Han declared, "Fellow citizens, as you know well, from the Korean War up until today, our alliance with the United States has been the basis of our national security, national defense, and economic development. The firm preservation of the ROK-U.S. alliance is necessary for our society and country's stability and development."[87] Emanating from the prime minister's office rather than the MND or MOFAT, the statement signified the seriousness of the South Korean government in pushing ahead with base relocation.

Denouement

The Pyeongtaek issue carried the attention of the national media for the next month. The prime minister also met with activist leaders in mid-May to discuss peaceful resolutions to the Pyeongtaek issue. Other than agreeing to restraint and nonviolence, however, the core differences between the government and activists remained the same. On June 5, Kim Jitae, Daechuri village head and chair of the Residents' Committee, turned himself in to local authorities as a condition for resuming talks between residents and the South Korean government. The government wanted to question Kim regarding his alleged role in fomenting illegal protests. Rather than being released after questioning, however, Kim was arrested and placed in prison until December 28. Kim's arrest dealt an incredible moral blow to the local residents. Although anti-base protests continued, by June 2006, various umbrella coalition groups, particularly the labor and farmers' groups, had shifted almost entirely away from the anti-base movement to prepare for protests against the upcoming U.S.–South Korea FTA negotiations.

[85] "Chungwahdae 'giji eejeon chajil obsi chujin-dwhe-ya'" [Blue House: "Base Relocation Must Progress without Setbacks], *Yonhap News Agency*, May 5, 2006.

[86] Joo-hee Lee, "Cheong Wa Dae Says No More Delays to Pyeongtaek Base Plan," *Korea Herald*, May 6, 2006.

[87] Transcript of Prime Minister Han Myeong-sook's national address, Seoul, South Korea, May 12, 2006. Available at http://www.chosun.com/politics/news/200605/200605120148.html.

The government again sent around 15,000 riot police on September 13 to destroy empty homes where activists and the handful of residents were residing.[88] In October 2006, workers began to level the land for construction as the government continued negotiating with the residents. The South Korean government and Daechuri residents finally signed an agreement on February 13, 2007, with the residents agreeing to move out by March 31 to nearby Paengseong Nowhari. With the village residents' decision made independently from the KCPT, the KCPT put forth a statement stating they would respect the agreement. However, the anti-base struggle, which had focused on Daechuri up to this point, now needed a new direction.[89]

The Pyeongtaek episode demonstrates the constraining role of the security consensus for South Korean anti-base movements in the politics of overseas military bases. The security consensus held by host-state elites created a situation where the South Korean government needed to balance its alliance obligations to the United States while staving off domestic pressure from anti-base movements. Responding to this dilemma, the South Korean government chose to drag its feet and temporarily delay the process of base expansion while co-opting local residents. Although it was the KCPT's residential "sit-in" that effectively blocked the MND from physically taking over the land for base expansion, the delay itself was a strategic response from the MND. The MND was aware that delaying the process in its interaction with the KCPT and residents, particularly through the winter, would keep the residents at bay without necessarily strengthening anti-base forces. However, foot-dragging for an extended period also raised diplomatic costs with the United States. Given the initial USFK transformation time line to relocate Yongsan Garrison and the 2nd Infantry Division to Camp Humphreys by 2008, the South Korean government did not want to jeopardize its alliance relations with the United States.[90] Thus the MND shifted tactics in April 2006. It used overwhelming power to block off protestors from the designated base expansion land and co-opted local residents while isolating national civic groups. Meanwhile, the use of radical tactics, which were effective in the 2000 Maehyangri anti-base movement, backfired for the KCPT. The MND's media campaign launched against anti-base movements after violent clashes on May 4–5, and its strategic efforts to isolate activists by only negotiating with residents, ultimately led to the devolution of the movement.

[88] Min-jung Lee and Hong-gi Ahn, "Doduri 32 chae modu cheolguh" [32 Buildings in Doduri All Destroyed], *OhMyNews*, September 12, 2006. http://www.ohmynews.com/articleview/article_view. asp?at_code=359437&ar_seq=2 (last accessed June 4, 2007); *Yonhap News Agency*, "Pyeongtaek binjib cheolguh" [Empty Houses in Pyeongtaek Destroyed], *Chosun Ilbo*, September 12, 2006. http:// news.chosun.com/site/data/html_dir/2006/09/13/2006091360124.html (last accessed June 4, 2007).
[89] See KCPT bulletin board, "KCPT Planned Project for 2007," February 13, 2007. http://www. antigizi.or.kr/zboard/zboard.php?id=notice&no=696 (last accessed June 28, 2007).
[90] Base relocation has now been pushed back to 2014.

CONCLUSION

Working under the constraints of a resilient elite security consensus, South Korean anti-base movements were relatively limited in their efforts to institute change in basing policy outcomes. Even though South Korean elites experienced some disagreement over policies related to the U.S. alliance, for the most part, the foreign policy and national security establishments continued to value the alliance and U.S. military presence. Similar to Japan and Italy, a strong consensus persisted, in part because the consensus had become embedded within domestic institutions and ideologies favoring close security ties to the United States. Additionally, an elite security consensus provided stability to U.S. basing arrangements, despite South Korea's democratization in the late 1980s. Consequently, the elite consensus challenged activists' ability to penetrate the state and form ties with influential elites. Thus, on the policy front, anti-base movements were unsuccessful in bringing about any significant changes to USFK basing decisions.

6

Alliance Relations and the Security Consensus Across Time

The previous chapters demonstrated how the degree of security consensus influenced basing policy outcomes by shaping the patterns of interaction between the host government, anti-base movements, and the United States. By process-tracing events in a single movement episode, the case examples provided a snapshot of anti-base movements in the Philippines, Japan, Italy, Ecuador, and South Korea. However, as snapshots in time, the security consensus assumed a fixed quality.

If the security consensus were to strengthen or weaken over time, would we expect variations in anti-base movement outcomes? For instance, how would increasing security ties between the Philippines and the United States in their fight against terrorism impact protests against the U.S. military presence in the southern Philippines? What if commonly shared beliefs about the U.S. alliance among South Korean political elites dissolved, with key elites advocating closer alignment with China? What if Japanese leaders decided to pursue a more independent security policy, resulting in an erosion of a previously strong security consensus? Based on the security consensus framework, activists should find it much more difficult to influence base policy outcomes if key elites coalesce more tightly around a security policy centered on the United States. Conversely, anti-base movements are more likely to have an impact on policy as the security consensus weakens.

Expanding the analysis to compare anti-base movement episodes across different time periods is important on two accounts. First, it allows us to test the robustness of the theory by adding within-country case comparisons. Shifts in the security consensus over time should lead to different configurations of state–society interaction, thus producing different policy outcomes over time. Second, a diachronic analysis highlights the predictive value of the security consensus framework. For example, under conditions of a weakened security consensus, we expect greater movement success as patterns of interaction between activists and security policymakers move from confrontation to greater cooperation. Conversely, even with a spike in anti-base movement opposition, base policies should remain unchanged if host-nation political elites continue to accept the U.S. alliance and U.S. bases as part of its greater national interest.

In this chapter, I examine the microfoundations of an elite security consensus to discuss both change and continuity in the consensus over time. I then explore how variation in the security consensus over time alters movement and government strategies, hence leading to different policy outcomes. I return to the Philippines and Japan/Okinawa in a paired comparison to demonstrate why the prospects for Philippine anti-base movement effectiveness decreased over time but remained fairly constant in Okinawa.

CONTINUITY AND CHANGE IN THE SECURITY CONSENSUS

Elites' perceptions of national security and their understanding of the U.S. alliance do not change overnight. As discussed in Chapter 1, institutional and ideational factors underlying the security consensus give the concept an inherent stickiness. Nevertheless, elite perceptions and beliefs about national security, and more specifically bilateral security alliances and U.S. bases, are mutable. What factors result in shifts in the security consensus? Specifically, what exogenous or endogenous changes alter political elites' perceptions and beliefs about the U.S. security alliance?

In Chapter 1, I argued that external threat perceptions bear significant weight in the formation and persistence of the elite consensus. In addition to material capabilities, threat perceptions are informed by domestic and ideational variables such as identity, ideology, and historical legacies. This suggests that ideational factors indirectly shape the security consensus via threat perceptions. However, factors such as historical legacies, beliefs, ideology, and domestic institutions may also directly feed into and reinforce the security consensus. Hence, a shift in any one or combination of these factors could potentially lead to shifts in the security consensus.

Continuity

Although the security consensus may shift for numerous reasons, a change in one particular variable does not necessarily produce a shift in the security consensus. The security consensus does not shift easily for two reasons. First, subfactors that provide depth to the security consensus, such as institutions, historical legacies, and ideology/identity, are themselves not easily mutable. For instance, historical legacies do not easily fade, even if they are reinterpreted over time, nor is their impact necessarily mitigated by generational change. As an example, Chinese leaders continue to invoke the hundred years of humiliation instigated by Western imperialism. The legacy of Nazi fascism also profoundly shapes how German political elites think about security policy and foreign affairs.[1] Thus, historical legacies and collective memory continue to shape the worldview of foreign policy elites and their interactions with the outside world.

---

[1] Thomas U. Berger, *Cultures of Antimilitarism: National Security in Germany and Japan* (Baltimore: The Johns Hopkins University Press, 1998).

Likewise, institutions, embedded with well-known beliefs and practices, do not easily change. The path-dependent logic of institutions enables policy continuity, even when elites are confronted with environmental change.[2] Of course, if we acknowledge that institutions are placed within "concrete temporal processes," as argued by historical institutionalists, change is plausible.[3] However, this implies a slow evolutionary process rather than sudden transformation.

Second, because the security consensus hinges on collective perceptions and ideas, a consensus, by definition, tends to be rigid. A shift in the consensus requires a shift in the ideas, beliefs, or perceptions of numerous individuals. If a large number of powerful elites all hold vested interests in maintaining the security consensus, one or two individuals transmitting alternative ideas will not easily shatter the existing order of beliefs. In short, the intersubjective nature of the security consensus provides the concept with a degree of stability over time.

Change

If shared perceptions and collective beliefs are relatively "sticky," what brings about change in the security consensus? I argued earlier that the variables that constitute the microfoundations of the security consensus are not easily mutable. But they do change. And like other ideational variables, the security consensus can shift over time. As suggested earlier, shifts often occur gradually. A change in external threat perceptions is the most obvious place to look when examining shifts in the security consensus. Elite attitudes and beliefs about bilateral alliances are likely to shift with changes in threat perceptions. This logic is supported by the correlation between threat perceptions and alliance durability found in the quantitative alliance literature.[4] A change in threat perceptions may itself be triggered by changes in the structural environment and shifts in the balance of power. For example, growing U.S. military and economic superiority over the Soviet Union by the mid-1980s corresponded with shifts in beliefs and attitudes about the Soviet threat. Germany's rapid rise at the turn of the century also heightened British threat perceptions. Faced with the German challenge to British naval superiority, British leaders warmed to the idea of an alliance with France. Casting aside their colonial bickering, the two sides signed the *Entente Cordiale* in 1904.

Shifts in the elite consensus may also be produced by domestic and institutional changes within the target state. Challenging structural accounts, Mark Haas argues that U.S. leaders' beliefs about the Cold War corresponded closely

---

[2] Mark Blyth, "The Transformation of the Swedish Model: Economic Ideas, Distributional Conflict, and Institutional Change," *World Politics* 54, no. 1 (2001): 1–26 at 4.

[3] Kathleen Thelen, "Historical Institutionalism in Comparative Politics," *Annual Review of Political Science* 2 (1999): 369–404 at 369.

[4] See Scott Bennett, "Testing Alternative Models of Alliance Duration, 1816–1984," *American Journal of Political Science* 41, no. 3 (1997): 846–78; and Brett Ashley Leeds and Burcu Savun, "Terminating Alliances: Why Do States Abrogate Agreements?" *Journal of Politics* 69, no. 4 (2007): 1118–32.

with domestic-ideological and institutional changes within the Soviet Union. Thus U.S. policymakers' belief that the Cold War had ended stemmed from their perception of Mikhail Gorbachev's reforms and his commitment to political liberalism.[5] Change within the system of internal political governance may also alter the relative strength of the security consensus among elites, and therefore elite attitudes toward alliance partners. For instance, regime change may bring leaders with a different set of beliefs and ideology into power. If ideology draws alliance partners together, regime change may potentially weaken (or strengthen) the security consensus among elites, leading to a new phase in alliance relations, or new alliance configurations altogether.[6] Regime change may also facilitate institutional shifts that alter elites' understanding of national security and U.S. relations over time.[7]

Although change is usually gradual, external shocks or major events, such as the collapse of the Cold War or the terrorist attacks of 9/11, function as critical points leading to shifts in the consensus. These "shocks" may cause elites to recalibrate (or, in extreme cases, fundamentally alter) their existing beliefs and perceptions about national security and the value of the U.S. alliance.[8] For instance, Chinese aggression in the Taiwan Straits or a successful North Korean nuclear test would likely strengthen the security consensus among host-government elites in the Asia-Pacific region.[9] Other "shocks," such as Korean reunification or Chinese democratization, on the other hand, would potentially weaken the security consensus with the reduced need for forward-deployed bases in the region.

Returning to anti-base movements in the Philippines and Okinawa, one should keep in mind that at any given moment elite ideas and perceptions regarding security relations with the United States and the U.S. military presence will vary slightly as a result of domestic politics, administration changes, international events, or shifts in the material environment. Of course, institutional and ideational constraints prevent the security consensus from roller-coasting erratically from strong to weak in a short span of time. However, evidence suggests that the security consensus among Philippine elites has strengthened since the closure of Subic Bay Naval Station in 1992. Meanwhile, Japanese support for

---

[5] Haas, *Ideological Origins of Great Power Politics*, 146.

[6] Leeds and Savun, "Terminating Alliances," 1121. The record here is mixed. Leeds and Savun do find a correlation between regime change and alliance termination, whereas other scholars, such as Bennett, do not. (See Bennett, "Testing Alternative Models of Alliance Duration.")

[7] In cases such as Italy or South Korea, the security consensus persisted despite regime change. Although regime change may alter the strength of the security consensus, it is neither a necessary nor a sufficient condition.

[8] Jeffrey Legro presents a more nuanced theory explaining how shocks lead to new thinking, or in this case a shift in the security consensus. Applying Legro's theory to my argument, if an external shock shatters the existing consensus and elites are able to consolidate around an alternative idea, a new consensus emerges. See Legro, *Rethinking the World*, 14.

[9] Shocks are more likely to produce conditions that immediately strengthen rather than weaken the security consensus. On the other hand, the security consensus is more likely to weaken gradually rather than abruptly.

the U.S. military presence has remained relatively strong since the mid-1990s despite more recent events within Japanese domestic politics that suggest elite divisions and a potential weakening of the security consensus.

RISING ELITE SECURITY CONSENSUS IN THE PHILIPPINES

As argued in Chapter 2, Philippine elites were divided in their position regarding U.S. bases and the future of U.S.-Philippine relations in 1991. Contributing to the lack of consensus was the popular belief that U.S. bases no longer played an important role in Philippine national security given the internal nature of security threats.[10] Yet, by the end of the decade, the majority of Philippine political elites eagerly awaited the return of U.S. "visiting forces." If elite discourse suggested a weak security consensus in the early 1990s, how did a consensus linking national security priorities with the U.S. alliance reemerge by the end of the decade? Why did Philippine elites, including several senators who voted to oust the Americans in 1991, later come to embrace the return of U.S. forces and strengthened security ties?

Several related issues transpired in the decade after Subic Bay Naval Station's closure that helped solidify the importance of the U.S. security alliance. First, the heavy financial burden of the Armed Forces of the Philippines (AFP) modernization program sent Manila scouring for additional economic assistance. Second, the Philippines faced increasing threats to national security in the late 1990s. A greater sense of vulnerability triggered by Chinese adventurism in the Spratly Islands increased the salience of external threats in the Philippines. Additionally, the Philippines experienced an upsurge in internal insurgencies from communists and Muslim separatist groups in the late 1990s. Increased threat perceptions and the demands of military modernization catalyzed the revival of U.S.-Philippine security relations in the late 1990s. New alliance commitments and an increasing U.S. military presence in the Philippines were institutionalized through the Visiting Forces Agreement (VFA), ratified by the Philippine Senate in 1999, and the Mutual Logistics Support Agreement (MLSA) in November 2002. If U.S.-Philippine relations had not warmed enough by the beginning of the twenty-first century, 9/11 and the global war on terror sealed the revitalized alliance by further consolidating elite support. Figure 6.1, based on my own qualitative assessment of U.S.-Philippine relations, provides an estimate of general trends in the security consensus after 1991.[11]

---

[10] Renato Cruz de Castro, "Twenty-First Century Philippine-American Security Relations: Managing an Alliance in the War of the Third Kind," *Asian Security* 2, no. 2 (2006): 102–21 at 107.

[11] My estimates are based on Philippine elite public statements, interviews, and a review of the secondary literature on Philippine national security. Granted, the concept of the security consensus is not easily quantifiable. However, this figure and other similar figures in this chapter are used only as heuristics to illustrate how the security consensus framework operates over time.

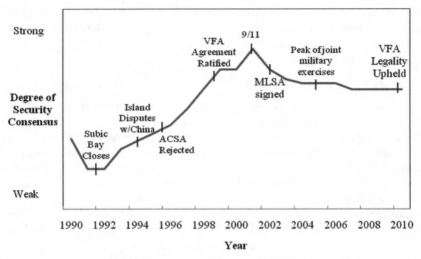

FIGURE 6.1. Security Consensus over Time in the Philippines.

The following sections describe in greater detail how an elite consensus regarding U.S.-Philippine security relations evolved following the withdrawal of U.S. forces in 1991.

AFP Modernization

U.S.-Philippine relations hit an all-time low after the Philippine Senate booted the Americans off the islands. Snubbed by the Philippines, the United States downgraded its political and military relations with Manila. With the loss of the U.S. security umbrella, the Philippines needed to quickly modernize its military.[12] To fill the security void, the Philippine government passed the Philippine Modernization Act in February 1995. The military modernization program shifted more emphasis toward external defense with military hardware and weapons systems upgrades for the Philippine Navy and Air Force.[13] After much wrangling in the Philippine Congress over the AFP's proposed budget, the Philippine government passed the AFP Modernization Act (Republic Act 7898) in February 1995. The Act proposed 331.62 billion pesos (about $13.24 billion in 1996 dollars) over a fifteen-year period for military modernization.

Even after the passage of Republic Act 7898, a new round of debate ensued about whether the Philippine economy could sustain such a hefty increase in

---

[12] The 1951 U.S.-Philippine Mutual Defense Treaty still remained in effect, however.
[13] The government planned to purchase fighter jets, air defense radar, offshore patrol vessels, and amphibious landing transport ships. See Renato Cruz de Castro, "Societal Forces as Sources of Military Doctrine and Posture: The Case of the AFP Modernization Program, 1991–2003," in *Asia in the New Millennium: APISA First Congress Proceedings*, edited by Amitav Acharya and Cai To Lee (Singapore: Marshall Cavendish International, 2004), 207.

military spending. Philippine legislators, concluding that the Philippine government would be unable to finance the modernization bill in its entirety, proposed a budget limit of 170 billion pesos. The Philippine Congress and the AFP finally reached a compromise and divided the modernization program into two subprograms. The appropriated budget would only cover subprogram 1, which would receive 164.55 billion pesos to develop the AFP's core capabilities.[14] Congress also set a ceiling of 50 billion pesos (about $2 billion in 1996 dollars) for the first five years of the fifteen-year program.[15] Just as the AFP and Congress ironed out cost issues, the Asian financial crisis presented a new challenge to military modernization. The peso depreciated by nearly 40 percent against the U.S. dollar, requiring the Air Force and Navy to suspend several weapons orders such as fighter planes and offshore patrol vessels.[16]

Increased Threats

Coincidentally, it was the conflict with China in the Spratly Islands that strengthened the Philippine government's resolve for military modernization. Tensions flared in February 1995 when the Chinese navy occupied Mischief Reef, territory in the Spratly Islands group claimed by the Philippines. In response to the construction of an alleged military outpost,[17] President Fidel Ramos dispatched warships and fighter jets to the area. The following month, the AFP seized several fishing boats, detaining sixty-two Chinese fishermen.[18] Although both sides sought diplomatic solutions to resolve the conflict, the Philippines remained wary of Chinese intentions in the South China Sea. Further sightings of Chinese naval vessels in the region, and the construction of a helicopter landing pad for the People's Liberation Army in 1997, continued to fuel tensions. Philippine policymakers now identified China as the primary long-term security threat.[19]

In addition to external threats posed by China, the Philippines faced an upsurge in several internal insurgencies in the late 1990s. Until at least 1995, the number of communist insurgents had been declining from a peak of 25,000 guerillas in 1988 to a low of 5,000 in 1995.[20] The number of Muslim

---

[14] AFP Modernization Program Management Office, *Armed Forces of the Philippines Modernization Program Primer* (Manila: AFP, n.d.). Information also available at http://www.afpmodernization.mil.ph/ (last accessed July 30, 2010).

[15] Congress of the Republic of the Philippines, Tenth Congress, Second Regular Session, Joint Resolution No. 28, "Joint resolution expressing the approval by both houses of congress of Republic Act No. 7898," December 19, 1996.

[16] De Castro, "Societal Forces as Sources of Military Doctrine and Posture," 210.

[17] China claimed the platforms were intended to provide shelter for fishermen.

[18] Philip Shenon, "Rival Claims to Island Chain Bring Edginess to Asia's Rim," *New York Times*, April 5, 1995, Section A-11, Column 1.

[19] Renato Cruz de Castro, "The Revitalized Philippine-U.S. Security Relations: A Ghost from the Cold War or an Alliance for the 21st Century?" *Asian Survey* 43, no. 6 (2003): 971–88 at 977.

[20] Morrison, *Asia Pacific Security Outlook 1997*, 97.

separatists had also declined sharply from approximately 26,000 fighters in 1987 to around 14,000 in 1991.[21] However, this trend reversed in the mid- to late 1990s. The number of NPA forces steadily increased, reaching 11,930 members in 2001. The number of guerilla fronts also expanded from fifty-eight in 1995 to seventy in 2000.[22] Regarding Muslim separatist groups, the Moro Islamic Liberation Front (MILF), a splinter group of the Moro National Liberation Front (MNLF), increased their level of violence, engaging in full-blown combat against the AFP by the end of the decade. Although MILF numbers continued to increase, a new Muslim separatist group, the Abu Sayyaf, posed an even greater security risk. Operating as a transnational network, the Abu Sayyaf successfully plotted several bombings and kidnappings in the southern Philippines.

In light of rising external threats and heightened internal disorder, improved security ties with the United States suddenly looked appealing. To Philippine elites, the Mischief Reef incident signaled revisionist intentions behind China's rise as a major regional power. If previously lost in impassioned debates against U.S. bases, Philippine elites now recognized the important balancing role served by the U.S. military presence in Asia. A renewed defense commitment between the two countries acted as a hedging strategy against Chinese incursion into the Spratlys. Furthermore, Philippine counterthreats against China rang hollow given the dismal state of the Philippine military. Thus, strengthening security ties with the United States offered a quick resource boost to the underfinanced, poorly equipped AFP.[23] Military assistance from the United States could also be directed against the communist and Muslim separatist insurgencies, freeing resources for AFP modernization.

To revive the U.S.-Philippine security alliance, officials began negotiating an agreement in 1996 that would legally enable U.S. troops and ships to operate on Philippine territory. After two years of negotiations, Washington and Manila signed the Visiting Forces Agreement (VFA) in 1998. Most immediately, the VFA guaranteed legal status to U.S. troops partaking in joint military exercises in the Philippines. In a mutually beneficial move, the VFA functioned as a means for Washington to help develop the AFP's operational strategy and create joint operability between the two forces. The VFA also opened access to air and naval facilities in the Philippines, facilitating rapid deployment of U.S. troops in the event of a crisis. The Philippine Senate subsequently ratified the VFA in 1999. The agreement not only permitted U.S. troops to take part in large-scale training exercises such as the *Balikatan* exercises in early 2000 but arranged a new framework for AFP modernization.[24]

---

[21] Ibid., 98.

[22] de Castro, "Twenty-First Century Philippine-American Security Relations," 109.

[23] de Castro, "Revitalized Philippine-U.S. Security Relations," 977–78.

[24] Ibid., 979. *Balikatan*, translated as "shoulder-to-shoulder," are annual joint exercises to improve combat planning, combat readiness, and interoperability in support of the 1951 Mutual Defense Treaty. The exercises had been suspended since 1993 but resumed in 2000 with 2,500 U.S. troops.

9/11 and the Global War on Terror

If events and circumstances in the late 1990s helped mend U.S.-Philippine relations, 9/11 provided the ideological glue. As the first Asian state to support the Bush administration's global war on terror, the Philippines immediately pledged to grant overflight rights and logistical support. In a State Department broadcast, Assistant Secretary of State James Kelly praised the Philippines for its "early, principled, and unequivocal support to the international fight against terrorism."[25] A joint statement produced during President Arroyo's November 2001 meeting with President Bush in Washington affirmed that both countries would "work on a vigorous, integrated plan to strengthen the Philippine security forces' capacity to combat terror and protect Philippine sovereignty."[26] The joint statement continued by offering an integrated plan that would "include a robust training package, equipment needed for increased mobility, a maintenance program to enhance overall capabilities, specific targeted law enforcement and counterterrorism cooperation, and a new bilateral defense consultative mechanism."[27] Bush also pledged to promote a tenfold increase in Foreign Military Financing (FMF) to $19 million for fiscal year 2002, an additional $10 million in military goods and services to assist the AFP, and another $10 million to support counterterrorism and law enforcement assistance.[28] Figure 6.2 indicates the amount of U.S. economic and military assistance given to the Philippines from 1993 to 2008. The two spikes beginning in the late 1990s and early 2000 roughly coincide with the onset of VFA negotiations and the war on terror, respectively.

Figure 6.3 provides a list of the number of publicly known joint military exercises between the U.S. military and the AFP, indicating the greater extent of military cooperation since the passage of the VFA.

In early 2002, 600 U.S. troops and special operations force members began training and conducting joint operations with the AFP to combat the Abu Sayyaf. After Afghanistan, the deployment to the southern Philippines marked the single largest deployment of U.S. forces in the war on terror since 9/11.[29] The impact of joint counterterrorist efforts received widespread praise after Philippine forces, with the assistance of the U.S. military, killed top Abu Sayyaf leader Abu Sabaya in a firefight. Abu Sabaya had masterminded the kidnapping of dozens of foreigners, including an American missionary couple in 2001.

---

[25] United States Department of State, Office of International Information Programs, "U.S. Official Praises Philippine Anti-Terrorism Effort," November 16, 2001. Available at http://www.global-security.org/military/library/news/2001/11/mil-011117-usia03.htm (last accessed March 4, 2008).

[26] White House, Office of the Press Secretary, "Joint Statement between the United States of America and the Republic of the Philippines," November 20, 2001. http://www.whitehouse.gov/news/releases/2001/11/20011120-13.html (last accessed March 4, 2008).

[27] Ibid.

[28] Ibid.

[29] Eric Schmitt, "U.S. and Philippines Setting Up Joint Operations to Fight Terror," *New York Times*, January 15, 2001, Section A-2, 1.

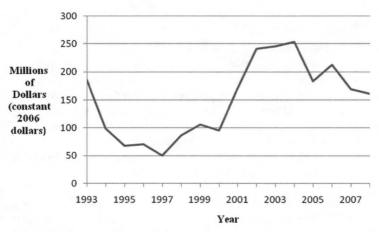

FIGURE 6.2. U.S. Military and Economic Assistance to the Philippines. *Source:* U.S. Agency for International Development (USAID), "U.S. overseas loans and grants." http:// gbk.eads.usaidallnet.gov/data/.

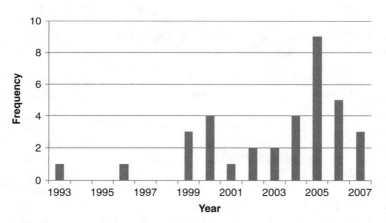

FIGURE 6.3. Number of Joint Military Exercises between the U.S. Military and the Armed Forces of the Philippines. *Source:* Docena, *At the Door of All the East*, 54–56.

By 2003, the fight against terrorism had cemented alliance relations, adding a new level of depth to the security consensus. In the first official state visit of a U.S. president to Manila in over 30 years, President Bush and President Macapagal-Arroyo confirmed that "the U.S.-Philippine partnership (had) taken on new vitality and importance in the context of the global war on terrorism."[30] This

---

[30] Republic of the Philippines, Malacanang Palace, Office of the Press Secretary, "Joint Statement between the Republic of the Philippines and the United States of America," October 18, 2003.

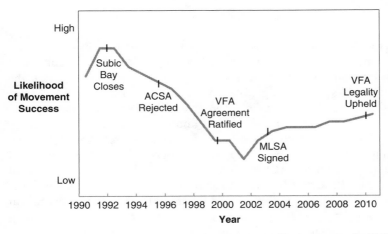

FIGURE 6.4. Probability of Anti-Base Movement Effectiveness in the Philippines.

echoed an earlier meeting in Washington where Bush reaffirmed the U.S. commitment to support the Philippines in destroying terrorist networks. In a joint statement, both sides confirmed that "the U.S.-Philippine security partnership has never been healthier."[31]

The shift in elite attitudes favoring a stronger U.S.-Philippine alliance was not limited to just a few elites at the top. Unlike in 1991, a widespread consensus existed within both the executive and legislative branches of government. This consensus was reflected in Manila's response to civil societal opposition against the VFA.[32] Although activists sustained numerous large, vocal protests against the VFA for over a year, very few elites were sympathetic to anti-VFA activist demands. Elites repeatedly stated that the VFA tied directly into the Philippines' national interest. The strong consensus favoring ratification of the VFA, and hence a strengthened U.S.-Philippine alliance, made it difficult for activists to gain any real traction in the VFA debate. As the security consensus solidified among Philippine elites, the likelihood of anti-base movement success declined in the late 1990s. This relationship is highlighted in Figure 6.4.

As with Figure 6.1, Figure 6.4 is a simple notional chart and only intended to demonstrate, ceteris paribus, the negative relationship between the strength of the security consensus and anti-base movement effectiveness in influencing basing policy outcomes. The following sections elaborate on how the shift in the political environment affected anti-base movements in the late 1990s.

---

[31] White House, Office of the Press Secretary, "Joint Statement between the United States of America and the Republic of the Philippines," May 19, 2003. http://www.whitehouse.gov/news/releases/2003/05/20030519-3.html (last accessed March 5, 2008).

[32] Although the anti-VFA protest was not directed against U.S. military bases, the arguments used by activists were similar to those found in anti-base protests. The VFA related directly to the U.S. military presence in the Philippines. Many activists also feared that the VFA would eventually lead to the return of permanent bases.

Anti-VFA Protests

Anti-base activists did not disappear with the closure of U.S. bases in 1992. Groups instrumental to the movement, such as Bayan and NFPC, continued their resistance against the U.S. military under new formations. For example, the NFPC helped establish a new organization, the People's Task Force for Bases Cleanup (PTFBC), to address environmental damages at the Subic Bay and Clark bases. In November 1994, the NFPC and other organizations, such as the League of Filipino Students, Gabriela, and Bayan, organized a rally during President Clinton's visit to the Philippines to oppose the Acquisition and Cross-Servicing Agreement (ACSA).[33] Although President Fidel Ramos and Foreign Secretary Roberto Romulo favored ACSA, the Senate viewed the proposal suspiciously. Senator Tañada and Senator Mercado (now the chair of the Defense Committee), who had voted "no" to bases earlier, questioned how the Philippine government could permit foreign troops and facilities to enter the Philippines without a treaty covering legal arrangements.[34] Proposals potentially suggesting the return of U.S. forces continued to evoke negative reactions among a significant number of elites. The Philippine government eventually rejected ACSA.[35]

Anti-base (or anti–U.S. military) groups mobilized in a similar fashion against the VFA. Mobilization took place as early as 1996, when rumors first circulated about possible negotiations granting U.S. troops legal status on Philippine soil. The NFPC again played a pivotal role, initiating the anti-VFA movement with Free Legal Assistance of Government (FLAG). After Manila and Washington signed "VFA-1,"[36] anti-VFA groups escalated their efforts as negotiations for "VFA-2" entered full swing. Political, social, and religious groups, led by Bayan, formed a broad coalition group known as "Junk VFA" to persuade the Senate not to ratify the VFA.[37] Activists held anti-VFA rallies and protests nearly weekly as the date of Senate deliberations edged closer.

---

[33] The proposed ACSA permitted the United States entry into Philippine ports to refuel and resupply ships. The United States could also spend up to $12 million on supplies and parts. See Daniel Boone Schirmer, *U.S. Bases by Another Name: ACSA in the Philippines* (Brooklyn, N.Y.: Philippines Bases Network, 1995), 7.

[34] Ibid.

[35] De Castro, "Revitalized Philippine-U.S. Security Relations," 977.

[36] "VFA 1" prescribes the legal status of U.S. troops in the Philippines. However, the Philippine government insisted that the VFA also address issues of reciprocity for Philippine defense and military officials visiting the United States. Thus, the two sides added a counterpart agreement – "VFA 2" – that guaranteed Filipino military personnel visiting the United States the same legal rights prescribed to U.S. military personnel training in the Philippines. See Republic of the Philippines, Department of Foreign Affairs, *The Visiting Forces Agreement (A Primer)* (Manila: Department of Foreign Affairs, 1998), 19.

[37] NFPC Secretary Cora Valdez-Fabros notes that a separate anti-VFA coalition, No to VFA, also formed as a result of ideological differences with members of Junk VFA. No to VFA was represented largely by the "rejectionist," or RJ, strand of the political left. The RJs splintered from the CPP in the early 1990s, rejecting the basic principles of Marxist-Leninist-Maoist

Protests took place on July 13, 1998, as Philippine negotiators under the new Estrada administration met their U.S. counterparts. Activists also planned a succession of protests near the U.S. Embassy to coincide with Secretary of State Madeline Albright's visit on July 21. Defense Secretary William Cohen was given the same courtesy a month later when activists protested outside AFP headquarters during his visit. In September, the Kilusansa Pambansang Demokrasya (KPD) rallied outside the Senate building and organized a caravan march from the former grounds of Clark Air Base to Subic Bay. The Junk VFA movement sponsored two days of protests in Manila and several other cities throughout the Philippines on September 15–16 to coincide with the date of the Senate's rejection of U.S. bases in 1991.[38] Protests continued throughout early 1999 as the Senate held VFA hearings. Activists highlighted the adverse social and environmental impact of even "visiting" troops, which they charged to be an affront to Philippine sovereignty.[39] Above all, activists feared that the VFA would eventually lead to the permanent stationing of U.S. troops and the return of permanent bases.[40]

State–Society Interaction

Similar to the base treaty in 1991, the VFA required ratification in the Philippine Senate. Before opening the VFA debate to the entire Senate, the VFA was sent to the Senate Foreign Relations Committee and the National Defense and Security Committee for their recommendation. Between January 26 and March 11, 1999, the Defense and the Foreign Relations Committees conducted six public hearings – three within the Senate and three in different cities around the Philippines – inviting nearly one hundred experts to share their reactions to the VFA. To gather a wide range of opinions, particularly those opposed to the VFA, the Senate invited academics, lawyers, activists, NGO workers, and local officials.

Anti-VFA activists attempted to counter government claims that linked VFA ratification to the national interest. Targeting elites, Junk VFA members devised strategies nearly identical to those used in the Anti-Treaty Movement.[41] However, activists found it nearly impossible to form ties with sympathetic elites as they had done only eight years earlier. Unlike in 1991, Philippine elites in 1999 had a much different perception of national security and the U.S. alliance.

---

thought. Of the two coalitions, the larger Junk VFA attracted significantly more publicity and media attention (interview with Cora Valdez-Fabros, Quezon City, Philippines, March 6, 2005).

[38] Although organizers expected a turnout of 30,000, only 1,000 protestors arrived in Manila as a result of torrential rains. See Tonia Macapagal and Angie Rosales, "Rains Fail to Dampen Rally Protesting VFA," *Manila Standard*, September 17, 1998.

[39] For a comprehensive list of reasons behind VFA opposition, see the "Arguments of Anti-VFA – De La Salle University Stand on VFA." http://poligov.tripod.com/antivfa.html (last accessed March 10, 2008).

[40] Interview with Herbert Docena, Quezon City, Philippines, March 13, 2006.

[41] Internal Junk VFA notes and documents. Copies obtained from personal collection of Corazon Fabros and NFPC Archives.

In 1991, elites were divided in their attitude toward the U.S. alliance. With supporters unable to justify the security logic behind U.S. bases, nationalist sentiments overpowered any justification to retain a U.S. military presence.

By 1999, the tide had changed. Eighteen of the twenty-three senators voted in favor of the VFA. In their deliberation speech, all eighteen pro-VFA senators pointed to the security benefits accrued from the VFA and strengthened U.S. alliance relations. Senate President Blas Ople, initially reluctant to approve the VFA, stated, "And because we remain a militarily weak nation, this security alliance with the United States remains a major anchor of our national safety, security, and freedom. How to give substance and effect to this treaty in a post–Cold War world that remains fraught with risks is the very aim and purpose of the Visiting Forces Agreement."[42] In a similar vein, Senator Franklin Drilon stated, "It will not be often that an opportunity to strengthen our capability to enforce our common interests with the United States will present itself. The VFA is one such opportunity we cannot afford to miss, for without the Visiting Forces Agreement, any thought of arming ourselves in defense of our interests or to deter aggression will be meaningless."[43]

To demonstrate the breadth and depth of the newfound security consensus among political elites, it is worth mentioning the shift in attitude of three members of the "Magnificent Twelve" who voted against U.S. bases in 1991: Joseph Estrada, Orlando Mercado, and Juan Ponce Enrile.[44] Now as president and national defense secretary, respectively, former senators Estrada and Mercado strongly endorsed the VFA, imploring the Senate to pass the agreement as a matter of national interest. Defense Secretary Mercado argued that the VFA "should not be considered a document independent of the country's national defense strategy ... but considered within the context of a more comprehensive policy on national defense and security."[45] The "turnabouts" of both Estrada and Mercado from their Senate days spurred the wrath of anti-VFA activists. Ironically, Senator Enrile, who eight years earlier vehemently denied any external security threat that justified the need for U.S. bases, spent a substantial portion of his speech evoking the China threat. He stated:

China ... has clearly and unequivocally initiated an aggressive move against our national interest and we are far too weak militarily and economically today to provide ourselves with an adequate defense against such a clear and present danger to us without the

---

[42] "The VFA: Paradigm Shifts in the Security and Freedom of Nations," speech by Senator Blas Ople, Senate President Pro Tempore and Chairman, Committee on Foreign Relations, May 3, 1999, in Republic of the Philippines, Senate Legislative Publications Staff, *The Visiting Forces Agreement: The Senate Decision* (Manila: Senate of the Philippines, 1999), 1.

[43] "A Choice of National Interest," speech by Senator Franklin Drilon, May 3, 1999, in Republic of the Philippines, Senate Legislative Publications Staff, *The Visiting Forces Agreement: The Senate Decision* (Manila: Senate of the Philippines, 1999), 52.

[44] In addition to Senator Enrile, two other members of the Magnificent Twelve still served in the Philippine Senate: Aquilino Pimentel, Jr., and Teofisto Guingona, Jr. Both senators voted against the VFA.

[45] Republic of the Philippines, Senate Legislative Publications Staff, *Visiting Forces Agreement*, 227.

assistance of our Mutual Defense Treaty with the United States of America; and so the need for the Visiting Forces Agreement to enable our military forces and those of the United States to work together.[46]

In almost direct contradiction to his speech in 1991, Enrile continued, "I am . . . constrained to admit that our defense alliance with the United States is probably the only viable security umbrella and certainly the only one we can count on today in the event of need."[47]

If most senators appeared staunchly in favor of the VFA, the consensus held even tighter in the executive branch of government. The executive summary of the VFA focused on the Agreement's "vital importance . . . to the continued potency of the Mutual Defense Treaty . . . and [its] effectiveness as a deterrent to a potential aggressor."[48] More concretely, the VFA "provide(d) the AFP with the opportunity to enhance its defense capabilities by taking part in [a] U.S. military assistance and training program."[49] Joint military exercises with U.S. troops enabled the AFP to adopt new strategies and technologies.[50] In other words, Philippine elites linked the VFA and strengthened security ties to the United States with AFP modernization. The VFA also minimized the cost of the AFP modernization program by improving external capabilities without expending exorbitant amounts on additional resources. During a public hearing, National Security Advisor Alexander Aguirre reminded the Senate that the country faced threats on two fronts, one internal and one external, but remained hindered in its security response because of limited resources. Therefore, the U.S. alliance remained the best option to deter potential aggressors.[51]

By the end of the decade, new external security threats and the sense of urgency felt by Philippine elites to modernize its military resulted in the reemergence of an elite security consensus. The consensus favored strengthened U.S. alliance relations and the return of "visiting" U.S. forces. Under this political environment, activist demands were drowned out by Philippine elites' insistence on VFA ratification. Granted, mobilization against the VFA did not reach the magnitude of protests in 1991. Unity was hampered by the split within the Philippine left, which resulted in two different anti-VFA coalitions. Nevertheless, protests continued frequently for over a year as the Philippine public awaited the Senate's verdict. Anti-VFA activists received the backing of several prominent Catholic leaders, including the outspoken moral leader of the People Power movement, Cardinal Jamie Sin. Yet, unable to penetrate the strong consensus and form ties with sympathetic senators as in 1991, the anti-VFA movement

---

[46] "Imperatives of National Survival," speech by Senator Juan Ponce Enrile, May 3, 1999, in Republic of the Philippines, Senate Legislative Publications Staff, *Visiting Forces Agreement*, 68.
[47] Ibid., 66.
[48] Republic of the Philippines, Senate Legislative Publications Staff, *Visiting Forces Agreement*, 195.
[49] Ibid., 205.
[50] Ibid., 205.
[51] Ibid., 228.

failed to translate their demands into actual policy outcomes.[52] Even if anti-VFA movements had reached levels of protest similar to those in 1991, the security consensus framework predicts that Philippine elites would have undermined activist mobilization.

Since 9/11, U.S. "visiting forces" have remained entrenched in the Philippines. The consensus, reformulated by national security threats in the mid- to late 1990s, has slowly become embedded within Philippine domestic institutions. Herbert Docena argues, "Although domestic opposition to U.S. presence remains strong, the political forces that favor the U.S. continue to dominate the country's political system." Activists opposed to the U.S military presence and joint exercises in the Philippines have thus found it much more challenging to influence security policy decisions pertinent to the U.S.-Philippines alliance.[53]

In 2009, several lawmakers, led by Senate Foreign Relations Committee chairwoman Miriam Defensor Santiago, called for a complete review, if not the abrogation, of the Visiting Forces Agreement. Legal opposition to the VFA coincided with renewed protests led by activists and former anti-base senators against the U.S. military presence following the acquittal of a U.S. soldier accused of rape. However, the Philippine government quickly defended the VFA's importance for continued military assistance and joint training and operations with the United States. In March 2010, the Philippine Supreme Court upheld the legality of the VFA. In sum, despite recurring cycles of protests against U.S. forces in the past few years, the strengthening of an elite security consensus over time has made it difficult for anti-base movements (or anti–U.S. military protests) from winning major concessions from host governments. Thus, in the post-9/11 period, even with other countries rejecting U.S. military requests for access, the Philippines has "repeatedly complied... explicitly endorsed... and actively supported" the U.S. military presence in the Philippines.[54] Activist calls to end military campaigns in Mindanao and immediately withdraw U.S. troops who have been "permanently" stationed in Mindanao since 2002 have largely gone unheeded.[55]

OKINAWA

Whereas the strengthening of the security consensus over time explains the change in movement outcomes in the Philippines, in Japan, the high degree of

---

[52] Public opinion regarding the VFA paralleled the opinion on U.S. bases in the early 1990s, with 36 percent against and 63 percent in favor of temporary visits of U.S. soldiers to participate in military exercises. See Social Weather Station Survey 1998, question on VFA.

[53] Activists note their success in the Angelo de la Cruz incident. Protestors pressured President Macapagal-Arroyo to withdraw Filipino troops from Iraq after Iraqi insurgents kidnapped a Filipino truck driver, Angelo de la Cruz. Iraqi insurgents threatened to execute de la Cruz unless Manila withdrew its fifty-one-member humanitarian force. Although the case was a clear victory for protestors, the issue did not apply directly to Philippine national security interests such as the VFA.

[54] Herbert Docena, *At the Door of All the East: The Philippines in United States Military Strategy* (Quezon City: Focus on the Global South, 2007), 106.

[55] Declaration signed by members of Stop the War Coalition – Philippines, April 17, 2007.

security consensus maintained since the mid-1990s should correspond to little change in the status quo regarding basing issues. That is, Okinawan anti-base movements continue to face significant challenges because of the U.S.-Japan alliance and the pervading consensus held by elites. Delays and co-optation through token concessions and economic incentives have helped Tokyo maintain positive alliance ties to the United States at the expense of Okinawan anti-base movements. In recent years, however, the downfall of the LDP has left some wondering whether the Democratic Party of Japan's (DPJ) 2009 electoral victory would herald a new era of U.S.-Japan relations reflecting a weakened security consensus and greater political opportunities for anti-base opponents.

Security Consensus in the Twenty-First Century

Chapter 3 argued that U.S.-Japan relations strengthened in the mid- to late 1990s despite brief tensions generated by the 1995 rape incident. The strong consensus showed little sign of waning entering the twenty-first century. Immediately after 9/11, Japan supported the U.S. "war on terror" by passing the Anti-Terrorism Special Measure Law. This law already extended Japan's offshore support for U.S. military activity based on the 1997 Guidelines for U.S.-Japan Defense Cooperation. However, Japan took this a step further by deploying SDF forces beyond Japanese waters.[56] For instance, Japan permitted Aegis destroyers to escort Japanese ships sent to provide logistical support to U.S. forces in the Indian Ocean. Security cooperation with the United States extended to other issue areas such as theater missile defense and the Iraq War. Supporting the U.S.-led invasion in Iraq, Japan dispatched a small contingent of ground forces to participate in reconstruction projects. According to Japan specialist Thomas Berger, "a broad spectrum of elite opinion [which] had solidified in support of the alliance" in the late 1990s enabled Japan to quickly adjust to the new U.S.-Japan alliance in the post 9/11 world.[57] Figure 6.5 highlights this persistence in the security consensus over time.

An analysis of Japan's domestic politics over the past decade supports the persistence of an elite security consensus. Richard Samuels's examination of domestic factions within the Japanese security debate reveals four broad camps: neoautonomists, pacifists, middle-power internationalists, and normal nationalists. Based on Samuels's typology, Figure 6.6 maps the various security camps found in Japan.[58]

Although multiple discourses exist, the normal nationalists and middle-power internationalists have alternated in power for the last six decades.[59]

---

[56] Thomas U. Berger, *Redefining Japan and the U.S.-Japan Alliance* (New York: Japan Society, 2004), 56.

[57] Ibid., 54.

[58] Ibid., 112.

[59] Samuels, *Securing Japan*, 197. The normal nationalists would like to see Japan return to the status of a "normal" nation – a nation that is capable of using its own military to defend itself against

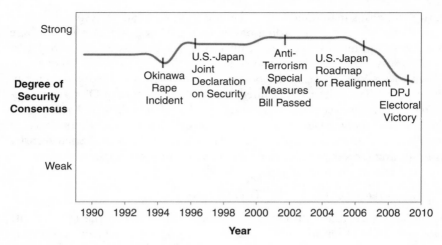

FIGURE 6.5. Security Consensus over Time in Japan.

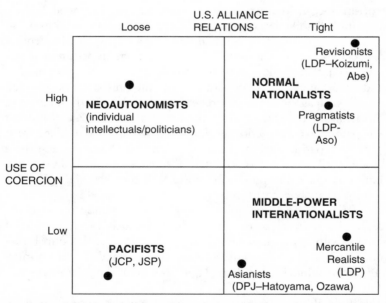

FIGURE 6.6. Typology of Security Camps within the Japanese Polity.

attacks. This group is divided between two groups: revisionists, who want to revise Article 9, legitimating the SDF with the use of force, and pragmatists (or realists), who view revisionists' provocation of Japan's Asian neighbors as unnecessary and instead provide for security without evoking Japan's imperial past. The middle-power internationalists are also internally divided between Asianists and mercantile realist strands. Middle-power internationalists are more cautious about expanding Japan's military role. Mercantile realists, questioning the growth of Japan's military role, continue to favor close ties to the United States. The Asianists, although accepting the U.S. alliance, argue at the same time that Japan should not ignore its Asian

Note how these two groups, located on the right half of the spectrum, are most closely aligned to the United States. From 2001 to 2007, the Koizumi-Abe strand of normal nationalists dictated security policy, followed by pragmatist LDP successors Yasuo Fukuda and Taro Aso.[60] Although the normal-nationalist camp, divided between revisionists and pragmatists, holds a different vision for the SDF, neither strand has ever been divided on the importance of the U.S.-Japan alliance.[61]

Under the leadership of former prime minister Junichiro Koizumi, the revisionists enhanced the salience of military power in Japanese national security. Symbolized by the JDA's elevated status to Ministry of National Defense in 2007, the transformation of Japanese security policy may have stretched the principles of the Yoshida Doctrine and Article 9 to its limits.[62] However, the strong security consensus built around the U.S.-Japan alliance remains intact. As Peter Katzenstein observes, "Japan has embraced what looks like a grand strategy of unquestioned security alignment with the United States. In an era in which the American imperium is under siege, Japan is deeply invested in enhancing its special relationship with the United States."[63] Japan's recent assertiveness may thus be interpreted as an updated version of the Yoshida Doctrine, with key elements such as the U.S. alliance and the hosting of U.S. bases in place. As Mike Mochizuki notes, even if constitutional revisions do take place, Japan will likely continue to restrain its use of military force in operations not directly impacting Japan's national security.[64]

Some skeptics question whether the consensus surrounding the U.S.-Japan alliance can continue now that the DPJ has broken nearly fifty-four years of continuous rule by the LDP. The DPJ, its main opposition, has distanced itself from the LDP's near unconditional support of the U.S.-Japan alliance, implying a narrower breadth in an elite consensus. For instance, in 2005, DPJ president Seiji Maehera argued, "In the future … it is quite conceivable that, despite our status as a close ally of the United States, Japan will refuse U.S. requests for cooperation if these involve international contributions that do not receive the understanding of the Japanese people."[65] During the 2009 election campaign,

---

neighbors. Both groups emphasize economic over military power and contend that Japan's security policy legitimacy should stem from international institutions. See Samuels, *Securing Japan*, 126–27.

[60] Considered a "revisionist" during his tenure as foreign minister, Aso was rebranded as a "pragmatist" as prime minister. See "The Return of Taro Aso," *New York Times*, September 24, 2008. On Fukuda's foreign policy, see Hitoshi Tanaka, "Japanese Foreign Policy under Prime Minister Yasuo Fukuda," *East Asia Insights* 5, no. 2 (2007): 1–4.

[61] Samuels, *Securing Japan*, 177.

[62] Ibid., Chap. 4. Thomas Berger, however, believes the Yoshida Doctrine makes "more sense today than ever," attested by Japan's ever-tighter coupling with the United States. See Berger, *Redefining Japan and the U.S.-Japan Alliance*, 54–55.

[63] Peter Katzenstein, *Japanese Security in Perspective* (London: Routledge, 2008), 31.

[64] Mike Mochizuki, "Change in Japan's Grand Strategy: Why and How Much?" *Asia Policy* 4 (2007): 191–96 at 195.

[65] Speech by Seiji Maehara, "The National Image and Foreign Policy Vision Aimed for by the DPJ," CSIS, Washington, D.C., December 8, 2005.

the DPJ demanded a more equal partnership with the United States, publicly declaring it would reject plans to relocate Futenma Air Station to northern Okinawa. And, as promised in his campaign, Prime Minister Yukio Hatoyama ended Japan's eight-year mission refueling U.S. warships in the Indian Ocean in January 2010.

Although the rise of the DPJ raises the possibility of a shift in Japanese security policy, three points are worth noting that indicate a wider breadth in the consensus than current events suggest. First, as Pekkanen and Krauss argue, the DPJ, composed of former LDP members, is "much closer [with the ruling party] on defense than pre-reform, opposition-party Diet members had been."[66] Second, the DPJ (as well as the LDP) is composed of several factions, some of which continue to wholeheartedly support the U.S.-Japan alliance. Third, although some DPJ factions oppose SDF deployment abroad and U.S. base realignment plans, the majority of DPJ members have no intention of weakening or abandoning alliance relations. Far from it, Seiji Maehara states: "In fact, as part of our commitment to long-term peace and stability of the Asian Pacific region, the DPJ supports a strengthening of the existing Japan-U.S. alliance."[67] In a March 2010 congressional hearing on U.S.-Japan relations, Representative Eni Faleomavaega, chairman of the House Foreign Affairs Subcommittee on Asia, the Pacific, and the Global Environment, stated, "Most of the issues on which the press has reported so breathlessly are relatively minor when viewed in the context of the *breadth and depth* [emphasis mine] of the bilateral relationship."[68] Broad agreement exists among Japanese and American leaders of "virtually all political persuasions" regarding the alliance, even as the DPJ and the Obama administration continue to determine what this means operationally.[69] As Prime Minister Hatoyama stated on the fiftieth anniversary of the signing of the Treaty of Mutual Cooperation and Security of Japan:

The U.S.-Japan security arrangements continue to be indispensable not only for the defense of Japan alone, but also for the peace and prosperity of the entire Asia-Pacific region. Under a security environment in which there still exist uncertainty and unpredictability, the presence of the U.S. Forces based on the Treaty will continue to function as a public good by creating a strong sense of security to the countries in the region.[70]

---

[66] Robert Pekkanen and Ellis S. Krauss, "Japan's 'Coalition of the Willing' on Security Policies," *Orbis* 49, no. 3 (2005): 429–44 at 437.
[67] Maehara, "National Image and Foreign Policy Vision Aimed for by the DPJ."
[68] Congressional testimony to United States House of Representatives, Subcommittee on Asia, the Pacific and the Global Environment, Committee on Foreign Affairs, on "U.S-Japan Relations: Enduring Ties, Recent Developments," Washington, D.C., March 17, 2010.
[69] Kent Calder, hearings on "Japan's Changing Role," testimony to United States House of Representatives, Subcommittee on Asia, the Pacific and the Global Environment, Committee on Foreign Affairs, Washington, D.C., June 25, 2009.
[70] Statement by Prime Minister Yukio Hatoyama on the fiftieth anniversary of the signing of the Treaty of Mutual Cooperation and Security of Japan and the United States of America, January 19, 2010. http://www.kantei.go.jp/foreign/hatoyama/statement/201001/19danwa_e.html (last accessed April 10, 2010).

Despite differences in policy objectives between the DPJ and LDP, the security consensus is still deeply entrenched in Japanese norms and institutions. Questions pertaining to the U.S alliance arise as Japanese officials periodically recalibrate national security policy to international events and domestic political trends. On the whole, however, the consensus surrounding the U.S.-Japan alliance and the role of U.S. bases in Japanese national security strategy remains relatively strong in the twenty-first century.

FROM SACO TO THE STRUGGLE IN HENOKO

Chapter 3 ended with a discussion of the SACO policy recommendations and the conditional return of Futenma Air Station, which amounted to token concessions and unfulfilled promises. The SACO report in December 1996 marked the conclusion of the first cycle of protest in the "third wave." Yet, even fifteen years after the SACO agreement, Futenma remains open as Washington, Tokyo, and anti-base Okinawans wrangle over the construction of Futenma's replacement facility in Henoko Bay. To understand why anti-base movements failed to make substantial progress on the Futenma issue a decade after SACO requires examination of additional movement episodes in the post-SACO period. In this section, I highlight how anti-base resistance, the pervading security consensus, and the use of compensation politics by the Japanese government led to a virtual standstill on the Futenma relocation issue. Figure 6.7 provides a notional graph demonstrating the negative relationship between the persistent security consensus among Japanese elites and the weak impact of anti-base movements in influencing major basing policy outcomes. Note how only in recent years have political opportunities opened at the national level, enabling anti-base Okinawans to work more closely with sympathetic political elites situated at the center of power.[71]

Nago City Elections

As noted earlier, Futenma's relocation did not amount to an anti-base victory. Outlined in the final SACO report, Futenma's return was contingent on the construction of an offshore replacement facility in the Henoko district of Nago City. By relocating Futenma within Okinawa, the Japanese government managed to split the anti-base struggle into internal local factions. As Miyume Tanji notes, "In the post-SACO period, the protest actors inevitably splintered into smaller, multiple groups ... [and] became geographically scattered and regionalized."[72] Specifically, Nago City residents were split between pro- and anti-base factions. Pro-base LDP members in Okinawa with close ties to Tokyo supported the offshore base, hoping to obtain large subsidies from the Japanese

---

[71] Activists have much more difficulty penetrating the bureaucracies that hold onto more traditional views of the U.S. alliance.

[72] Tanji, *Myth, Protest and Struggle in Okinawa*, 163.

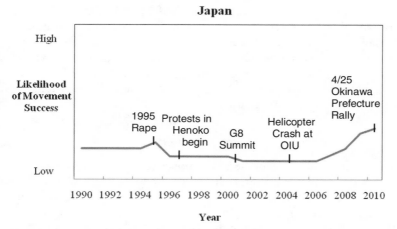

FIGURE 6.7. Probability of Anti-Base Movement Effectiveness in Japan.

government. Although these members supported the mayor of Nago City, the mayor initially supported the anti-base position. Hoping to shift Mayor Tetsuya Higa's position on the bases, several officials from Tokyo met Nago city officials in a closed-door meeting to persuade Higa to support the offshore facility. Indeed, Higa emerged from the meeting with a different attitude. Although not explicitly endorsing the base, he allowed Tokyo to begin topographical surveys in preparation for base construction.[73]

The Henoko district in Nago City became the focal point of post-SACO anti-base movements in Okinawa. Political parties, labor unions, teachers' associations, women's groups, and environmental groups launched a fresh campaign aimed at blocking the construction of the offshore facility. Unlike earlier Okinawan anti-base movements directed by political parties and unions, however, *shimin*, or local citizens, carried the anti-base mantle forward. At the core of this *shimin* struggle was the Henoko Life Protection Society, a committee formed in January 1997 by twenty-seven residents opposed to the offshore heliport.[74] The group pitched a large tent (later replaced by a prefabricated structure) by Henoko's fishing port, naming their makeshift headquarters the "struggle hut." The Society was based on the identity of local Henoko residents and characterized by the participation of older residents who had experienced the Battle of Okinawa.

Several other anti-base groups in Nago and northern Okinawa organized in solidarity with the Society in opposing the heliport construction. Four labor unions in Nago formed the Five Party Coalition in February 1997 with the specific goal of supporting the Henoko Life Protection Society and enlarging its support base. This coalition was joined by Okinawa Peace Center, an island-wide

[73] Ibid., 164.
[74] Ibid.

coalition of labor unions, in hopes of drawing in support from trade unions in various areas of Okinawa. Two more anti-base groups formed in April: the Society of Nago Citizens Opposed to the Heliport and the All-Nago Citizens' Group Against the Heliport.[75] Like the Henoko Life Protection Society, these two groups defined themselves as "citizens" movements, distancing themselves from any political affiliation. The *shimin*-led anti-base movement represented local residents rather than any political group or ideological position. Of course, political parties and unions still served an important role by bringing in mobilization resources and experience. However, they played more of a supporting rather than a lead role in the post-SACO anti-base movement.[76]

As the number of anti-base groups in Nago City proliferated, activists organized a broader coalition composed of twenty-one groups to promote a referendum in an effort to derail base relocation plans. Named the Nago Citizens' Referendum Promotion Council, the coalition channeled anti-base opposition into the political process by proposing a citywide referendum to vote in favor of or against the offshore facility. The anti-base coalition used multiple frames to draw attention to the struggle against the offshore base.[77] Anti-base literature and flyers evoked anti-Japanese sentiment. Okinawans were reminded of Tokyo's past deceitfulness: Japan's sacrifice of Okinawa during World War II, and the continued presence of the U.S. military even after Okinawa's reversion in 1972. By highlighting the fact that Futenma's replacement facility represented U.S. rather than Okinawan interests, activists contradicted official statements that Tokyo was working to address Okinawan grievances. The anti-base coalition also adopted an environmental frame by focusing on the dugong – a sea mammal related to the manatee. Realizing that the endangered dugong inhabited Henoko Bay, activists claimed that the offshore base would destroy the dugong population. The dugong became the unofficial symbol of the anti-base struggle during this phase of the movement, which helped draw in environmental NGOs and other activists from mainland Japan. The dugong appeared on anti-base flyers, T-shirts, and badges with slogans such as "Money disappears in a moment, but nature, if protected, lasts forever" or "On the beautiful sea and beautiful island that cultivates life, we do not need the offshore base."[78]

In December 1997, 51.3 percent of Nago residents voted against the offshore heliport in Henoko.[79] Despite this victory for the anti-base coalition, Tokyo, weighing the importance of the U.S. alliance, continued to skirt around anti-base opposition. The central government refused to openly discuss base issues with any top officials in the Okinawan prefectural government for nearly

---

[75] Ibid., 165.
[76] Ibid., 168.
[77] For instance, flyers produced by the Japanese Communist Party (February 2000) and the Okinawa Committee for Struggles against the Kyushu-Okinawa Summit addressed multiple grievances stemming from U.S. bases.
[78] Inoue, *Okinawa and the U.S. Military*, 177.
[79] Yonetani, "Playing Base Politics in a Global Strategic Theater," 78.

ten months after Governor Ota rejected Prime Minister Hashimoto's appeal for the construction of the offshore heliport.[80] The Futenma relocation issue was eventually transferred down to the next governor, the LDP-backed Keiichi Inamine, and the new administration headed by Prime Minister Keizo Obuchi. With new leadership in Okinawa, Prime Minister Obuchi reopened financial flows, pledging 10 billion yen to Inamine's government and making a personal pledge to find a solution to Futenma's relocation.[81] To further placate anti-base opposition, Obuchi announced in April 1999 that Nago City (along with Kyushu) would host the 2000 G-8 summit. In preparation for the summit, Tokyo pledged an annual 100 billion yen stimulus package to northern Okinawa (where Nago City was located) for the next ten years, with the first 100 billion yen redirected to Okinawa beginning in 2000.[82] The economic incentives worked their magic. In December 1999, Nago City consented to the construction of an offshore heliport under the stipulation that Tokyo meet several conditions, including a fifteen-year limit on military use of the offshore base. Tokyo had again played its hand well, relying on compensation packages and other economic incentives to soothe anti-base opposition. By inducing local communities to accept large-scale public works and providing additional material incentives, Tokyo pacified anti-base opposition. Economic incentives helped separate more radical elements among the anti-base opponents from those who were willing to tolerate bases so long as they were well compensated.[83]

Rifts within the Nago anti-base movement deepened, with more grassroots movements overshadowed by party political machines in the 1998 Nago City mayoral election. As the movement gained exposure globally, the tension between pro-base residents' material interests and the global aspirations of anti-base Okinawans trying to reach out to a broad, international audience became more pronounced. For instance, when environmental and peace groups from mainland Japan arrived in Henoko wearing "Save the Dugong" buttons, Henoko residents retorted, "Our life is more important than the dugong's."[84] Masamichi Inoue notes, "Tokyo's carrots and sticks, when fused with the pro-base group's desire to revitalize the local economy, slowly but steadily permeated from the top to the bottom of Nago's pyramid-like pro-base mobilization structure."[85] Of course, Tokyo exploited these tensions through compensation politics. With indirect support from Tokyo, pro-base groups captured the mayoral race, whereas the Nago anti-base coalition withered as a cohesive movement.

---

[80] Ibid., 78.
[81] Ibid., 80.
[82] Ibid.
[83] For a discussion on compensation politics as a government strategy in Okinawa, see Mulgan, "Managing the U.S. Base Issue in Okinawa."
[84] Inoue, *Okinawa and the U.S. Military*, 188.
[85] Ibid., 166.

Into the Twenty-First Century

Fifteen years have passed since the SACO agreement, yet Futenma Air Base continues to operate. Have anti-base movements completely failed in their struggle against U.S. bases? Table 6.1 highlights several movement episodes in Okinawa since 1995.

At the very least, it is safe to conclude that anti-base movement outcomes over the past decade have been mixed. Over the course of several episodes, anti-base

TABLE 6.1. *Anti-Base Movement Episodes in Okinawa*

Date	Event	Movement's Immediate Goal	Government Response
September 1995 to December 1996	Rape of 12-year-old schoolgirl	Base reduction/SOFA revision	SACO recommendations: base land return, including Futenma Air Station; noise-reduction policies
June 1997 to December 1997	Announcement of Henoko as replacement facility site of Futenma	Referendum in Nago City to block construction of offshore replacement facility	Government officials sent to influence referendum outcome
July 2000	Upcoming G-8 summit	Raise international attention about Okinawan bases; stop offshore facility plan.	Government pledges massive economic subsidies and public works projects
August 2004	Helicopter crash at Okinawa International University	Compensation for crash; suspend military flights over civilian areas; early return of Futenma Base	Government investigates crash, pledges to push forward with relocation plans
April 2004 to September 2005	Drilling surveys in Henoko Bay	Block geological survey and drilling of seabed through canoe protest	Government cancels offshore plan, announces new plan expanding Camp Schwab
November 2009–	DPJ electoral victory	Immediate and unconditional return of Futenma	Under U.S. pressure, return to 2006 plan after Hatoyama's political fall?

Note: This list excludes anti-base mobilizations aimed at influencing election outcomes, such as the 1998 and 2006 Nago City mayoral elections or the 1998 and 2006 gubernatorial elections. The distinction between formal and informal politics regarding bases in Okinawa is often blurred.

movements were able to win tactical concessions, such as the inclusion of Futenma's relocation in the 1996 SACO report, the rejection of an offshore heliport in the 1997 referendum, and the blocking of Tokyo's attempt to push ahead with the "coral reef" base plan in 2005. At each point of "victory," however, the Japanese government countered the activists' tactical gains by putting forth new proposals keeping U.S. bases in Okinawa and managing positive alliance relations with the United States. As activists correctly pointed out, the Futenma agreement originally outlined under the SACO report amounted to base relocation rather than reduction.[86] In a catch-22, activists may successfully block new base plans in northern Okinawa but in doing so enable Futenma Air Station to remain open.

To their credit, anti-base activists were effective in blocking the offshore replacement facility plan. In April 2004, a group of activists paddled into Henoko Bay in canoes to physically prevent the DFAA from conducting geological drilling surveys. After five hundred consecutive days of resistance, local Henoko activists prevailed as the government removed the scaffolds from the water in September 2005. However, as activists valiantly "paddled" against the government, Tokyo and Washington entered negotiations to discuss U.S. military realignment in Okinawa. In October 2005, the United States and Japan announced they would scrap the offshore facility plan. Rather than building on top of a reef as engineered in the offshore plan, the two sides agreed to a "coastal plan" that would expand nearby Camp Schwab. To accommodate the functions of Futenma, the government planned to build a V-shaped runway extending Camp Schwab into the sea.[87] In addition, the United States announced the relocation of 7,000 U.S. marines to Guam on the condition of Futenma's relocation. Prime Minister Koizumi and President George W. Bush signed the USFJ realignment plan, committing Japan to take on a greater role in the U.S.-Japan security alliance.[88] Tokyo, however, forged this new agreement without any consultation with the local or prefectural governments in Okinawa. Okinawans, including the LDP governor Keiichi Inamine, were outraged that Tokyo had again neglected their voice.

---

[86] On the contrary, Japan and the United States believe this relocation is tantamount to a reduction. As one U.S. official stated, "The Futenma base will be moved from an area where 80,000 live to one where only less than 2,000 reside. You cannot say this is not burden reduction. If the return of the base is realized, a military base that is located in a densely-populated area will be moved to the north, where there is a small population. ... This will be very beneficial for Okinawa." Interview with Naha U.S. Consul General Thomas G. Reich by Tsuyoshi Matsumoto of the *Ryukyu Shimpo*, November 22, 2005. Transcript available on Naha Consulate Web site as "Consul General Speaks to Ryukyu Shimpo on DPRI." http://naha.usconsulate.gov/wwwh-interview20051122.html (last accessed November 23, 2007).

[87] Yoshikazu Makishi, "U.S. Dream Come True? The New Henoko Sea Base and Okinawan Resistance," *Japan Focus* no. 502 (2006). http://www.japanfocus.org/products/details/1819 (last accessed November 15, 2007).

[88] See Japan Ministry of National Defense, *Defense of Japan 2006*, Chap. 4, Sec. 2. http://www.mod.go.jp/e/publ/w_paper/pdf/2006/4-2-1.pdf (last accessed November 23, 2007). Later the United States announced it planned to withdraw 8,000 Marines.

The DPJ electoral victory in August 2009 helped renew island-wide opposition to U.S. bases. Today, anti-base movements in Okinawa are in a unique position, with near unanimous support from local government officials. Additionally, Okinawans have found elite allies not only among the ruling party's more progressive coalition partners – the SDP and the People's New Party – but from sympathetic DPJ members as well, including DPJ powerbroker Ichiro Ozawa. This raises two important questions. First, are we experiencing a decline in an elite security consensus regarding the U.S.-Japan alliance? And, if so, will the outcome mark a major success for Okinawan anti-base movements as the security consensus framework predicts?

As Tokyo and Washington resume negotiations over Futenma's replacement, one should keep in mind that, in a broad sense, the DPJ continues to support the U.S.-Japan alliance, even if new ruling elites hold different positions regarding the implementation of specific alliance policies. The dilemma that faced the DPJ-led government under former prime minister Hatoyama highlights the nature of base politics, where political elites must juggle domestic and international pressures. Okinawans, sensing that the new government might renege on its campaign pledge regarding Futenma, mobilized mass protests as a stark reminder of the DPJ's promise.[89] On November 8, 2009, approximately 6,000 citizens participated in the "All-Okinawa Mass Meeting" in Ginowan City, demanding the unconditional return of Futenma Air Station.[90] This was followed by a No Bases solidarity rally in Okinawa in April 2010, with an estimated 90,000 participants.[91] Expressing his difficulty in maneuvering between Okinawan resistance and U.S. pressure, Foreign Minister Katsuya Okada asked Okinawans for their understanding in handling the alliance crisis and difficult negotiations.[92] If the security consensus is resilient, Tokyo will agree to relocate most of Futenma's functions within Okinawa prefecture, disappointing anti-base activists and local residents once again. This outcome would parallel anti-base movement episodes in South Korea and Italy in the mid-2000s; both countries experienced a shift toward left-leaning governments initially considered less amicable to U.S. alliance policies but ultimately decided to support U.S. base initiatives.

On the other hand, Futenma's relocation outside of Okinawa would constitute the long-awaited victory for anti-base movements. This outcome is possible,

[89] As late as March 2010, Japanese officials asserted that Japan would meet U.S. requests, even if it meant alienating coalition partners and locals. See John Brinsley and Sachiko Sakamaki, "U.S. Base to Stay on Okinawa, Japanese Official Says," *Bloomberg News*, March 3, 2010. http://www.bloomberg.com/apps/news?pid=20601101&sid=a5yLx1.IMP8I (last accessed April 12, 2010).

[90] David Allen and Hana Kusumoto, "Protesters Rally against Okinawa Base Plans," *Stars and Stripes*, November 10, 2009.

[91] Martin Fackler, "90,000 Protest U.S. Base on Okinawa," *New York Times*, April 25, 2010. Additional solidarity rallies took place in various locations in the United States and Japan.

[92] Gavan McCormack, "The Travails of a Client State: An Okinawan Angle on the 50th Anniversary of the US-Japan Security Treaty," *The Asia-Pacific Journal*, March 8, 2010. http://japanfocus.org/-Gavan-McCormack/3317 (last accessed December 16, 2010).

but only if the depth of the security consensus deteriorates, thereby giving activists greater political leverage on base issues. This weakened security consensus would be marked by shifts in elite strategic thinking within the bureaucracies, as well as more fundamental changes to Japanese security institutions. Prior to Hatoyama's political fall, rumors had circulated that Tokyo would propose Tokunoshima Island in Kagoshima Prefecture to the United States as a solution to the Futenma relocation issue. It is unclear, however, whether the United States would accept an alternative site outside of Okinawa. Moreover, mayors on Tokunoshima Island drafted a letter directed at President Obama that voiced their opposition to U.S. bases, making it uncertain whether residents would accept a U.S. base. The DPJ chose Naoto Kan to succeed Hatoyama, with the understanding that his government would cooperate with the United States and return to a relocation plan similar to the 2006 design. At the time of publication, however, Washington and Tokyo had not come to any firm agreement.

More than a decade after the 1996 SACO agreement, Futenma Air Base continues to operate. Ironically, persistent anti-base opposition in northern Okinawa contributed to this stalemate. However, the strong security consensus regarding the U.S.-Japan alliance posed a formidable obstacle for activists. Today, Okinawan anti-base activism sits at a crossroad, with greater political opportunities opened by the DPJ victory. If entrenched ideas and domestic institutional constraints in support of the U.S. alliance prevail, Tokyo will likely continue its strategy of economic co-optation and political coercion to maintain positive alliance relations. If the DPJ's victory signals a more fundamental shift not only in the breadth but in the depth of the security consensus as well, the power of movements in Okinawan base politics will rise.

CONCLUSION

This chapter demonstrated the relationship between the security consensus and movement effectiveness diachronically in the Philippines and Japan. By allowing "variability" in the security consensus, particularly in the Philippine case, I showed how changes in the security consensus over time resulted in different patterns of action between the state and society, thereby producing different outcomes. As an elite security consensus regarding U.S. relations strengthens over time, movement effectiveness should decrease as patterns of interaction between activists and security policymakers move from cooperation to greater confrontation. Thus, in the Philippines, anti-base activists who found allies within the Philippine Senate in 1990–91 became increasingly marginalized as Philippine elites tightened their alliance with the United States. In the security-scarce environment of the 1990s, Philippine elites embraced the U.S. alliance as the best guarantee against national security threats.

Although not discussed at length in this chapter, we should expect greater movement "success" when the security consensus weakens over time. As the host government moves away from a security policy centered on the U.S.

alliance, political space opens for activists to penetrate the state and form ties with elites while reframing the public debate and discourse on bases. For anti-base movements to achieve success, however, activists must still employ the right strategies and frames while taking advantage of the available political opportunity to "penetrate" the state. In Japan, some see the DPJ's victory foreshadowing the beginning of a decline in a U.S.-centered security consensus. However, as movement episodes in South Korea and Italy might suggest, the security consensus often remains resilient in the wake of a domestic regime shift. If this holds true in Japan, Okinawan anti-base movements will continue to face formidable obstacles from Tokyo and Washington in the future.

7

Activists, Alliances, and the Future of U.S. Basing Strategy

This book addressed two key questions. First, when and how did anti-base movements affect U.S. base policy decisions? Second, how did host governments maneuver between domestic politics and U.S. relations in the wake of anti-base opposition? The central claim was that elite beliefs and perceptions regarding U.S. relations in the context of national security (a) functioned as a political opportunity structure inhibiting or facilitating movements and (b) influenced patterns of movement–government interaction leading to particular policy outcomes.

As highlighted in the Philippine and Ecuadorian cases, anti-base movements were more likely to influence basing policy outcomes under conditions of weak security consensus. A weak consensus, leading to policy incoherence and division among elites, enabled activists to penetrate the state. With easier access to elites, anti-base forces presented an alternative security agenda by demanding the removal of U.S. bases. Not only did anti-base activists challenge elites advocating a pro-U.S. foreign policy stance, but their demands resonated with several key elites responsible for base policy decisions. Therefore, by forming ties with sympathetic elites and shaping the public discourse on bases, activists played an important role in pushing for major base policy changes.

Conversely, as demonstrated by Okinawan, Italian, and South Korean anti-base movements, activists often faced stiff resistance from governments under a strong, resilient security consensus. Shaped by and embedded within historical legacies, anticommunist ideology, and domestic institutions, a core consensus favoring alliance relations with the United States persisted among key elites in Tokyo, Rome, and Seoul. Moreover, in Japan and South Korea, heightened external threat perceptions stemming from the North Korean nuclear threat and China's regional ascension helped solidify a consensus favoring U.S. bases in the post–Cold War era. Voices demanding the withdrawal of U.S. forces certainly existed within the polity. However, these alternative views, often carried by elites on the political fringe, were typically isolated or ignored. Facing major anti-base protests, host governments attempted to diffuse domestic pressure to prevent U.S.–host-state alliance relations from deteriorating.

In crisis situations created by powerful anti-base opposition, host governments occasionally provided limited concessions in an effort to quell protests. For example, Tokyo and Washington commissioned the SACO report in response to intense protests triggered by the 1995 rape incident in Okinawa. On the whole, however, the presence of a strong or even moderate security consensus reduced anti-base movement effectiveness. Despite large-scale mobilization, basing policies remained virtually unchanged. When concessions were provided by host governments, they were often token in nature. Prioritizing national security, host governments thwarted anti-base pressure by using a range of strategies from delay, to co-optation, to coercion. In sum, a dominant elite consensus favoring a U.S. force presence and strong ties to the United States functioned as a powerful ideological barrier against anti-base movements.

THEORETICAL ISSUES

My argument embraces insights from both international relations and social movement theories. The security consensus framework draws from the political process model found in the social movement literature. It also resonates with arguments presented by statist realists addressing the role of domestic politics in international relations. Additionally, the concept of "security consensus," constituted by ideas, institutions, and ideology as well as material-based threat perceptions, borrows extensively from insights found in constructivist international relations. By selectively drawing on insights across different subfields and paradigms, I have adopted a problem-driven research approach to the study of overseas U.S. military bases and anti-base protests.[1]

A potential challenge for scholars conducting research at the nexus of different subdisciplines is the levels-of-analysis problem. As this book demonstrates, however, drawing social movement analysis into international relations theory creates space for intellectual innovation in the choice of a proper unit of analysis. Shifting the unit and level of analysis below the level of states to movement episodes opens the door for a more complex set of explanations. At the same time, this analytical move does not negate the important role of the state, or the national context in which anti-base movements are embedded. By thinking about anti-base movements at the level of countries and movement episodes, this book is able to address important theoretical and empirical questions across disciplines.

The security consensus framework is open to criticism that I present an overwhelmingly structural account of base politics. The security consensus, as a "super-variable," creates an excessively parsimonious argument, determining base policy outcomes simply by the presence or absence of elite ideational cohesion. This criticism is echoed more generally by social movement scholars

---

[1] This approach is referred to by some as analytic eclecticism. See Peter J. Katzenstein and Nobuo Okawara, "Japan, Asian-Pacific Security, and the Case for Analytical Eclecticism," *International Security* 26, no. 3 (2001): 153–85 at 154.

who find fault with the political process model. Critics contend that political opportunity structure promises to explain too much while at the same time ignoring the role of agency.[2] As Gamson and Meyer argue, "The concept of political opportunity structure is ... in danger of becoming a sponge that soaks up every aspect of the social movement environment."[3]

The empirical chapters assuage any appearances of advocating a purely structural account of base politics. In the case studies, I described movement mobilization in detail, building evidence that activists achieved moderate to high levels of mobilization strength in all the cases. In the Philippines and Ecuador, I showed how anti-base activists actively supported and formed ties with sympathetic elites. Penetrating the state, activists presented an alternative security discourse eventually adopted by enough key elites to change basing policy outcomes.[4]

A purely structural argument would directly link a weak security consensus to changes in base policies. My analysis suggests that the link and underlying causal mechanisms are more complicated. Nor is it inevitable that a weak security consensus always leads to base withdrawals or other major changes. For example, despite the weak security consensus in Ecuador, Washington and Quito would likely have re-signed the Manta base agreement had anti-base activists not escalated the issue into a national controversy. One might counter this claim by arguing that a leftist president, such as Rafael Correa, would not have accepted a U.S. military presence. However, careful process tracing of events shows that the shift against Manta, which took place even before Correa's election, rose from the bottom up. In short, the Manta case was not a pure elite-driven process dictated by a weak security consensus. Movement strategies, such as the decision to host the International No Bases Conference in Quito or the dissemination of information to elites based on extensive research in Manta and the Colombia-Ecuador border, also played an important role in outcomes.

Even under conditions of strong security consensus where movements seem to demonstrate significantly less impact, outcomes were still dependent on the actions of agents. For instance, government elites in South Korea could have used force earlier to remove local residents in Pyeongtaek. However, the government, partially out of fear of escalating anti-American sentiment, opted to delay coercive tactics until the spring of 2006. The MND's public relations campaign

---

[2] David Meyer, "Protest and Political Opportunities," *Annual Review of Sociology* 30 (2004): 125–45 at 126. Also see Jeff Goodwin and James Jasper, *Rethinking Social Movements: Structure, Meaning, and Emotion* (Oxford: Rowman and Littlefield, 2004).

[3] William Gamson and David Meyer, "Framing Political Opportunity," in *Comparative Perspectives on Social Movements: Political Opportunities, Mobilizing Structures, and Cultural Framings*, edited by Doug McAdam, John D. McCarthy, and Mayer N. Zald (Cambridge: Cambridge University Press, 1996), 275.

[4] An alternative discourse against U.S. bases already existed in the Philippines prior to the formation of anti-base movements in the early 1980s. This position was magnified by the Anti-Treaty Movement. Although the anti-base faction was never in the majority, it had built enough momentum in the elite Senate to reject U.S. bases.

prior to the dispatch of riot police also worked brilliantly in undercutting public support for the KCPT. Hence, even though a strong security consensus significantly shaped the patterns of engagement between state and society, the choices of actors still mattered. Using brute force during the development phase of the KCPT in 2005 or failing to adequately explain and interpret government actions in Pyeongtaek to South Korean citizens could potentially have altered outcomes. Derailing the entire relocation process may have been a stretch, but greater concessions to the KCPT, such as a reduction in base size, were in the realm of possibility.[5] In sum, although the consensus constrains or facilitates what actors can or cannot do, it does not determine outcomes itself. A larger part of the story revolves around the choices of movement and government actors within structural boundaries.

ADDRESSING REGIME TYPE IN THE BASE POLITICS LITERATURE

Scholars of base politics, most notably Alexander Cooley and Kent Calder, have pointed to regime type as a major factor influencing base politics. Base agreements appear most stable in consolidated democracies and most unstable during periods of democratization.[6] In various sections of the book, I have discussed regime type as a potential confounding or alternative explanation to my security consensus argument. Indeed, given the correlation between democratic transitions and mass mobilization, one might find it surprising that regime type did not play a larger role in my argument. This section addresses the issue of regime type head on and demonstrates how the security consensus holds up against regime-based explanations for base policy outcomes.

The relationship between regime type and base politics is most succinctly put forth by Alexander Cooley.[7] Cooley develops a compelling theory explaining "when and why bilateral military basing agreements become accepted, politicized, or challenged by host countries."[8] Although the argument rests on two interacting variables – the regime's political dependence on U.S. bases and the contractual credibility of political institutions – the latter variable, understood through variations among regime types, provides much of the analytical heavy lifting. For Cooley, consolidated democracies provide the most credible institutions and therefore the most stable environment for basing agreements. The institutional features of consolidated democracies – procedural legitimacy, institutional stability, and consolidated party systems – help

---

[5] Although U.S. and Korean officials stated that this was a nonoption, in the face of unrelenting anti-base opposition and a resurgence of anti-U.S. public opinion, I presume both governments would have been more amenable to KCPT demands. For instance, the KCPT wanted both governments to reassess base location plans, questioning the need for the entire relocation of the 2nd Infantry Division to Pyeongtaek or the addition of recreational facilities such as a golf course.

[6] Cooley, *Base Politics*, 16–17; Calder, *Embattled Garrisons*, 112–14.

[7] Cooley, *Base Politics*.

[8] Ibid., 3.

"lock-in" basing commitments.[9] Under consolidated democracies, basing agreements are accepted when host governments remain dependent on security contracts. Even when host governments are not dependent on U.S. bases for political, economic, or security benefits, the institutional features of democracies help depoliticize base issues. As a set of broader routine bilateral security arrangements, basing issues "are generally removed from everyday party politics and debates."[10]

Conversely, base agreements are most unstable during phases of democratic transition when contractual institutions are least credible. The lack of procedural legitimacy, jurisdictional ambiguity, and weak party systems that reward ideological or nationalist mobilization in democratizing countries all bode poorly for U.S. bases.[11] Basing agreements are highly politicized during regime shifts. In particular, host regimes not dependent on base contracts for security or other benefits "are . . . the most likely of all base hosts to unilaterally abrogate the contract and evict the U.S. military."[12]

Lastly, authoritarian regimes provide a mixed bag. The lack of independent institutions allows a central figure to dictate the terms of basing agreements. As long as the regime remains dependent on the security contract and feeds political, economic, and/or security benefits to the ruler, basing agreements remain relatively stable. However, the lack of independent institutions also places the future of bases directly at the whims of dictators. As a regime's dependence on U.S. security contracts decreases, the leverage of dictators increases vis-à-vis the United States. Base issues therefore become politicized, characterized by increasing demands from host governments. These demands may include greater economic compensation, revisions to SOFA, or a reduction in the number of troops or bases.

On one level, Cooley's analysis of base politics and my own are not competing explanations because we focus on different questions, looking at slightly different outcomes. First, my analysis focuses on a narrower aspect of base politics: the impact of anti-base movements. Second, although Cooley and I are both interested in basing policy outcomes, our dependent variables mean different things. For Cooley, outcomes refer to the politicization and stability of basing contracts. In my analysis, policy outcome is taken as a measure of movement effectiveness or movement success.

Disclaimers aside, how does the security consensus framework address the question of regime type in base politics? While acknowledging that both

---

[9] Ibid., 15–16. Procedural legitimacy refers to institutional procedures, such as legislative ratification, that give basing contracts greater domestic credibility. Institutional stability refers to the delegation of basing issues to bureaucracies. The base policymaking process becomes "entrenched" by the increasing number of "veto players" who have a stake in maintaining bases. Lastly, consolidated party systems "tend to moderate the political stance of controversial foreign policy and sovereignty issues."

[10] Ibid., 21.

[11] Ibid., 18.

[12] Ibid., 21.

approaches offer a unique contribution to our understanding of base politics, I contend that, more often than not, the security consensus subsumes regime type explanations. For the security consensus framework to hold up against Cooley's argument, the empirical cases need to demonstrate that major domestic opposition to bases and base policy changes were determined by anti-base movement pressure under conditions of weak security consensus rather than weak domestic political institutions. Conversely, the stability of base agreements should derive from the security consensus rather than the contractual credibility of political institutions under democracies. I test the weight of both arguments by briefly investigating base politics in Italy, South Korea, and the Philippines, which appear in both our works. I also include an analysis of base politics in Spain, reinterpreting Cooley's analysis through the security consensus framework.

Italy

According to Cooley's theory, during the Cold War, Italian acceptance of U.S. bases stemmed from two factors: Christian Democrat dependence on U.S. security contracts and the credibility of domestic political institutions. The democratic nature of Italian politics kept basing issues depoliticized even after the Cold War and the decline of the Christian Democrats. Although Italy's reliance on U.S. bases significantly diminished without the Soviet threat, democratic institutions helped legitimize the U.S. military presence in Italy.

Offering a different explanation, in Chapter 4 I argued that the stability of U.S. bases on Italian soil rested with the security consensus, not the political institutions associated with regime type. The high degree of regime dependence on U.S. security contracts during the Cold War, noted by Cooley, is reflected in the existence of a strong security consensus. Key elites shared a common understanding that U.S. bases functioned as a necessary component of Italian national security. Over time, Italian elites internalized the norms and values shared under the Atlantic alliance, transforming NATO into a key pillar of Italian foreign policy. The strong consensus persisted despite Italy's fragmented, and at times unstable, political party system. For example, on the eve of Prodi's 2006 electoral victory, U.S. officials feared the Italian government would renege on the Vicenza base expansion agreement signed by Prodi's conservative predecessor and political rival, Silvio Berlusconi. That he did not is more a testament to the security consensus and Italian elite understanding of the Atlantic alliance than democratic political institutions.

On the other hand, the contractual environment in Italy may be less stable than Cooley acknowledges because of frequently changing electoral laws and the disproportionate strength of minor parties. Moreover, even under consolidated democracies such as Italy, security contracts are less transparent and credible than Cooley assumes. In interviews with U.S. Consulate and Italian security experts, no one was able (or perhaps willing) to verify the existence of an overarching bilateral agreement guaranteeing Dal Molin airfield for the expansion of the 173rd Airborne Brigade.[13] In fact, No Dal Molin activists cited the lack of transparency and the central government's failure to inform Vicenza citizens about base expansion in a timely fashion as major grievances.[14] In sum, the democratic institutional logic put forth by Cooley fails to explain the politicization of the recent Vicenza movement episode and the continuity of favorable U.S. basing policies in Italy.

In the Italian case, it appears that the security consensus subsumes regime type. The moderation of left parties on foreign policy issues is explained by the dominance of the security consensus and reinforced by democratic institutions and party politics. In other words, stable, democratic institutions feed into the security consensus. Moreover, Italian elites may exhibit greater support for U.S. security relations and bases precisely because they share the same democratic principles. Contrary to Cooley's interpretation, bases are not necessarily depoliticized in Italy, as witnessed by major anti-base protests from 2006 to 2007. However, we expect basing policy outcomes to remain relatively unchanged because of the strong degree of security consensus held by Italian political elites. Because it places a high value on U.S.-Italian relations and the NATO alliance, Italy will continue to play a critical role in U.S. overseas basing strategy for the foreseeable future.

South Korea

The South Korean case also reveals discrepancies between Cooley's theory and my own. Cooley links greater politicization of USFK-related issues from 1996 to 2002 to Korea's relatively recent democratization and the uncertain contractual environment in South Korea. Democratization indeed empowered civil society to intensify criticism without having to fear a brutal government crackdown. Despite greater politicization, however, the presence of U.S. forces, SOFA, and other base-related issues remained relatively intact.

Cooley interprets the contractual environment in South Korea from 1996 to 2002 as unstable, with democratic institutions still undergoing the consolidation process. I offer a different interpretation. Strong alliance ties and the persistence of the security consensus helped South Korea weather much of the political storm, leading to few changes on basing policy issues. Cooley is correct in noting the politically charged issue of the U.S. military presence from 1996 to 2002. Perhaps this resulted from the unstable contractual environment given the democratizing nature of South Korea's political institutions, as argued by Cooley. Analyzing anti-base movements using Cooley's theory, as South

---

[13] As one Italian security expert and Ministry of Defense advisor argued, most documents related to U.S. bases had been kept secret until recently. The few documents that are available tend to be vaguely worded. Interviews with activists also corroborated this statement (interview with Italian security expert, January 22, 2008, Rome, Italy).

[14] The lack of transparency and the undemocratic nature of basing agreements were also listed as major grievances by South Korean anti-base activists in Pyeongtaek.

Korea moves toward greater democratic consolidation, we should observe a decrease in anti-base protests. Yet, in 2006, South Korea once again witnessed major clashes between the South Korean government and civil society over U.S. military issues.[15] Will base politics become routine in South Korea or, as Katharine Moon has argued, will South Korea's vibrant, growing civil society suggest even greater politicization of U.S. base issues in a period of consolidated democracy?[16] If the security consensus persists at moderate to high levels, anti-base protests will only have a limited impact on base policy outcomes. However, if we begin to see a gradual ebbing of the consensus, as many believed was the case in the early 2000s, we should expect to see not only greater contestation from civil society, but greater changes in base policy outcomes as well.

Philippines

The Philippines in 1991, marked by conditions of weak security consensus, corresponds to the unstable contractual environment found in Cooley's argument. The overthrow of Marcos and low contractual credibility of political institutions in the aftermath helped politicize U.S. bases, leading to the ouster of U.S. forces. My argument explains this outcome and the pivotal role of anti-base movements on the basis of the weak security consensus held by elites. Which interpretation provides a closer fit between theory and evidence?

Examining the Philippine case longitudinally gives us some leverage. Both Polity IV scores, which evaluate "concomitant qualities of democratic and autocratic authority in governing institutions," and Freedom House scores, which measure the degree of political and civil liberties, have remained fairly constant since 1990.[17] If the contractual environment of U.S. bases remains unchanged as indicated by measures of democracy for the Philippines, we should expect the same level of base politicization in 1991 as 2001.

What are the legitimating mechanisms that have helped depoliticize the U.S. military presence in the Philippines today?[18] With constant threats of coups, and the fluidity of party politics, it is unclear whether credible political institutions are intact in the Philippines. The acceptance of U.S. forces since 1999 therefore is better explained by the reemergence of the security consensus among key Philippine elites, as argued in Chapter 6. Thus, the stable contractual environment guaranteeing U.S. military-related agreements today, such as the 1999

---

[15] A democratic institutional argument would counter this criticism by arguing that base policy outcomes remained unchanged during this period.

[16] Moon, "Korean Nationalism, Anti-Americanism, and Democratic Consolidation."

[17] Polity IV scores have been locked at 8 (out of 10, with 10 being most democratic) since 1987. Freedom House scores have generally hovered between 2 and 3 (on a 1–7 scale, 1 being most free) since 1987.

[18] The absence of permanent bases may be the simplest answer. Moreover, U.S. troops are primarily located in the southern Philippines, far from the political capital. However, as Herbert Docena notes, the constant rotation of U.S. forces has de facto reestablished a permanent U.S. presence in the Philippines, even without U.S. bases. See Docena, *At the Door of All the East.*

VFA and the 2002 Mutual Logistics Support Agreement (MLSA), is shaped more by the strong security consensus than by consolidated democratic institutions.

Spain

A case study in Cooley's research not found in my book is the Spanish case. Does the security consensus framework apply to additional cases found in Cooley's work but not my own? Rather than challenging the institutional argument presented by Cooley, I use his analysis to probe whether my framework applies to Spanish anti-base movements in the 1980s.

The security consensus was relatively weak in Spain in the early 1980s. Spain was loosely aligned with the West during the early years of the Cold War. However, unlike other strong U.S. allies such as Germany and Italy, Spain remained outside NATO until 1981. The ideological and institutional ties shaping elite perceptions and beliefs regarding the U.S. alliance were not fully developed during this period. This is reflected in the 1982 presidential election, where Felipe Gonzalez of the Socialist Party (PSOE) ran on an anti-NATO party platform. While Gonzalez remained ambivalent about a U.S. base presence, other PSOE and Communist (PCE) members voiced their opposition to both NATO and U.S. bases.[19] Meanwhile, anti-base activists routinely organized large demonstrations outside U.S. bases in Rota, Zaragoza, and Madrid.

Gonzalez eventually backtracked from his initial anti-NATO stance, successfully guiding Spain's entry into the Atlantic community in 1982. However, base issues remained unsettled. In the mid-1980s, the PSOE pushed for more favorable basing terms. Spanish base negotiators listed the closure of the Torrejón Air Base as a high priority. After two years of negotiations, the United States and Spain concluded a new basing arrangement that reduced the U.S. troop presence in Spain by 40 percent. Furthermore, Spanish negotiators extracted additional economic and military benefits. Most importantly, the United States agreed to withdraw forces from bases in Torrejón and Zaragoza.[20]

Cooley attributes the politicization and outcome of base politics during this period to the instability of political institutions resulting from Spain's recent democratization. I do not necessarily counter this explanation. However, the correlation between strong anti-base mobilization, a weak security consensus, and major shifts in base policy outcomes makes it worth exploring the security consensus framework in the Spanish case. Did anti-base movements and the conditions of weak security consensus contribute to base closures during the 1986–88 negotiations? A fundamental question is whether anti-base movements helped Gonzalez solidify his position entering base negotiations with the United States in 1986. Did anti-base activists work with sympathetic elites, pushing the government to negotiate more favorable base terms?

---

[19] Cooley, *Base Politics*, 76.
[20] Ibid., 79.

On the one hand, base policy outcomes may have been purely elite driven. Even without major protests, the PSOE likely would have pushed for a new basing agreement. A movement-based account, however, posits that, absent major protests, PSOE members would not have formulated and sustained a coherent position challenging current basing arrangements. A weak security consensus enabled activists to work in tandem with anti-base elites to push forward an alternative basing agreement. Even if activists and elites shared the same preferences, it may have required anti-base movements to help elites project and clarify their true positions publicly. My discussion does not challenge Cooley's interpretation of the Spanish case per se. It only suggests reconsidering the case from the vantage point of social movements, evaluated in the context of U.S.-Spain relations and the elite security consensus prevailing at the time.

In sum, I differ from Cooley by arguing that bilateral relations and the salience of national security weigh heavily in the politics of military bases. The security consensus conditions elite responses to domestic base opposition irrespective of regime type. I argue that the depoliticization of U.S. bases has less to do with the consolidated nature of democratic institutions and more to do with the existing security consensus permeating key elites in host countries.

Despite empirical discrepancies between Cooley's analysis and my own work, the two theories are not necessarily incompatible. In certain respects, the two arguments may complement one another since Cooley does not specifically address anti-base movements in his own theory nor do I specifically discuss regime type in my own argument.[21] It may be beyond mere coincidence that allied countries where the security consensus remains strongest – Germany, Italy, Japan, and South Korea – also happen to be consolidated democracies. On closer examination, the three mechanisms discussed by Cooley that help depoliticize U.S. basing issues – procedural legitimacy, internal jurisdiction, and party politics – actually feed into the sources of security consensus.[22] For example, the bureaucratization of base politics in countries like Japan helps perpetuate and institutionalize elite perceptions and beliefs about U.S. bases and the U.S.-Japan alliance. Likewise, the consolidation of political parties helps solidify the dominant position of elites favoring a strong security consensus. Thus elite attitudes and beliefs, buffered by the institutional mechanisms suggested by Cooley, help stabilize basing agreements despite the presence of major anti-base protests.

---

[21] Regime type is taken for granted in my analysis, partly because the phenomenon of anti-base movements is most acute in post-democratized societies. Regime type matters when exploring anti-base movements because it affects the probability of successful mobilization (i.e., authoritarian regimes tend to quash civil societal attempts at collective action) as well as the degree of state penetration. Anti-base movements will find it more difficult to penetrate strong, autocratic states compared with democratic states, which provide access through institutional procedures and formal channels. Kent Calder also addresses the interaction between anti-base movements and regime type, examining the distinction between centralized and decentralized democracies as an intervening variable on policy outcomes. See Calder, *Embattled Garrisons*, 123.

[22] The impact of institutions in Cooley's argument corresponds to the dimension of "depth" in my coding of the security consensus.

THE FUTURE OF U.S. BASING STRATEGY

In 2004, the Pentagon's Global Defense Posture Review (GDPR), the blueprint behind overseas U.S. military base realignment, called for a shift from large, permanent bases to lighter facilities such as forward operating bases or cooperative security locations (CSLs).[23] Representing the first major transformation of U.S. global force posture since the post–World War II era, the GDPR reflected not only a change in strategic thinking but the increasing political and diplomatic difficulties stemming from American bases.[24]

Although the GDPR revealed the future of U.S. overseas basing strategy, initial adjustments to base realignment were already in motion with the end of the Cold War. Following strategic and operational changes outlined in the Pentagon's 2001 Quadrennial Defense Review (QDR), the Bush administration mandated a thorough review of U.S. global force posture. In particular, the review addressed the shift from static defense to expeditionary operations, new advances in military technology and capabilities, and increasing uncertainty in the strategic environment.[25] Thus, the Pentagon began its review process *prior* to the events of 9/11. However, this cataclysmic event reinforced the dire need for a flexible strategy and new global force posture. An overseas basing strategy needed to reflect "new" threats such as terrorism, the proliferation of weapons of mass destruction, and insurgency movements unfolding in Afghanistan and Iraq.[26] Additionally, the strategy needed to contend with the possible realignment of traditional alliances and the addition of new strategic partners.[27]

As discussed in this book and other volumes addressing the politics of bases, a central characteristic of base politics is its two-level nature. The international

[23] Kurt Campbell and Celeste Johnson Ward, "New Battle Stations?" *Foreign Affairs* 82, no. 5 (2003): 95–103. Forward operating sites are installations with pre-positioned equipment ready for use and a minimal troop presence. Cooperative security locations are created through prearranged agreements with the host state. This arrangement provides the United States access to host-government facilities for training and operations purposes but requires little or no permanent troops in peacetime. The new basing arrangements along the "arc of instability" provide greater flexibility in meeting new global security threats. See United States Department of State, Foreign Press Center Briefing, "Senior Administration Officials from the Departments of State and Defense," Washington, D.C., August 16, 2004. http://fpc.state.gov/fpc/35246.htm (accessed October 18, 2006).

[24] The GDPR is also known as the Integrated Global Presence and Basing Strategy (IGPBS). Global defense posture "comprises the size, location, types, and capabilities of forward military forces. It constitutes a fundamental element of our ability to project power and undertake military actions beyond our borders." See United States Department of Defense, "Strengthening U.S. Global Defense Posture: Report to Congress," Washington, D.C., September 17, 2004, 4.

[25] Ibid.

[26] The OBC acknowledged new threats along the "arc of instability" spanning West Africa, the Middle East, Southeast Asia, the Pacific, and the Andes. However, the OBC also cautioned against ruling out traditional great power rivalries in Asia or Europe. Additionally, the OBC's review of U.S. global force posture recommended adopting a comprehensive definition of threats, taking into account human rights violations, natural disasters, and epidemics.

[27] United States Department of Defense, "Strengthening U.S. Global Defense Posture," 2.

environment shapes bilateral relations, which in turn establishes the permissive conditions for U.S. bases in host countries. However, the domestic politics of host nations also has an enormous bearing on the status and operation of U.S. forces. Thus, well before President Bush's August 2004 message on global defense posture, the United States had already embarked on an ambitious diplomatic campaign, consulting with dozens of allies about changes in U.S. overseas force deployment.[28]

The Overseas Basing Committee (OBC) took a positive step by identifying the political risks associated with the current direction of U.S. global force posture. Currently, the United States relies on a mix of traditional alliances and new partners to hedge against future threats. The former provides predictability and greater reliability for cooperation and access in the event of conflict. The latter gives the United States improved access and proximity to global hotspots. In the final review, the OBC reiterated the importance of traditional alliance partners and advised the DOD to reassess the timing of troop withdrawals in major host countries, particularly Germany. At the same time, the OBC called for caution when relying on new alliance partners. Specifically, the United States should not assume the possibility of long-term relations prior to any formalized agreement.[29] Bilateral arrangements with new partners lack a mutual history of support. Furthermore, new partners characterized as fledgling democracies or autocracies, particularly those concentrated in Africa and Central Asia, do not guarantee long-term political stability. Admitting that U.S. soft power is on the decline, the OBC correctly suggested that base planners consider the motives behind new basing agreements, such as short-term economic gains versus long-term national interests.[30] In light of domestic anti-base opposition, then, the security consensus framework offers four sets of policy implications related to U.S. overseas basing strategy.

1. Managing and Strengthening the Security Consensus

While the OBC recognizes domestic instability as an issue affecting U.S. force presence and basing access, particularly with new security partners, it also assumes that our traditional allies will generally accept U.S. basing arrangements. This assumption is warranted if we accept the security consensus hypothesis. Even when faced with serious civil societal pressure against U.S. forces, host-government elites are likely to stave off movement pressure and manage their alliance relations with the United States if a security consensus exists.

Unfortunately, global attitudes regarding U.S. leadership have shifted in recent years, suggesting a decline in the security consensus in some parts of the

---

[28] Ibid., 14.
[29] Overseas Basing Committee, *Interim Report of the Commission on Review of Overseas Military Facility Structure of the United States*, 8.
[30] Ibid., 10.

world.[31] As argued throughout this book, an eroding security consensus enables activists to exploit elite divisions, magnifying domestic opposition against the U.S. military presence. This was illustrated in the Philippines, where a weak security consensus, undoubtedly accelerated by the democratization movement and the post–Cold War security environment, led to base closure. Turkey is another case where the lack of elite consensus and domestic opposition resulted in the rejection of base access and overflight passes for Operation Iraqi Freedom.

The United States has little direct control over the degree of security consensus within host governments. The consensus shifts with changes in the external security environment and internal domestic political factors that Washington may or may not be able to influence. Where possible, however, the United States can take action by promoting policies that foster mutual trust, respect, and transparency among alliance partners. If host-nation acceptance of U.S. forces rests on shared national interests, Washington must demonstrate to its allies that they, too, have a stake in the U.S. global defense posture. Quid pro quos function as effective leveraging tools in base politics, but a stable network of overseas bases cannot be sustained entirely through compensation politics. The U.S. military presence and foreign bases must also fit into the host nation's national interest and overarching security framework.

A common perception among anti-base activists (and some host-government elites) is that the U.S. global defense posture exists *solely* for the benefit of U.S. interests – that the United States' strategic imperatives trump all other motives behind the planning of its overseas basing strategy. And reflecting on some questionable U.S. foreign policy behavior in the past – meddling in domestic affairs, propping up dictatorships, or circumventing human rights conventions – anti-base activists have good reason to believe that a U.S. military presence functions more as a force of evil rather than good.[32] Often missed from this perspective, however, is the understanding of security as a collective good and the possibility that U.S. bases at times function as a stabilizing, balancing force. For instance, in the Asia-Pacific, a region plagued with historical animosities, mutual distrust, and relative insecurity, the U.S. military may function as a stabilizing linchpin. As Singapore's prime minister Lee Kwan Yew argued, the United States is often perceived by Asian leaders as the "least distrusted actor" in the region.[33]

---

[31] Pew Research Center, Pew Global Attitudes Project, "America's Image Slips, but Allies Share U.S. Concerns Over Iran, Hamas," June 15, 2006; Stephen Walt, *Taming American Power: The Global Response to U.S. Primacy* (New York: W.W. Norton, 2005); and Chalmers A. Johnson, *Nemesis: The Last Days of the American Republic* (New York: Metropolitan Books, 2007).

[32] This view was apparent in Kyrgyzstan in 2010 when opposition leaders criticized the United States for ignoring the abuses and corruption of former president Kurmanbek Bakiyev to avoid jeopardizing U.S. basing access. Although the acting prime minister reassured the United States continued use of Manas Air Base as a transit hub for the war in Afghanistan, the fate of Manas remained precarious. Domestic issues fueled the violent protests that deposed the Bakiyev government. Had the energy of antigovernment protestors also been directed toward the Manas base, opposition leaders would have certainly been less accommodating to U.S. strategic concerns.

[33] Thomas Christensen, "Fostering Stability or Creating a Monster?" *International Security* 31, no. 3 (2006): 81–126 at 87.

Strengthening the security consensus requires greater diplomatic effort on the part of the United States in clarifying its strategic goals and objectives to host-nation partners. This warrants a larger role for the State Department on overseas basing issues and more generally in international affairs. More specifically, the United States needs to bolster public diplomacy. One possible solution is the resurrection of the United States Information Agency (USIA). Until its closure in October 1999, USIA used a wide range of overseas information programs to foster mutual understanding between the United States and other nations. Before its functions were transferred to the State Department's Bureau of Public Affairs, USIA maintained 190 offices in 142 countries, with the broad goal of explaining and supporting American foreign policy and promoting U.S. national interests.[34] Unfortunately, as Senator John McCain argued, "Dismantling an agency dedicated to promoting America and Americans amounted to unilateral disarmament in the struggle of ideas."[35] Under Secretary of State Hillary Clinton's leadership, the Obama administration has taken steps to improve America's image abroad. As the GAO recommended to the incoming Obama administration in 2009, "In today's highly volatile global environment, it is more critical than ever that the United States effectively coordinate, manage, and implement its public diplomacy and strategic communications activities to affect foreign public opinion."[36] Whether conducted by the State Department and Pentagon or an independent agency such as USIA, the United States needs to communicate its strategy and values clearly and persuasively to other nations. The information disseminated should be factual and objective, not deliberately spun to put the United States in a favorable light, which will only arouse suspicion.[37]

To manage the security consensus, the United States should also consider extending its network ties to opposition political members in host countries.[38] The goal is to demonstrate to both incumbent and opposition political leaders that host countries have a national security stake in maintaining close security ties to the United States. Alexander Cooley has advocated a "political hedging" strategy by maintaining contacts with opposition political groups and actors. A hedging strategy ultimately lowers the risk of major base policy upheavals in the event of regime change or other domestic political windfalls.[39] We cannot assume that our traditional allies will indefinitely accept or refrain from seriously challenging U.S. strategic imperatives when contingency plans implicate host countries.

---

[34] See archived Web site of the former United States Information Agency. http://dosfan.lib.uic.edu/usia/usiahome/factshe.htm (last accessed April 3, 2008).

[35] John McCain, "Hone U.S. Message of Freedom," *Orlando Sentinel*, June 28, 2007.

[36] Walter Pincus, "GAO Calls for a New Priority on Public Diplomacy," *Washington Post*, January 12, 2009.

[37] American Political Science Association, *Task Force on U.S. Standing in World Affairs. 2009. U.S. Standing in The World: Causes, Consequences, and the Future* (Washington, D.C.: American Political Science Association, 2009).

[38] This prescription is also advocated by Alexander Cooley and Kent Calder. See Cooley, *Base Politics*, 273; and Calder, *Embattled Garrisons*, 239.

[39] Cooley, *Base Politics*, 273; and Calder, *Embattled Garrisons*, 239.

2. New Allies, Bad Friends?

I echo the words of caution issued by the OBC as the United States signs basing agreements with new allies and partners. As Alexander Cooley argues, weak institutions and the political uncertainty of democratic transitions create an unstable environment for U.S. bases. Therefore, the United States should weigh other options before signing deals with authoritarian regimes, or even nascent democracies.[40] Along similar lines, Kent Calder predicts an increase in "bazaar politics" – when host nations "haggle and play aggressive dual games" in an effort to extract as much as possible from the United States – as Washington forges new ties with regimes in Central Asia and the Middle East.[41] I offer a somewhat different explanation (but arrive at the same conclusions as Calder and Cooley) why some of our new allies may not make the best friends in the long term.

Unlike agreements with Washington's traditional alliance partners, new security agreements forged with volatile regimes lack the long-standing historical legacy, ideology, or institutional mechanisms that help reinforce a strong security consensus among government elites. Newer basing agreements, such as the CSLs negotiated in Uganda, Kenya, Ghana, and Zambia, are signed by host states under the pretense of short-term gains through foreign aid, military assistance, or political legitimacy. The lack of deeper security interests or shared values suggests a precarious bilateral relationship.

A weak or absent consensus makes basing arrangements much more susceptible to change based on events and circumstances. Diplomatic confrontation, civil societal opposition, or base-related accidents that normally would not warrant the abrogation of base agreements under conditions of a strong security consensus could potentially trigger major base policy changes. The diplomatic fallout between the United States and Uzbekistan and the ouster of U.S. forces from the K2 base in 2005 is instructive. U.S. criticism of the Karimov regime's brutal crackdown against protestors in Andijon resulted in restricted nighttime flights and heavy airlifts from K2. Eventually, the Uzbekistan government terminated the SOFA, resulting in the withdrawal of U.S. forces.[42]

The news is not all bad regarding new alliance partners. Although elites in African or Central Asian states lack a strong consensus supporting U.S. security arrangements, we should expect more favorable attitudes toward U.S. bases in Eastern Europe.[43] In recent years, the United States has negotiated basing arrangements with Romania, Bulgaria, and Poland. As these countries are members of NATO, their elites are generally supportive of U.S. policies and

---

[40] Cooley, "Base Politics."

[41] Calder, *Embattled Garrisons*, 140, 113.

[42] Cooley, *Base Politics*, 230–31.

[43] Cooley also finds greater stability in Bulgaria and Romania as a result of their consolidated democratic status and the stability of domestic political institutions. See Cooley, *Base Politics*, 244–46.

place a high value on their strategic partnership with Washington.[44] Elites perceive NATO membership and close ties to the United States not only as a means of boosting international reputation but also as a deterrent against Russian influence.

In sum, DOD plans to expand its overseas basing network in regions such as Africa, Central Asia, and Eastern Europe have resulted in several new basing agreements since 2001 – some with democracies, others with states having more questionable democratic credentials. The United States should exercise caution when selecting new partners for basing agreements. States with similar regional security goals, interests, and values as the United States, shared by the majority of host-government political elites, make the best partners for a U.S. overseas basing strategy.

There is some truth that basing agreements are unstable under weak democracies. Unfortunately, the United States cannot simply avoid dictatorships or fledgling democracies across the board. On occasion, strategic interests necessitate working with less than ideal regimes to secure larger objectives. Difficult trade-offs must be made. On the one hand, by adopting what other nations perceive as hypocritical policies, the United States creates the potential for "blowback." On the other hand, the international environment is constantly changing. Basing arrangements critical today may be unnecessary ten years from now, enabling base planners to discount longer-term basing arrangements.

Perhaps the best strategy is a diversified portfolio of bases. The United States should maintain several main operating bases with traditional allies or new partners where the security consensus runs high. When securing basing agreements with new partners, the United States should weigh in on domestic political factors affecting the mid- to long-term stability of agreements. The United States should clarify the role of the U.S. presence with host nations. Money talks, and quid pro quos may initially attract political elites. But, for longer-term arrangements, the United States will have to foster stronger diplomatic ties to host states so that elites themselves perceive a security stake in their partnership with the United States.

3. Afghanistan and Iraq

What implications can be drawn for U.S. bases in Afghanistan and Iraq? Even if the United States denies the "permanent" status of these bases or presents a timetable for troop withdrawal, it is unclear whether some bases will remain in place for at least the mid- to long term.[45] The Obama administration announced in December 2009 that it would increase the number of U.S. forces in

---

[44] This does not mean, however, that anti-base opposition will not take place in NATO countries. This was the case in the Czech Republic, where anti-base protestors mobilized to block the establishment of a missile defense radar installation in 2009.

[45] Carl Hulse, "House Resolution Rejects Permanent Bases in Iraq," *Washington Post*, July 26, 2007; and Cooley, *Base Politics*, 266.

Afghanistan by 30,000 troops, bringing the total number of U.S. troops in Afghanistan to nearly 100,000 by late 2010.[46] Prior to this announcement, the Pentagon was already building $1.1 billion worth of military bases in Afghanistan to accommodate the previous surge of U.S. forces in 2008–9. The cost of constructing new barracks, airfields, training areas, and warehouses is projected to reach $4 billion.[47]

However, protests and violent armed opposition against the U.S. military have erupted on numerous occasions. For example, protests erupted in May 2006 when a U.S. military convoy truck recklessly slammed into traffic, killing several people. Aggravating the situation, U.S. soldiers fired into a crowd as angry Afghans rioted on the streets.[48] Civilian fatalities stemming from controversial airstrikes, most notably in August 2008, have deepened levels of fear and resentment against U.S. and NATO forces.[49]

At least within Kabul, however, Afghan leaders share the belief that U.S. military and NATO forces must remain in Afghanistan if the regime is to survive. Thus, the central government is not likely to push for major changes on base-related issues until the country stabilizes. With that said, U.S. planners should remain wary of political instability and insecurity outside of Kabul. Afghanistan's fragmented provinces and President Harmid Karzai's inability to influence warlords outside of Kabul make predictions on base politics difficult. One of Washington's priorities in Afghanistan is to assist Kabul in expanding its capacity to govern beyond the capital region. A true security consensus cannot exist as long as provinces function independent of Kabul.

In Iraq, anti-U.S. forces – both the violent and nonviolent variants – put pressure on the fragile Iraqi government to draw down the U.S. military presence as quickly as possible. Noteworthy were influential religious clerics such as Muqtada al-Sadr, who repeatedly demanded the withdrawal of U.S. occupation forces. Civilian casualties, abuse scandals, and the recklessness of private military contractors also pushed Iraqi officials to demand greater regulations against the U.S. military as well as private military corporations. Despite ongoing security concerns, it is difficult to argue that a strong consensus favoring permanent bases or a long-term U.S. military presence exists in Iraq. This was attested by the Iraqi government's eagerness to assume primary security control in June 2009.

[46] Ian S. Livingston, Heather L. Messera, and Michael O'Hanlon, *Afghanistan Index*, April 8 (Washington, D.C.: Brookings Institution, 2010).

[47] Ann Tyson, "U.S. Commanders Request 10,000 Additional Troops for Afghanistan," *Washington Post*, April 1, 2009; and Walter Pincus, "U.S. Construction in Afghanistan a Sign of Long Commitment," *Washington Post*, January 13, 2009.

[48] Carlotta Gall, "Afghans Raise Toll of Dead from May Riots in Kabul to 17," *New York Times*, June 8, 2006. The death toll eventually climbed to twenty.

[49] See United Nations Assistance Mission to Afghanistan, *Afghanistan: Annual Report on Protection of Civilians in Armed Conflict, 2008* (Kabul: United Nations Assistance Mission to Afghanistan, 2009).

The withdrawal of "combat troops" brought total U.S. troop levels to just under 50,000 in September 2010. President Obama intends to follow through on his goal of removing the remaining U.S. forces by the end of 2011. However, the majority of Iraqis recognize that a continued U.S. military presence is contingent on whether Iraqi forces are capable of handling security on their own.[50] Only at the fringes do we find Iraqis either in full support of a permanent presence or wanting an immediate withdrawal of U.S. forces at all costs. As Kenneth Pollack of the Brookings Institution argues, "The vast majority fall in the middle – determined that U.S. troops should leave, but only after a certain period of time."[51] The preceding statement provides ample wiggle room, but it is quite conceivable that a small contingent of U.S. forces will remain in Iraq even after the war ends. Under this scenario, several U.S. bases may remain open in Iraq. Although Iraqi political elites will likely see a major long-term U.S. presence as a political liability, they could accept a smaller number of troops to continue training and advising Iraqi security forces beyond 2011. If an elite consensus linking the U.S. military presence with Iraqi national security strengthens over time, the United States may be able to retain its bases within the region. However, if political elites remain split over competing visions of Iraq's long-term security relationship with Washington, anti-base elements may gain leverage and increase the political costs of keeping American bases inside Iraq.

4. U.S. Bases and the Local Community

Base politics scholars have recommended that policymakers address the "micro-politics" of bases that adversely impact bilateral relations.[52] This includes addressing base issues at the local level, where most anti-base movements are rooted.[53] Currently, the U.S. military hosts numerous community relations programs that enable local residents and U.S. military members to interact through sports, community service, and cultural activities. Members of the U.S. military visit local schools and provide free tutoring or English language instruction.

Although these programs improve community relations between the U.S. military and local residents, they tend to draw in community members from the "pro-base side." Base commanders and public affairs officers do not necessarily avoid dialogue and discussion with anti-base residents. However, an attitude persists among base officials that everybody who can be potentially persuaded has already been persuaded, with the remainder opposing U.S. bases

---

[50] Kenneth Pollack, "Five Myths about the Iraq Troop Withdrawal," *Washington Post*, August 22, 2010. http://www.washingtonpost.com/wp-dyn/content/article/2010/08/19/AR2010081905642_2.html (last accessed September 4, 2010).

[51] Ibid.

[52] Cooley, *Base Politics*, 272.

[53] Smith, *Shifting Terrain*; and Lutz, *Bases of Empire*.

for ideological reasons.[54] As one commanding officer wrote to an activist, "We have to agree to disagree."[55] My own observations of relations between local residents and the U.S. military corroborate the sentiments of base officials. Understandably, base commanders do not want to spend time and energy interacting with those who resent their presence and refuse to listen to the "voice of reason." Community networks, however, are an important part of base politics. Implementing concrete measures addressing (or preventing) problems arising from the base presence, such as crime, pollution, or noise, help build credibility and trust behind U.S. intentions within the local community. If directly meeting anti-base residents and activists is a nonstarter, working with local community leaders to explain the reasons and benefits behind the U.S. military presence may work as an indirect method of disseminating information.[56]

ANTI-BASE MOVEMENTS: LOCAL AND GLOBAL

Finally, we return to the central topic of this book: anti-base movements. Where do anti-base movements fit into base politics and overseas basing strategy? Anti-base protests are only one component of base politics. At times, however, they exert a powerful impact on base policy decisions. Unfortunately, the patterns, motives, and behavior of anti-base movements and their ability to undermine bilateral relations and U.S. basing strategy are not always clearly understood. U.S. base officials, diplomats, and policymakers often evaluate anti-base movements as a monolithic entity. In reality, anti-base movements, as described in the empirical sections of this book, are comprised of different actors. Each addresses the issue of bases from a slightly different angle. The variety of anti-base protestors range from local residents focused on NIMBY issues to "professional" activists deeply engaged in broader, transnational social justice movements. Likewise, activists with different political agendas join anti-base movements to assert their particular cause, such as the environment, sexual crimes and abuse, or demilitarization. When mobilized effectively, civil society not only creates tension between alliance partners but threatens the permissive environment for a U.S. global force posture.

In the previous section, I covered several policy implications and prescriptions for U.S. overseas basing strategy. What insights and lessons can be drawn for anti-base movements? I offer four sets of recommendations for activists regarding anti-base movement strategy and advocacy. The first suggestion stems directly from the security consensus framework: when possible, activists should

---

[54] Interview with base officials at Yongsan Garrison and Camp Humphreys in South Korea and Camp Ederle in Vicenza.

[55] Letter from Major General Frank Helmick, Commanding General, United States Army Southern European Task Force, to a Vicenza activist, November 19, 2007.

[56] This point was raised by the base commander at Camp Humphreys in an interview conducted on December 7, 2005.

form ties with political elites. As discussed in the introductory chapter, U.S. base policies are ultimately decided by government officials. Therefore, anti-base movements gain greater leverage and influence on basing policy outcomes when they form ties with key elites. This was certainly the case with successful anti-base movements such as the Anti-Treaty Movement in the Philippines and the No Bases Coalition in Ecuador. Although not included in this volume, ties between Puerto Rican anti-base activists and several U.S. congressional representatives helped activists shut down Roosevelt Roads Naval Station in Vieques in 2001. The support of several prominent U.S. political figures such as Hillary Clinton and Jesse Jackson, and the direct involvement of U.S. representatives such as Nydia M. Velazquez and Luis V. Gutierrez, increased publicity and political leverage for the Vieques movement.[57]

Encouraging anti-base movements to form ties with sympathetic elites seems self-evident. Yet, one might find surprising the level of resistance to this suggestion by some activists. Ties to political elites raise the specter of co-optation. The lack of trust in politicians, the political establishment, or more generally formal politics often stems from activists' own experience and interaction with government officials over the course of several movement episodes. This attitude was expressed by several anti-base activists in South Korea, Japan, and even the Philippines. Activists in Vicenza also faced heated discussions over strategy: Should they maintain support for radical left parties? At the local level, should movement leaders move from informal to more formal avenues of politics?[58] Although the wariness of movements in engaging formal political actors is understandable, research across several anti-base movement episodes suggests that movements that form alliances with political elites and engage base politics through both formal and informal channels tend to have a greater impact on basing policy outcomes.

Second, activists must seek broad coalitions with diverse groups, even at the risk of intercoalition division and factionalism. Although no strict formula for anti-base coalition formation exists, the trajectory of most anti-base movements begins at the local level, eventually shifting scale to the national or transnational level. Scale shift occurs when movement leaders at the local level, acting as brokers, contact or reach out to outside civil societal groups and NGOs.[59] Broad anti-base coalitions are advantageous through their greater mobilizing capacities, which in turn generate greater publicity and media attention. This was the case in the movement to shut down the Kooni Firing Range in Maehyangri, described briefly in Chapter 5. Maehyangri was virtually unheard of, despite protests by local villagers to close the Kooni Range since the late

---

[57] See Katherine T. McCaffrey, *Military Power and Popular Protest: The U.S. Navy in Vieques, Puerto Rico* (New Brunswick, N.J.: Rutgers University Press, 2002).

[58] E-mail correspondence with No Dal Molin activist Enzo Ciscato, May 15, 2008.

[59] Activists representing organizations at the regional or national levels may also act as brokers, offering their support even before local movement leaders reach out to outside groups. See Yeo, "Not in Anyone's Backyard."

1980s. Without the involvement of numerous NGOs and civic groups, the bombing accident in Maehyangri in 2000 would likely have gone unnoticed. Fortunately, a year before the accident, a documentary about the plight of Maehyangri residents in 1999 drew the attention of several NGOs, including Green Korea United (GKU). After the accident, GKU and other civic groups involved in the PAR-SOFA campaign latched onto the Maehyangri issue, committing their support to local anti-base leaders. Local anti-base activists alone would not have been able to build the pressure necessary to force U.S. and South Korean officials to the negotiating table.

Third, and related to the previous point, activists need to adopt framing strategies that attract a broad formation but at the same time minimize (1) potential factionalism within the group and (2) the alienation of local anti-base groups within the larger coalition. Anti-base movements in the Philippines or the SOFA revision movement in South Korea led to full or partial concessions formed under politically neutral campaign banners, such as the Anti-Treaty Movement or People's Action for Reform of the Unjust SOFA. These neutral slogans helped draw in other civil societal actors who were often wary of joining anti-base groups associated with groups on the Far Left.[60] Friction between local and national groups also loomed large in several anti-base coalitions, such as those in Okinawa. Successful movements in the Philippines and Ecuador were able to avoid these tensions, partially because the movement's center of gravity began at the national rather than local level. For other coalitions with a strong local base, however, such as those in Vicenza and Pyeongtaek, "outside" groups worked to ensure that local grievances were not neglected by the broader framing of the movement. The length and scale of mobilization experienced by the KCPT and the No Dal Molin campaigns would not have taken place unless the more abstract claims for peace and sovereignty had been bridged with more tangible frames such as forced eviction or environmental destruction.

Fourth, what should activists do when confronted with a strong security consensus? Rather than abandon all hope, activists must remain cognizant of political opportunities and the importance of timing. Although the security consensus acts as a powerful ideational barrier, political opportunities operating at the subnational level still allow activists to exert pressure on governments. These political opportunities arise during election periods, during the run-up to base renegotiations, or at more unexpected moments following base-related tragedies. Even if activists are unable to accomplish the ultimate goal of shutting down existing U.S. bases or preventing the construction of new ones, a well-organized campaign in a limited time frame can (1) put pressure on the alliance, forcing the U.S. and host governments to modify existing base plans; (2) pressure

---

[60] Debate over the use of moderate versus radical tactics took place within the ATM and PAR-SOFA. By and large, however, the overarching strategies called for moderation, thus providing political space for more politically neutral NGOs, such as environmental organizations, to enter the coalition.

governments to accept greater accountability and transparency on U.S. base issues; and (3) give voice to local residents who would otherwise suffer in silence. This was the case in protests against the Kooni Firing Range in South Korea and, to a lesser extent, the 2009 fiasco over Futenma's relocation. Intense anti-base opposition in Japan, South Korea, and Italy has also required host governments to conduct additional studies on the environmental impact of bases resulting in modifications to initial base plans.

In studying anti-base movements in different parts of the world, I noticed many striking similarities and patterns. Anti-base activists used similar frames, often a mixture of local rights and justice claims embedded within more abstract peace and sovereignty frames. Movements relied on loose coalition structures as their mode of organization. Although opposed to U.S. bases and U.S. policies, activists targeted the host government rather than the United States. Perhaps the least profound but most symbolically meaningful similarity was the anti-base movements' predilection for large tents. My first visit to the Presidio – the large white tent functioning as the headquarters of the No Dal Molin campaign – evoked earlier memories of candlelight vigils in the Pyeongtaek greenhouse or conversations in the tentlike structure at Henoko. The Tuesday night public forum I witnessed inside the Presidio felt surreal, as if the same discussions of strategy, same criticisms against U.S. bases, and same words of hope and encouragement had been transported from Pyeongtaek in 2005 to Vicenza in 2008.

These similarities and patterns warrant further research on anti-base movements as a global or transnational phenomenon. This book has focused almost entirely on domestic anti-base movements. However, a growing transnational anti-base network also exists. As "rooted cosmopolitans," many local anti-base activists have formed ties with other anti-base campaigns facing similar struggles in an effort to reduce or abolish U.S. bases around the world.[61] From a policy perspective, U.S. officials may brush aside transnational anti-base movements for now. However, if local grievances remain unaddressed, anti-base activists will win additional support for their cause. They will continue to deepen ties not only among themselves but with the unmobilized mass public and political elites. For example, peace activists across Europe mobilized to support anti-base initiatives in the Czech Republic before the Obama administration decided to cancel plans for a missile defense radar base in that country. Populist support for left-leaning elites in Ecuador, Bolivia, and Venezuela also complicated U.S. basing initiatives in Latin America.[62]

Chalmers Johnson writes, "The American network of bases is a sign not of military preparedness but of militarism, the inescapable companion of imperialism."[63] Although it may be a stretch to equate the U.S. global force posture with

---

[61] Tarrow, *New Transnational Activism*, 28–29.

[62] Mahyar A. Amouzegar, *Evaluation of Options for Overseas Combat Support Basing* (Santa Monica, Calif.: RAND, 2006), xxxv.

[63] Johnson, *Sorrows of Empire*, 24.

formal empires of the past, this is exactly how many opponents of military bases interpret the network of U.S. overseas bases. As visible symbols of U.S. power abroad, bases, at times, elicit intense political reactions. For sure, we can expect more anti-base protests in the future. The global anti-base movement strives to channel and transform the local NIMBY nature of anti-base protests into a transnational "not in anyone's backyard" movement. The key question is whether anti-base movements progress to the point where an overseas basing strategy becomes increasingly costly or untenable because of political opposition in critical combat support or access regions.[64] Relying more heavily on lighter facilities, joint-use bases, or nonpermanent access agreements may help address or avoid NIMBY grievances. However, beyond these "creative" military arrangements, the United States will need to diligently pursue parallel political and diplomatic solutions if it wishes to sustain its network of overseas bases in the future. Both U.S. and host-government officials need to understand why anti-base opposition erupts. Although co-optation and coercion might serve as quick fixes to stave off domestic pressure and preserve alliance relations, in the long run these strategies do little to promote U.S. standing abroad. There are, of course, no easy or permanent solutions.

---

[64] On the importance of strategic access, see Eric V. Larson, *Assuring Access in Key Strategic Regions: Toward a Long-Term Strategy* (Santa Monica, Calif.: RAND, 2004).

Appendix

Selected List of Interviews

I conducted interviews with activists, government and military officials, politicians, policymakers, and academics between September 2005 and April 2010. The majority of interviews were conducted from 2005 to 2006 and in 2008. A number of activists and government officials interviewed agreed to follow-up interviews or engaged in an ongoing conversation about U.S. bases and anti-base opposition with myself and each other in more informal settings. Several interviewees chose not to be named. With a few exceptions, the list here represents those interviewees cited in the book. Those who are included in the list but not cited have been added to reflect my efforts to present a balanced view of base politics. Unless stated otherwise, affiliations are listed as current at the time of the interview.

1. Jose Almonte, former national security advisor. Manila, Philippines, March 21, 2006.
2. Edgardo Angara, former senator. Manila, Philippines, March 14, 2006.
3. Ma Socorro Diokno, Anti-Base Coalition and Anti-Treaty Movement activist leader. Quezon City, Philippines, April 10, 2006.
4. Corazon Fabros, co-chair of Nuclear-Free Philippines Coalition and anti-base activist. Quezon City, Philippines, March 6, 2006, and April 18, 2006.
5. Miriam Ferrer, professor, UP-Diliman. Quezon City, Philippines, February 23, 2006.
6. Eugene Martin, former political officer, U.S. Embassy, Manila. Washington, D.C., September 2, 2005.
7. Lidy Nacpil, former secretary of Bayan and anti-base activist. Quezon City, Philippines, April 28, 2006.
8. Orlando Mercado, former Senate Defense Committee chairman and Secretary of Defense under President Joseph Estrada. March 21, 2006 (e-mail interview and correspondence).
9. Leticia Ramos-Shahani, former Senate Foreign Relations Committee chairwoman. Manila, Philippines, March 15, 2006.
10. Rene Saguisag, former senator. Manila, Philippines, March 22, 2006.
11. Jovito Salonga, former senate president. Pasig City, Philippines, March 4, 2006.

12. Herbert Docena, Focus on Global South. Quezon City, Philippines, April 5, 2006.
13. Roland Simbulan, co-chair of Nuclear-Free Philippines Coalition, professor and Faculty of Regents, University of the Philippines, and anti-base activist. Manila, Philippines, March 10, 2006.
14. Wigberto "Bobby" Tañada, former senator. Quezon City, Philippines, March 19, 2006.
15. Yongsan USFK official no. 1. Seoul, South Korea, October 5, 2005.
16. Yongsan USFK official no. 2. Seoul, South Korea, October 8, 2005.
17. Kun-young Park, Catholic University of Korea. Seoul, South Korea, May 30, 2006.
18. Young-kwon Yoon, former foreign affairs and trade minister. Seoul, South Korea, May 26, 2006.
19. Peter Yu, community relations officer, Camp Humphreys, USFK. Pyeongtaek, South Korea, January 6, 2006.
20. Group of grassroots activists from KCPT. Pyeongtaek, South Korea, October 19, 2005.
21. Hee-ryong Won, National Assembly Foreign Affairs Committee member. Seoul, South Korea, June 19, 2006.
22. Youkyoung Ko, secretary general of National Campaign for Eradication of Crime by U.S. Troops in Korea. January 8, 2006.
23. Yu-jin Lee, director, Green Korea United. December 21, 2005.
24. Assistant for international relations, Office of the Deputy Commander, USFK. Seoul, South Korea, September 25, 2005.
25. Robert Ogburn, public affairs, U.S. Embassy. Seoul, South Korea, October 15, 2005.
26. KCPT steering committee member. Pyeongtaek, South Korea, November 6, 2005.
27. Hangchonryon member from Hanshin University. Pyeongtaek, South Korea, November 6, 2005.
28. Yong-han Kim, Pyeongtaek Labor Party official and activist. Pyeongtaek, South Korea, November 7, 2005.
29. Jung-hyeon Mun, anti-base movement leader. Pyeongtaek, South Korea, November 7, 2005.
30. Young-jae Yoo, KCPT Policy Committee chair and Solidarity for Peace and Reunification of Korea member. Seoul, South Korea, August 22, 2005.
31. South Korean National Security Council official. Seoul, South Korea, May 30, 2006.
32. Young-koo Cha, director for policy planning in the MND. Seoul, South Korea, December 19, 2006.
33. Pyeongtaek city official no. 1, Office of ROK-U.S. Relations. Pyeongtaek, South Korea, February 9, 2006.
34. Pyeongtaek city official no. 2, Office of ROK-U.S. Relations. Pyeongtaek, South Korea, February 9, 2006.

35. PeaceWind activist. KCPT headquarters, Pyeongtaek, South Korea, December 12, 2005.
36. Doo-hui Oh, KCPT Steering Committee. Pyeongtaek, South Korea, November 6, 2005, and December 9, 2005.
37. Camp Humphreys USFK official no. 3. Pyeongtaek, South Korea, February 3, 2006.
38. Joung-bin Lee, former foreign affairs and trade minister. Seoul, South Korea, June 22, 2006.
39. U.S. Embassy official, political-military affairs. Seoul, South Korea, October 13, 2005.
40. Chuck Jones, former senior country director of Korea, Office of Secretary of Defense. September 1, 2005.
41. John Hill, principal director for East Asia, Office of the Under-Secretary of Defense for Policy. Washington, D.C., May 5, 2010.
42. Masahiro Tomiyama, Okinawan activist. Seoul, South Korea, December 12, 2005 (translator Kyonga Kim).
43. Hiroshi Ashitomi, Okinawan activist. Nago City, Japan, January 21, 2006 (translator Kyung-mi Lee).
44. Okinawan activist no. 1. Pyeongtaek, South Korea, December 10, 2005.
45. Masaaki Gabe, professor, Department of Political Science, University of the Ryukyus. Nishihara, Japan, January 19, 2006.
46. Joseph Nye, former assistant secretary of defense for policy planning. April 7, 2010 (e-mail correspondence).
47. Adrian Bonilla, FLACSO-Ecuador director. Quito, Ecuador, March 9, 2006.
48. Helga Serrano and Ecuador No Bases Coalition members (via e-mail). August 31, 2007.
49. Stefano Osti, No Dal Molin activist. Vicenza, Italy, January 16, 2008.
50. Wilbert van der Zeijden, International No Bases secretary general. Quito, Ecuador, March 8, 2008.
51. Camp Ederle base official no. 1. Vicenza, Italy, January 16, 2008.
52. Camp Ederle base official no. 2. Vicenza, Italy, January 16, 2008.
53. Enzo Ciscato, No Dal Molin activist. Vicenza, Italy, January 15, 2008.
54. U.S. Consulate official. Milan, Italy, January 18, 2008.
55. Guido Lanaro, No Dal Molin activist. Vicenza, Italy, January 14, 2008.
56. Piero Maestri, antiwar activist. Milan, Italy, January 17, 2008.
57. Stephanie Westbrook, U.S. Citizens for Peace & Justice in Rome. Rome, Italy, January 23, 2008.
58. Roberto Menotti, Aspen Institute Italia. Rome, Italy, January 22, 2008.
59. Advisor to Italian Ministry of Defense. Rome, Italy, January 22, 2008.
60. Paolo Costa, extraordinary commissioner of the government, and Italian delegate to EU Parliament. January 23, 2008 (e-mail correspondence).
61. Filippo Andreatta, professor, University of Bologna, and foreign policy advisor to Prime Minister Romano Prodi. Bologna, Italy, January 6, 2008 (telephone interview).

Bibliography

Abinales, Patricio, and Donna J. Amoroso. *State and Society in the Philippines*. Lanham, Md.: Rowman and Littlefield, 2005.

American Political Science Association. *Task Force on U.S. Standing in World Affairs*. *2009*. *U.S. Standing in The World: Causes, Consequences, and the Future*. Washington, D.C.: American Political Science Association, 2009.

Amouzegar, Mahyar A. *Evaluation of Options for Overseas Combat Support Basing*. Santa Monica, Calif.: RAND, 2006.

Aquino, Belinda. *Reflections on the U.S. Bases in the Philippines*. Transcript of the Pansol Reflections Series, Calamba, Laguna, Philippines, August 5. Manila: Senate Legislative Publications Staff, 1990.

Ball, Desmond. *U.S. Bases in the Philippines: Issues and Implications*. Canberra: Strategic and Defence Studies Centre, 1988.

Barnett, Michael. "Identity and Alliances in the Middle East," in *The Culture of National Security: Norms and Identity in World Politics*, edited by Peter J. Katzenstein, 400–50. New York: Columbia University Press, 1996.

Bello, Walden. "Moment of Decision: The Philippines, the Pacific, and U.S. Bases," in *The Sun Never Sets: Confronting the Network of Foreign U.S. Military Bases*, edited by Joseph Gerson and Bruce Birchard, 149–66. Boston: South End Press, 1991.

Bengzon, Alfredo R. A. *A Matter of Honor: The Story of the 1990–1991 R.P.-U.S. Bases Talks*. Manila: Anvil, 1997.

Bennett, Scott. "Testing Alternative Models of Alliance Duration, 1816–1984." *American Journal of Political Science* 41, no. 3 (1997): 846–78.

Berger, Thomas. "Norms, Identity, and National Security in Germany and Japan," in *The Culture of National Security: Norms and Identity in World Politics*, edited by Peter Katzenstein, 316–56. New York: Columbia University Press, 1996.

Cultures of Antimilitarism: National Security in Germany and Japan. Baltimore: The Johns Hopkins University Press, 1998.

Redefining Japan and the U.S.-Japan Alliance. New York: Japan Society, 2004.

Berman, Sheri. *The Social Democratic Moment: Ideas and Politics in the Making of Interwar Europe*. Cambridge, Mass.: Harvard University Press, 1998.

Blyth, Mark. "The Transformation of the Swedish Model: Economic Ideas, Distributional Conflict, and Institutional Change." *World Politics* 54, no. 1 (2001): 1–26.

Braumoeller, Bear. "Causal Complexity and the Study of Politics." *Political Analysis* 11, no. 3 (2003): 209–33.

Calder, Kent E. *Embattled Garrisons: Comparative Base Politics and American Globalism.* Princeton, N.J.: Princeton University Press, 2007.

Campbell, Kurt, and Celeste Johnson Ward. "New Battle Stations?" *Foreign Affairs* 82, no. 5 (2003): 95–103.

Caouette, Dominique. "Persevering Revolutionaries: Armed Struggle in the 21st Century, Exploring the Revolution of the Communist Party of the Philippines." PhD dissertation, Cornell University, 2004.

Castro-Guevara, Maria, ed. *The Bases Talks Reader: Key Documents of the 1990–91 Philippine-American Cooperation Talks.* Manila: Anvil, 1997.

Center for International Policy. *Just the Facts: A Civilian's Guide to U.S. Defense and Security Assistance to Latin America and the Caribbean.* Washington, D.C.: Center for International Policy, 2003.

Chiozza, Giacomo. *Anti-Americanism and the American World Order.* Baltimore: Johns Hopkins University Press, 2009.

Christensen, Thomas J. *Useful Adversaries: Grand Strategy, Domestic Mobilization, and Sino-American Conflict, 1947–1958.* Princeton, N.J.: Princeton University Press, 1996.

"Perceptions and Alliances in Europe: 1865–1940." *International Organization* 51, no. 1 (1997): 65–97.

"Fostering Stability or Creating a Monster?" *International Security* 31, no. 1 (2006): 81–126.

Congressional Budget Office. *Options for Changing the Army's Overseas Basing.* Washington, D.C.: CBO, 2004.

Congressional Quarterly. "Philippine Base Closings, 1991–1992 Legislative Chronology," in *Congress and the Nation.* Washington, D.C.: CQ Press, 1992.

Cooley, Alexander. "Base Politics." *Foreign Affairs* 84, no. 6 (2005): 79–92.

Base Politics: Democratic Change and the US Military Overseas. Ithaca, N.Y.: Cornell University Press, 2008.

Cortes, Rosario Mendoza, Celestina Puyal Boncan, and Ricardo Trota Jose. *The Filipino Saga: History as Social Change.* Quezon City: New Day Publishers, 2000.

Croci, Osvaldo. "The Second Berlusconi Government and Italian Foreign Policy." *International Spectator* 37, no. 2 (2002): 89–105.

Davidson, Jason W. "Italy-U.S. Relations since the End of the Cold War: Prestige, Peace, and the Transatlantic Balance." *Bulletin of Italian Politics* 1, no. 2 (2009): 289–308.

de Castro, Renato Cruz. "Adjusting to the Post-US Bases Era: The Ordeal of the Philippine Military's Modernization Program." *Armed Forces and Society* 26, no. 1 (1999): 119–38.

"The Revitalized Philippine-U.S. Security Relations: A Ghost from the Cold War or an Alliance for the 21st Century?" *Asian Survey* 43, no. 6 (2003): 971–88.

"Societal Forces as Sources of Military Doctrine and Posture: The Case of the AFP Modernization Program, 1991–2003," in *Asia in the New Millennium: APISA First Congress Proceedings*, edited by Amitav Acharya and Cai To Lee, 229–47. Singapore: Marshall Cavendish International, 2004.

"Twenty-first Century Philippine-American Security Relations: Managing an Alliance in the War of the Third Kind." *Asian Security* 2, no. 2 (2006): 102–21.

Del Pero, Mario. "Containing Containment: Rethinking Italy's Experience during the Cold War." Working Paper no. 2. New York: New York University, International Center for Advanced Studies, 2002.

Dionisio, Josephine. *Enhanced Documentation on National Peace Coalitions and Citizens' Groups Peace-Building Experiences in the Philippines.* Manila: UNDP, 2005.

Docena, Herbert. *At the Door of All the East: The Philippines in United States Military Strategy.* Quezon City: Focus on the Global South, 2007.

"Plenary Panel Four Presentation: How Do We Strengthen the International Network for the Abolition of Foreign Military Bases?" Quito, Ecuador, 2007.

Ecuador No Bases Coalition. *Base de Manta: Ojos y oidos del Plan Colombia.* Quito: Ecuador No Bases Coalition, 2007.

Eldridge, Robert D. *The Return of the Amami Islands: The Reversion Movement and U.S.-Japan Relations.* Lanham, Md.: Lexington Books, 2004.

Evangelista, Matthew. *Unarmed Forces: The Transnational Movement to End the Cold War.* Ithaca, N.Y.: Cornell University Press, 1999.

Ferrer, Miriam. "The Dynamics of the Opposition to the US Bases in the Philippines." *Kasarinlan* 7, no. 4 (1992): 62–87.

"Anti-Bases Coalition," in *Studies on Coalition Experiences,* edited by C. Cala and J. Grageda, 4–27. Manila: Bookmark, 1994.

Foreign Service Institute, Department of Foreign Affairs. *Primer on the R.P-U.S. Military Bases Agreement.* Manila: FSI, 1989.

Forsyth, Douglas. "The Peculiarities of Italo-American Relations in Historical Perspective." *Journal of Modern Italian Studies* 3, no. 1 (1998): 1–21.

Friends of the Filipino People. *For Philippine Survival: Nationalist Essays by Claro Recto and Renato Constantino.* Manila: Friends of the Filipino People, n.d.

Funabashi, Yoichi. *Alliance Adrift.* New York: Council on Foreign Relations Press, 1999.

Gamson, William, and David Meyer. "Framing Political Opportunity," in *Comparative Perspectives on Social Movements: Political Opportunities, Mobilizing Structures, and Cultural Framings,* edited by Doug McAdam, John D. McCarthy, and Mayer N. Zald, 275–90 Cambridge: Cambridge University Press, 1996.

Giugni, Marco, Doug McAdam, and Charles Tilly. *How Social Movements Matter.* Minneapolis: University of Minnesota Press, 1999.

Golay, Frank H. *Face of Empire: United States-Philippine Relations, 1898–1946.* Madison: University of Wisconsin–Madison Center for Southeast Asian Studies, 1998.

Goldstein, Judith, and Robert O. Keohane. *Ideas and Foreign Policy: Beliefs, Institutions, and Political Change.* Ithaca, N.Y.: Cornell University Press, 1993.

Goodwin, Jeff, and James Jasper. *Rethinking Social Movements: Structure, Meaning, and Emotion.* Oxford: Rowman and Littlefield, 2004.

Greco, Ettore. *Italy's European Vocation: The Foreign Policy of the New Prodi Government.* U.S.-Europe Analysis Series. Washington, D.C.: Brookings Institution, 2006.

Haas, Mark L. *The Ideological Origins of Great Power Politics, 1789–1989.* Ithaca, N.Y.: Cornell University Press, 2005.

Hahm, Chaibong. "The Two South Koreas: A House Divided." *Washington Quarterly* 28 (2005): 57–72.

"South Korea's Progressives and the U.S.-ROK Alliance." *Joint U.S.-Korea Academic Studies* 17 (2007): 187–202.

Harkavy, Robert E. *Bases Abroad: The Global Foreign Military Presence.* Oxford: Oxford University Press, 1989.

Strategic Basing and the Great Powers, 1200–2000. London: Routledge, 2007.

Harrison, Selig. "South Korea-U.S. Alliance under the Roh Government." *Nautilus Policy Forum Online* 06–28A, April 11, 2006. http://www.nautilus.org/fora/security/0628Harrison.html.

Ina, Hisayoshi. "The Japan-U.S. Security Alliance in a New Era of International Relations," in *Japan-U.S. Security Alliance for the 21st Century: Cornerstone of Democracy, Peace and Prosperity for Our Future Generations*, edited by Japanese Ministry of Foreign Affairs, 3–14. Tokyo: Overseas Public Relations Division, Ministry of Foreign Affairs, 1996.

Inoue, Masamichi. *Okinawa and the U.S. Military: Identity Making in the Age of Globalization*. New York: Columbia University Press, 2007.

Iversen, Paul. "The Consequences of Bushismo in Vicenza, Italy." March 2005. http://www.peaceandjustice.it/vicenza-dal-molin.php.

Jacobs, Lawrence, and Benjamin Page. "Who Influences U.S. Foreign Policy?" *American Political Science Review* 99, no. 1 (2005): 107–23.

Japan Ministry of Foreign Affairs. "The Japan-U.S. Special Action Committee (SACO) Interim Report," in *Japan-U.S. Security Alliance for the 21st Century: Cornerstone of Democracy, Peace and Prosperity for Our Future Generations*, edited by Japan Ministry of Foreign Affairs, 83–84. Tokyo: Overseas Public Relations Division, Ministry of Foreign Affairs, 1996.

"Japan-U.S. Declaration on Joint Security – Alliance for the Twenty-First Century." April 16, 1996. http://www.mofa.go.jp/region/n-america/us/security/security.html.

"Report on the Interim Review of the Guidelines for U.S.-Japan Defense Cooperation." June 17, 1997. http://www.mofa.go.jp/region/n-america/us/security/guideline.html.

Japan Ministry of National Defense. *Defense of Japan 2006*. Japan Ministry of National Defense, 2006. http://www.mod.go.jp/e/publ/w_paper/pdf/2006/4-2-1.pdf.

Johnson, Chalmers A. *Blowback: The Costs and Consequences of American Empire*. New York: Metropolitan Books, 2000.

The Sorrows of Empire: Militarism, Secrecy, and the End of the Republic. New York: Metropolitan Books, 2004.

Nemesis: The Last Days of the American Republic. New York: Metropolitan Books, 2007.

Jung, Wook-Shik. *Dongmaeng-ae dut* [Alliance Trap]. Seoul: Samin Press, 2005.

Kane, Tim. *Global Troop Deployment Dataset 1950–2005*. Washington, D.C.: Heritage Foundation, 2006.

Karnow, Stanley. *In Our Image: America's Empire in the Philippines*. New York: Foreign Policy Association, 1989.

Katzenstein, Peter. *Cultural Norms and National Security: Police and Military in Postwar Japan*. Ithaca, N.Y.: Cornell University Press, 1996.

Japanese Security in Perspective. London: Routledge, 2008.

Katzenstein, Peter J., and Robert O. Keohane. *Anti-Americanisms in World Politics*. Ithaca, N.Y.: Cornell University Press, 2007.

Katzenstein, Peter, and Nobuo Okawara. "Japan's National Security: Structures, Norms, and Policies." *International Security* 17, no. 4 (1993): 84–118.

"Japan, Asian-Pacific Security, and the Case for Analytical Eclecticism." *International Security* 26, no. 3 (2001): 153–85.

Keck, Margaret E., and Kathryn Sikkink. *Activists Beyond Borders: Advocacy Networks in International Politics*. Ithaca, N.Y.: Cornell University Press, 1998.

Kim, Mikyoung. "The U.S. Military Transformation and Its Implications for the ROK-U.S. Alliance." *IFANS Review* 13, no. 1 (2005): 15–39.

Kim, Yong-han. "Juhan-migun bandae tujaeng-ui haet-bul, Maehyang-ri" [Maehyangri, the sunshine of the opposition struggle against United States Forces, Korea], in

Jae-sook Kang, *Nogunri ae-seo Maehyangri kkaji* [From Nogunri to Maehyangri], 243–70. Seoul: Deep Freedom Press, 2001.

King, Gary, Robert O. Keohane, and Sidney Verba. *Designing Social Inquiry: Scientific Inference in Qualitative Research.* Princeton, N.J.: Princeton University Press, 1994.

Kitschelt, Herbert. "Political Opportunity Structures and Political Protest: Anti-Nuclear Movements in Four Democracies." *British Journal of Political Science* 16, no. 1 (1986): 57–85.

Ko, Youkyoung. "Hanguk-ui banmi-gun-giji undong-gwa dongasia yundae" [Anti-U.S. military base movements and East Asian solidarity], in *Bipan Sahoehak Daehoe* (8th Meeting, November 4–5), 297–310. Seoul: College of Social Science, Seoul National University, 2005.

Krasner, Stephen D. *Defending the National Interest: Raw Materials Investments and U.S. Foreign Policy.* Princeton, N.J.: Princeton University Press, 1978.

Larson, Eric V. *Assuring Access in Key Strategic Regions: Toward a Long-Term Strategy.* Santa Monica, Calif.: RAND, 2004.

Larson, Eric V., Norman D. Levin, Seonhae Baik, and Bogdan Savych. *Ambivalent Allies? A Study of South Korean Attitudes Toward the U.S.* Santa Monica, Calif.: RAND, 2004.

Lee, Nae-Young. "Changing South Korean Public Opinion on the U.S. and the ROK-U.S. Alliance." Paper prepared for a workshop on "America in Question: Korean Democracy and the Challenge of Non-Proliferation on the Peninsula." Seoul, South Korea, May 10–11, 2005.

Lee, Sook-Jong. *The Transformation of South Korean Politics: Implications for U.S.-Korea Relations.* Washington, D.C.: Brookings Institution, Center for Northeast Asian Policy Studies, 2005.

Leeds, Brett Ashley, and Burcu Savun. "Terminating Alliances: Why Do States Abrogate Agreements?" *Journal of Politics* 69, no. 4 (2007): 1118–32.

Legro, Jeffrey. *Rethinking the World: Great Power Strategies and International Order.* Ithaca, N.Y.: Cornell University Press, 2005.

Livingston, Ian S., Heather L. Messera, and Michael O'Hanlon. *Afghanistan Index*, April 8. Washington, D.C.: Brookings Institution, 2010.

Lutz, Catherine. *The Bases of Empire: The Global Struggle against U.S. Military Posts.* New York: New York University Press, 2009.

McAdam, Doug. "Political Opportunities: Conceptual Origins, Current Problems, Future Directions," in *Comparative Perspectives on Social Movements: Political Opportunities, Mobilizing Structures, and Cultural Framings*, edited by Doug McAdam, John D. McCarthy, and Mayer N. Zald, 23–40. Cambridge: Cambridge University Press, 1996.

   "Legacies of Anti-Americanism: A Sociological Perspective," in *Anti-Americanisms in World Politics*, edited by Peter J. Katzenstein and Robert O. Keohane. Ithaca, N.Y.: Cornell University Press, 2007.

McAdam, Doug, John D. McCarthy, and Mayer N. Zald, eds. *Comparative Perspectives on Social Movements: Political Opportunities, Mobilizing Structures, and Cultural Framings.* Cambridge: Cambridge University Press, 1996.

McAdam, Doug, Sidney Tarrow, and Charles Tilly. *Dynamics of Contention.* Cambridge: Cambridge University Press, 2001.

McCaffrey, Katherine T. *Military Power and Popular Protest: The U.S. Navy in Vieques, Puerto Rico.* New Brunswick, N.J.: Rutgers University Press, 2002.

McCarthy, John D., and Mayer N. Zald. "Resource Mobilization and Social Movements: A Partial Theory." *American Journal of Sociology* 82, no. 6 (1977): 1212–41.

McCormack, Gavan. "The Okinawan Election and Resistance to Japan's Military First Politics." *Japan Focus* no. 688, November 15, 2006. http://www.japanfocus.org/products/details/2275.

"Abe and Okinawa: Collision Course?" *Japan Focus* no. 914, September 1, 2007. http://www.japanfocus.org/products/details/2512.

Client State: Japan in American Embrace. London: Verso, 2007.

Mearsheimer, John J. *The Tragedy of Great Power Politics.* New York: Norton, 2001.

Meyer, David. *A Winter of Discontent: The Nuclear Freeze and American Politics.* New York: Praeger, 1990.

"Political Opportunity and Nested Institutions." *Social Movement Studies* 2, no. 1 (2003): 17–35.

"Protest and Political Opportunities." *Annual Review of Sociology* 30 (2004): 125–45.

Meyer, David, and Debra Minkoff. "Conceptualizing Political Opportunity." *Social Forces* 82, no. 4 (2004): 1457–92.

Miranda, Felipe. "Filipino Public Opinion on the Issue of American Facilities in the Philippines." *Quezon City: Social Weather Station*, 1989.

Mitchell, Derek, ed. *Strategy and Sentiment: South Korean Views of the United States and the U.S.-ROK Alliance.* Washington, D.C.: CSIS, 2004.

Mochizuki, Mike. *Toward a True Alliance: Restructuring U.S.-Japan Security Relations.* Washington, D.C.: Brookings Institution Press, 1997.

"Change in Japan's Grand Strategy: Why and How Much?" *Asia Policy* 4 (2007): 191–96.

Monteleone, Carla. "The Evolution of the Euro-Atlantic Pluralistic Security Community." *Journal of Transatlantic Studies* 5, no. 1 (2007): 63–85.

Moon, Katharine H. S. "Korean Nationalism, Anti-Americanism, and Democratic Consolidation," in *Korea's Democratization*, edited by Samuel Kim, 135–58. Cambridge: Cambridge University Press, 2003.

"South Korean Civil Society and Alliance Politics," in *Strategy and Sentiment: South Korean Views of the United States and the U.S.-ROK Alliance*, edited by Derek Mitchell, 50–58. Washington, D.C.: CSIS, 2004.

Morrison, Charles, ed. *Asia Pacific Security Outlook 1997.* Honolulu: East-West Center, 1997.

Mulgan, Aurelia George. "Managing the U.S. Base Issue in Okinawa: A Test for Japanese Democracy." Working Paper no. 2000/1, Department of International Relations, Australian National University, Canberra, January 2000.

National Democratic Front. *Our Vision of a Just and Democratic Society.* Philippines: Gintong Tala, 1987.

Nuti, Leopoldo. "The Role of the U.S. in Italy's Foreign Policy." *International Spectator* 38, no. 1 (2003): 91–101.

Oh, Doo-hui. "A-jik kkeun-naji ahn-eun SOFA gaejeong undong" [The unfinished SOFA revision movement], in Jae-sook Kang, *Nogunri eseo Maehyangri kkaji* [From Nogunri to Maehyangri], 200–42. Seoul: Deep Freedom Press, 2001.

O'Hanlon, Michael. *Unfinished Business: U.S. Overseas Military Presence in the 21st Century.* Washington, D.C.: Center for a New American Security, 2008.

Okamoto, Yukio. "Searching for a Solution to the Okinawan Problem," in *Japan-U.S. Security Alliance for the 21st Century: Cornerstone of Democracy, Peace and Prosperity for Our Future Generations*, edited by Japanese Ministry of Foreign

Affairs, 43–60. Tokyo: Overseas Public Relations Division, Ministry of Foreign Affairs, 1996.

Ota, Masahide. *The Battle of Okinawa: The Typhoon of Steel and Bombs*. Tokyo: Kume Publishing Company, 1984.

Essays on Okinawa Problems. Okinawa: Yui Shuppan, 2000.

Overseas Basing Committee. *Interim Report of the Commission on Review of Overseas Military Facility Structure of the United States*. Arlington, Va.: Overseas Basing Committee, 2005.

Park Kun-Young. "80 nyun-dae hanguk-ui banmijoo-ui, byun-hwa, jeonmang, geuligo ham-eui" [South Korean anti-Americanism, change, prospects, and togetherness]. Presented at Perspectives of Social Science in the 1980s from a 21st Century Perspective. Seoul, South Korea, October 7, 2005.

A New U.S.-ROK Alliance: A Nine Point Policy Recommendation for a Reflective and Mature Relationship. Washington, D.C.: Brookings Institution, Center for Northeast Asian Policy Studies, 2005.

Pekkanen, Robert, and Ellis S. Krauss. "Japan's 'Coalition of the Willing' on Security Policies." *Orbis* 49, no. 3 (2005): 429–44.

Pew Research Center, Pew Global Attitudes Project. "America's Image Slips, but Allies Share U.S. Concerns Over Iran, Hamas." June 15, 2006.

Pineo, Ronn F. *Ecuador and the United States: Useful Strangers, The United States and the Americas*. Athens: University of Georgia Press, 2007.

Price, Richard. "Reversing the Gun Sights: Transnational Civil Society Targets Landmines." *International Organization* 52, no. 3 (1998): 613–44.

"Transnational Civil Society and Advocacy in World Politics." *World Politics* 55, no. 4 (2003): 579–606.

Pyle, Kenneth B. *Japan Rising: The Resurgence of Japanese Power and Purpose*. New York: Public Affairs, 2007.

Republic of Ecuador. Letter from Rafael Correa to participants of the International No Bases Conference. Official letter no. DPR-0-07-8, March 6, 2007.

Republic of Ecuador, Ministry of Foreign Affairs. *Plan Nacional de Política Exterior*. http://www.mmrree.gov.ec/mre/documentos/ministerio/planex/planex_esp.htm.

Republic of Korea, Ministry of National Defense. News Release. "*Pyeongtaek – Giji pok-ryuk si-wui-dae-ae jangbyung soo-sib-myung boo-sang*" [Pyeontaek Base, soldiers injured by violent protestors], May 5, 2006.

Defense White Paper, 2006.

Republic of Korea, National Assembly Records, Unification and Foreign Affairs Committee, 250th Assembly, 16th Meeting, December 7, 2004.

Republic of Korea, National Assembly Records – Main Assembly. 250th Assembly, 14th Meeting, December 9, 2004.

Republic of the Philippines. *Record of the Senate*. Fifth Regular Session, July 22 to September 30, 1991, Vol. 1, nos. 1–27. Manila: Senate Legislative Publications Staff, 1992.

Republic of the Philippines, Congress. Tenth Congress, Second Regular Session. Joint Resolution No. 28, "Joint resolution expressing the approval by both houses of congress of Republic Act No. 7898," December 19, 1996.

Republic of the Philippines, Department of Foreign Affairs. *The Visiting Forces Agreement (A Primer)*. Manila: Department of Foreign Affairs, 1998.

Republic of the Philippines, Department of National Defense. In *Defense of the Philippines: 1998 Defense Policy Paper*. Quezon City: DND, 1998.

Republic of the Philippines, Malacanang Palace, Office of the Press Secretary. "Joint Statement between the Republic of the Philippines and the United States of America," October 18, 2003.

Republic of the Philippines, Senate Legislative Publications Staff. *The Bases of Their Decisions: How the Senators Voted on the Treaty of Friendship between the Government of the Republic of the Philippines and the Government of the United States of America.* Manila: Senate of the Philippines, 1991.

The Visiting Forces Agreement: The Senate Decision. Manila: Senate of the Philippines, 1999.

Rimanelli, Marco. *Italy between Europe and the Mediterranean: Diplomacy and Naval Strategy from Unification to NATO, 1800–2000.* New York: P. Lang, 1997.

Rochon, Thomas, and David Meyer, eds. *Coalitions and Political Movements: The Lessons of the Nuclear Freeze.* Boulder, Colo.: Lynne Rienner, 1997.

Saavedra, Luis Ángel. *Operaciones De Avansada O Base Militar Operativa? Un Análisis De La Base De Manta.* [Operations of Outpost or Operative Military Base? An Analysis of the Manta Base]. Quito: Fundación Regional de Asesoría en Derechos Humanos, INREDH, 2007.

"The Manta Base: A U.S. Military Fort in Ecuador." *Fellowship* 73, no. 1 (2007): 20–21.

Salonga, Jovito R. *The Senate That Said No: A Four-Year Record of the First Post-EDSA Senate.* Quezon City: University of the Philippines Press, 1995.

Samuels, Richard J. *Securing Japan: Tokyo's Grand Strategy and the Future of East Asia.* Ithaca, N.Y.: Cornell University Press, 2007.

Samuels, Richard J., and Patrick Boyd. "Prosperity's Children: Generational Change and Japan's Future Leadership." *Asia Policy* 6 (2008): 15–51.

Sandars, C. T. *America's Overseas Garrisons: The Leasehold Empire.* Oxford: Oxford University Press, 2000.

Schirmer, Daniel Boone. *U.S. Bases by Another Name: ACSA in the Philippines.* Brooklyn, N.Y.: Philippines Bases Network, 1995.

Schweller, Randall L. *Unanswered Threats: Political Constraints on the Balance of Power.* Princeton, N.J.: Princeton University Press, 2006.

Shin, Gi-Wook, and Kristine Burke. "North Korea and Contending South Korean Identities: Analysis of the South Korean Media; Policy Implications for the United States." *KEI: Academic Paper Series* 2, no. 4 (2007): 1–12.

Sikkink, Kathryn. *Ideas and Institutions: Developmentalism in Brazil and Argentina.* Ithaca, N.Y.: Cornell University Press, 1991.

Silliman, Sidney G., and Lela Garner Noble, eds. *Organizing for Democracy: NGOs, Civil Society, and the Philippine State.* Honolulu: University of Hawaii Press, 1998.

Simbulan, Roland G. *A Guide to Nuclear Philippines: A Guide to the U.S. Military Bases, Nuclear Weapons, and What the Filipino People Are Doing About These.* Manila: IBON Databank Philippines, 1989.

"September 16, 1991: The Day the Senate Said 'No!' to Uncle Sam – An Insider's Account." NFPC Library Archives, September 11, 2002. Also found at http://www.yonip.com/main/articles/september_16.html.

Singer, J. David. "The Level-of-Analysis Problem in International Relations." *World Politics* 14, no. 1 (1961): 77–92.

"Bringing the State Back In: Strategies of Analysis in Current Research," in *Bringing the State Back In*, edited by Peter B. Evans, Dietrich Rueschemeyer, and Theda Skocpol, 3–43. Cambridge: Cambridge University Press, 1985.

Smith, Sheila A. "Challenging National Authority: Okinawa Prefecture and the U.S. Military Bases," in *Local Voices, National Issues: The Impact of Local Initiative in Japanese Policy-making*, edited by Sheila A. Smith, 75–114. Ann Arbor: University of Michigan Press, 2000.

 Shifting Terrain: The Domestic Politics of U.S. Military Presence in Asia. Honolulu: East-West Center, 2006.

Snow, David, Burke Rochford, Steven Worden, and Robert Benford. "Frame Alignment Processes, Micromobilization, and Movement Participation." *American Sociological Review* 51, no. 4 (1986): 464–81.

Snyder, Jack L. *Myths of Empire: Domestic Politics and International Ambition*. Ithaca, N.Y.: Cornell University Press, 1991.

Sobel, Richard. *The Impact of Public Opinion on U.S. Foreign Policy since Vietnam*. New York: Oxford University Press, 2001.

Steinberg, David I. *Korean Attitudes Toward the United States: Changing Dynamics*. Armonk, N.Y.: M. E. Sharpe, 2004.

Straub, David. "U.S. and ROK Strategic Doctrines and the U.S.-ROK Alliance." *Joint U.S.-Korea Academic Studies* 17 (2007): 165–86.

Suh, Jae-Jung. "Persistence and Termination of Military Alliances: NATO, the Soviet Union-Egypt, and the United States-Iran." Unpublished dissertation chapter, University of Pennsylvania, 2000.

 "Bound to Last? The U.S.-Korea Alliance and Analytical Eclecticism," in *Rethinking Security in East Asia: Identity, Power and Efficiency*, edited by Jae-Jung Suh, Allen Carlson, and Peter Katzenstein, 131–71. Stanford, Calif.: Stanford University Press, 2004.

Tanaka, Hitoshi. "Japan-U.S. Alliance for the 21st Century – President Clinton's Visit to Japan," in *Japan-U.S. Security Alliance for the 21st Century: Cornerstone of Democracy, Peace and Prosperity for Our Future Generations*, edited by Japanese Ministry of Foreign Affairs, 3–14. Tokyo: Overseas Public Relations Division, Ministry of Foreign Affairs, 1996.

 "Japanese Foreign Policy under Prime Minister Yasuo Fukuda." *East Asia Insights* 5, no. 2 (2007): 1–4.

Tanji, Miyume. *Myth, Protest and Struggle in Okinawa*. London: Routledge, 2006.

Tarrow, Sidney G. *Power in Movement: Social Movements and Contentious Politics*, 2nd ed. Cambridge: Cambridge University Press, 1998.

 The New Transnational Activism. Cambridge: Cambridge University Press, 2005.

Thelen, Kathleen. "Historical Institutionalism in Comparative Politics." *Annual Review of Political Science* 2 (1999): 369–404.

Tilly, Charles, and Sidney G. Tarrow. *Contentious Politics*. Boulder, Colo.: Paradigm Publishers, 2007.

United Nations Assistance Mission to Afghanistan. *Afghanistan: Annual Report on Protection of Civilians in Armed Conflict, 2008*. Kabul: United Nations Assistance Mission to Afghanistan, 2009.

United States CINPAC Virtual Information Center. "Special Press Summary: Land Partnership Plan and Yongsan Relocation," January 31, 2002.

United States Department of Defense. "Strengthening U.S. Global Defense Posture: Report to Congress," Washington, D.C., September 17, 2004.

 Base Structure Report: A Summary of the Department of Defense's Real Property Inventory. Washington, D.C.: Office of the Deputy Under-Secretary of Defense, 2009.

United States Department of State. "U.S. Troop Relocation Shows Strength of U.S.-Korea Alliance." Transcript of U.S. and ROK representatives discussing the Alliance Policy Initiative, July 28, 2004. http://usinfo.org/wf-archive/2004/040728/epf307.htm (last accessed May 10, 2007).

"Senior Administration Officials from the Departments of State and Defense." Foreign Press Center Briefing, Washington, D.C., August 16, 2004.

United States Department of State, Office of International Information Programs. "U.S. Official Praises Philippine Anti-Terrorism Effort," November 16, 2001. Available at http://www.globalsecurity.org/military/library/news/2001/11/mil-011117-usia03.htm.

United States General Accounting Office. *Overseas Presence: Issues Involved in Reducing the Impact of the U.S. Military Presence on Okinawa.* Washington, D.C.: U.S. General Accounting Office, 1998.

Briefing Report to the Chairman, Caucus of International Narcotics Control, U.S. Senate: Drug Control, International Counterdrug Sites Being Developed. Washington, D.C.: GAO, 2000.

Defense Infrastructure: Basing Uncertainties Necessitate Reevaluation of U.S. Construction Plans in South Korea." Washington, D.C.: GAO, 2003.

United States House of Representatives, Committee on Armed Services. *Military Installations and Facilities Subcommittee: Hearings on Military Construction, H.R. 1208.* Washington, D.C.: U.S. Government Printing Office, 1992.

United States House of Representatives. "Counter-drug Implications of the U.S. Leaving Panama." Prepared testimony by Deputy Assistant Secretary of Defense for Drug Enforcement Policy and Support Ana Marie Salazar, House Committee on Government Reform, Subcommittee on Criminal Justice, Drug Policy, and Human Resources, June 9, 2000.

United States Information Service. *Background on the Bases: American Military Facilities in the Philippines.* Manila: United States Information Service, 1988.

In Our Mutual Interest: U.S. Military Facilities in the Philippines. Manila: United States Information Service, 1990.

University of Bologna, Master's in International Relations Students 2005–06. "Italian Foreign Policy." Working Paper for the course on Analisi della Politica Estera [Foreign Policy Analysis], July 27, 2006.

Walt, Stephen. *The Origins of Alliances.* Ithaca, N.Y.: Cornell University Press, 1987.

Taming American Power: The Global Response to U.S. Primacy. New York: W.W. Norton, 2005.

Waltz, Kenneth. *Theory of International Politics.* Reading, Mass.: Addison-Wesley, 1979.

Weitsman, Patricia A. *Dangerous Alliances: Proponents of Peace, Weapons of War.* Stanford, Calif.: Stanford University Press, 2004.

Weldes, Jutta. "Constructing National Interests." *European Journal of International Relations* 2, no. 3 (1996): 275–318.

Wendt, Alexander. *Social Theory of International Politics.* Cambridge: Cambridge University Press, 1999.

White House, Office of the Press Secretary. "Joint Statement between the United States of America and the Republic of the Philippines," November 20, 2001. http://www.whitehouse.gov/news/releases/2001/11/20011120-13.html.

"Joint Statement between the United States of America and the Republic of the Philippines," May 19, 2003. http://www.whitehouse.gov/news/releases/2003/05/20030519-3.html.

Wohlforth, William. *The Elusive Balance: Power and Perceptions during the Cold War.* Ithaca, N.Y.: Cornell University Press, 1993.

Wui, Marlon, and Glenda Lopez, eds. *State–Civil Society Relations in Policy-making.* Quezon City: University of the Philippines Press, 1994.

Yee, Albert. "The Causal Effects of Ideas on Policies." *International Organization* 50, no. 1 (1996): 69–108.

Yeo, Andrew. "Local National Dynamics and Framing in South Korean Anti-Base Movements." *Kasarinlan* 21, no. 2 (2006): 34–69.

"Not in Anyone's Backyard: The Emergence and Identity of a Transnational Anti-Base Network." *International Studies Quarterly* 53, no. 3 (2009): 571–94.

Yonetani, Julia. "Playing Base Politics in a Global Strategic Theater." *Critical Asian Studies* 33, no. 1 (2001): 70–95.

"Future 'Asset,' But at What Price? The Okinawa Initiative Debate," in *Islands of Discontent: Okinawan Responses to Japanese and American Power*, edited by Laura Hein and Mark Selden, 243–72. Lanham, Md.: Rowman and Littlefield, 2003.

Yoon, Kwang-Ung. "Migoon-giji ijeong sa-eob gwal-lyeon beu-ri-ping" [Briefing on issues related to the USFK base relocation project], Ministry of National Defense, May 3, 2006. Available at http://www.mnd.go.kr/cms.jsp?p_id=03406000000000.

"Pyeongtaek migoon giji eejeon jaegeumtoh opda" [No Reevaluation of Pyeongtaek Base Relocation]. Special Statement Prepared by the MND Minister of Defense, May 4. *MND News Brief*, May 3, 2006. Available at http://mnd.news.go.kr/warp/webapp/news/print_view?id=5ae9967224cc3de6665c2c17.

Newspapers and News Services

Asahi News Service
Asahi Shimbun
Associated Press
BBC Monitoring
Bloomberg News
Chosun Ilbo
Corriere della Sera
Daily Yomiuri
Financial Times
Hankyoreh
Hankyoreh21
Inter-Press Service
ISN Security Watch
Joongang Ilbo
KCPT/Village Voice
Korea Herald
Latin America Regional Reports
Manila Standard
Minjung ae sori
MND News Brief
Navy NewsStand
New York Times

OhMyNews
Orlando Sentinel
Reuters
Ryukyu Shimpo
Stars and Stripes
The Times (London)
Washington Post
Yomiuri Shimbun
Yonhap News Agency

Index